SO FAR, SO GOOD

River Teeth Literary Nonfiction Prize

SERIES EDITORS:

*Daniel Lehman*, Ashland University
*Joe Mackall*, Ashland University

The River Teeth Literary Nonfiction Prize is
awarded to the best work of literary nonfiction
submitted to the annual contest sponsored by
*River Teeth: A Journal of Nonfiction Narrative.*

# So Far, So Good

RALPH SALISBURY

UNIVERSITY OF NEBRASKA PRESS | LINCOLN AND LONDON

Library of Congress
Cataloging-in-Publication Data
Salisbury, Ralph J.
So far, so good / Ralph Salisbury.
p. cm. —
(River Teeth Literary Nonfiction Prize)
ISBN 978-0-8032-4592-1 (pbk.: alk. paper)
1. Salisbury, Ralph J. 2. Poets, American—
20th century—Biography. 3. College teachers—United States—Biography.
4. Racially mixed people—United
States—Biography. 5. Cherokee Indians—Biography. 6. Irish Americans—
Biography. 7. Social values. 8. Civilization, Modern—20th century. I. Title.
PS3569.A4597Z46 2013
818'.5403—dc23 [B] 2012035280

Set in Minion by Laura Wellington.
Designed by Nathan Putens.

*To my wife and fellow writer,*
*Ingrid Wendt; to Jeff, Brian, and*
*Martina, my children; and to*
*Connor, Travis, Gemma, and*
*Gavino, my grandchildren.*

SO FAR, SO GOOD

# PROLOGUE

Bullet-shattered glass clattering onto my baby bed, I awake and cry, into darkness, for help.

Do I remember this? Or do I remember being told? I will feel it, whichever it is. I will feel it, chill bomb-bay wind buffeting my eighteen-year-old body, a mile above an old volcano's jagged debris; feel it, seeing photos of Jewish concentration camp children, huddled together for warmth, photos of Korean orphans, huddled together, homeless in blizzard after American bombing—bombing in which, twenty-five, I had refused an order to join.

Ma snatches my blanket-swaddled body up, to shield me against whatever might come next, and glass shards pierce her arms. Pa lunges out into the night, gripping a pistol, with which he'd once wounded an armed robber and had too many times drunkenly terrorized his own family.

Pa, alert to shoot whoever is attacking our home, finds only snow—snow a mass killer that will, scientists tell us, bury the last child to be born on earth.

Targeting a farmhouse window would be a "drive-by shooting" in today's news—news meant to arouse fear—fear, which seems to sell medications, deodorants, conformist designer clothes, manipulative political candidates, and an economically disastrous, bad-for-everyone's-physical-and-mental-health, materialistic, militaristic imperialism.

Bombs exploding, hundreds of babies cremated alive—what did my experience of the world's violence amount to really? A racially motivated harassment? A neighborhood grudge? Or, maybe, a drunken young stranger saw our dimly lighted farmhouse windows as an opportunity to outdo pals, who'd shot holes into road signs, meant to keep people from being lost or from losing their lives on dangerous curves.

A drive-by shooting—a mystery.

A drive-on shooting—not mystery but history: Giddyap, oxen, mule, horse—and drive, drive, drive on, to the last acre of free-for-the-taking land—on, on, on, to extermination of the last of the Mohicans—of tribe after tribe after tribe.

A ride-by shooting—motivation: an Easterner's urge to imitate fictional Wild West heroes, by aiming out of a train window and killing a buffalo or an Indian.

I think of my brother Bob's telling me that another American soldier shot an Arab off his horse, in Algeria, during World War II, just for the hell of it.

In this rambling, free-associational placement of electronic impulse on screen, ink on page, there will be some accounts of terror and death. Few compared to those on TV news but more than I, or you, might wish.

A survivor of one lightning strike, some car and plane mishaps, some explosions, a few bullets, a heart attack, cancer, and other human afflictions, I ask myself, as readers may well be asking, why should anyone read this?

Maybe for warnings implicit in my confessed mistakes. Maybe for what little wisdom my many years have bestowed. Maybe for the story of someone who grew up without indoor plumbing or electricity and worked—despite hunger—in often above 100-degree heat and often 30-below-zero cold, from lantern-lit predawn to lantern-lit late night, on a Mississippi River Valley farm, beside a narrow, dusty, muddy, or snow-choked dirt wagon trail, which had become an auto road.

If you had walked that road with me from my fourth through my eleventh years—stamping with one booted heel, maybe, to crack yesterday's footprint's ice into zig-zag lightning—you would have found yourself in a one-room school's smells of chalk dust, glue, and the seldom bathed bodies of children.

If you had joined me in visiting my father's mother, you would have hiked several miles along a creek, on a generations-worn footpath, until you reached the small hill farm, to which our outgunned and outnumbered Cherokee-Shawnee forebears had fled, abandoning rich valley plantations to murderous, government-sanctioned mobs.

Someone who hunted first with bow and arrow and then, starting at age twelve, with rifle and shotgun, and helped to keep his family alive, I might belong in a museum, among stuffed animals, but I have learned to use this computer, more complex than those with which I aimed the cannon and machine guns of a B-29 bomber—same type plane as the two that ended lives in Hiroshima and Nagasaki and changed all of our lives.

I was seventeen when I enlisted in what was then the army air corps. I was twenty when World War II ended, and I was twenty-five when I refused orders to join in the fire-bombing of North Korean cities and only escaped prison because a computer failed to extend my enlistment and sent my World War II honorable discharge the week before I was to be arrested. Seventy-five now, in a year when Muslim martyrs' suicide attacks have destroyed the U.S. World Trade Center and much of the Pentagon and killed thousands, I have started this day, as I have started most days for most of my life, by trying to write.

Why?

Yesterday I would have given the honest answer Socrates was executed for giving to most questions worth asking, "I do not know."

Today, my life—and the lives of all living things—soon to end, I do know why I am beginning to try to write a hop-skip-and-jumps-and-maybe-some-dancing memoir. My daughter, to whom I read or told stories nearly every night of her childhood, has asked me to put some of our family's realities down, with no fictionalizing and no poeticizing, just things as they were. I am trying, although, for most of my life, I have depended on imagination as an astronaut depends on a heat shield, imagination protecting me from the painful realities I have needed to reenter.

Free association, spontaneity, a wholeness of the moment, a union of past and present, of childhood and after—these are what I seek, and the result may be as random and unorganized as my bank account and my life. Whether or not I live to finish and publish this manuscript, here are some memories of a poverty-stricken, malnourished, sometimes nearly fatally ill, and mostly mysteriously happy child, memories of a mixed-race, somewhat educated world citizen. And memories of an individual seeking what seems to be best for himself, for his loved ones, and for other individuals.

Whatever is here I offer to the world, knowing that my life is but one of a multitude of lives, all doomed to undergo change and, I believe, to go on and on, in the Great Plan, which, perhaps, we humans can, in our best moments, somewhat sense.

# 1

It is January 24, 1926, and the third child of an Irish American mother and an English-Cherokee-Shawnee father has killed his mother and himself.

That would have been my life's story had not my father, the son of a Cherokee medicine man, left his suffering wife in her sister's care, harnessed horse to sled, and braved blizzard winds in search of a university-trained doctor.

The sled runners pass swiftly over ice-crusted snow, until what seems to be just another drift proves to be a hidden rock — one of the many dropped, like a sleepy child's toys, when a glacier slipped back into its hibernation dream after failing to reach the equator.

Thrown from Dad's sled, the doctor has to tape his own cracked ribs before sleighing on to save my mother from being killed by her twisted-around-backward baby and saves me from hanging myself with the cord that had been, for nine months, a lifeline.

Eight and a half pounds of centuries of Native American–European mating happenstance are yanked into the world, dangled head down, and whacked on the butt. This first of a lifetime of blows inspires the first of a lifetime of protests, a lung-clearing squall.

Maybe my books are self-administered, lung-clearing, mind-clearing shocks — WHACK!

On 1929 newspapers' picture pages lords of commerce were attempting wingless flight from skyscrapers, whose heights mocked cathedrals' centuries of pitiful attempts to reach Heaven.

Money had been squandered to buy guns and ammunition and explosives and poison gas. The stock markets of the world had collapsed, and millions, including my three-year-old self, were hungry, too hungry to fight off disease. Fever burned into my brain the dark shape of our huge barn teetering on my little thumb. My gasping breath told a doctor to tell my worried parents that I would probably not live to blow out four birthday candles—which wouldn't be there in any case, because there was little flour for bread, none for cake.

Dad drove his Model T Ford through a blizzard. When he returned, he held, in his numbed hands, ice cream, which he'd sacrificed badly needed food money to buy. Ice cream was something he'd never had in his hard childhood. A younger brother's taking the risk of catching scarlet fever to offer a bit of boiled potato was a precious early memory.

From Mom's story my ravenous ears received again and again the gift that Dad had risked his life on icy roads to bring. I was too sick to eat, but the ice cream melts, now, on my storytelling tongue, and it will melt again and again and again in the ears of my children and grandchildren, though TV hypnotically sounds and shows the glory of slim actors' salty, grease-flavored, fast-food gluttony and the joys of school cafeteria food fights.

During a visit to my family's farm this year, 2001, I discovered that my sister, Ruth, had bought an electric range and a microwave to replace the wood-burning stove. When we were children, Ruth, my brothers Ray and Rex, and I all took pride in carrying the kindling, with which our mother's cooking fires were started. Our half brother, Bob, was big enough to chop or saw wind-felled maple limbs into chunks short enough to fit into the stove. We children knew that we had to work to stay alive. Winter was not a movie monster, against which well-groomed men and women gracefully struggled on camera. Winter froze the birds cats hunted and froze any cats that ventured too far from the barn, which was heated by the big bodies of horses and cows. Winter was cruel, but it also kept meat from spoiling. It supplied ammunition for snowball wars. It provided snow for igloos and for Eskimo statues, as pale as polar bears.

I remember my pride in cradling more and more, heavier and heavier, stacks of kindling in my arms, then carrying the load to the kitchen porch, where, stamping snow from rubber boots, I'd wait until Ma opened the door, took the wood, and praised me. Praise was important, and so was the reward of standing by the stove, chilled fingers tingling as they thawed. Fire, its heat greater than that exuded by thousands of horses and cows, cooked the potatoes Ma and Aunt Jennie had planted and harvested and piled in a wooden bin in our dark, rat-infested cellar. Fire cooked the rabbits, wild ducks, and pheasants Dad and big brother Bob hunted, after the last scraps of butchered hog were gone.

Fire kept us alive until the sun was warm again, but fire had burned my pet kittens in the blazing barn and burned men, women, and children to death in a war, in the newspaper, which my mother lit with a match, to ignite kindling to ignite chunks of wood.

From the black earth of my home rain would wash up white skulls and body bones of varmints, cats, dogs, and cows—whatever had been too humble to merit deep burial. Playing Indian pursued by cowboy, nostrils flared wide from running hard, I would sometimes scent the recently dead—from sickness, old age, or attack—slowly, too slowly, becoming bones, and I would run harder, over the centuries of life and the eons before life, which had become the dirt under my tingling feet. Rover, the big dog, on whose warmth I often pillowed my sleepy face, sometimes smelled of the corpses in which he'd wallowed.

Helping big brother Ray to scatter oats for chickens was one of my jobs, and sometimes, the brood hens off their nests, I'd see chickens' birth. It was nothing like my butt-first, reluctant, self-centered entrance into life. Tiny beaks pecked windows into the shells of eggs. Then, windows widening to doors, out would come slimy, loathsome little morsels, which would dry and be cute yellow chicks.

Ducklings were also cute, but at age two or three I whacked fluffy little ducks with a stick and got whacked myself. I cannot remember my slaughter of the innocents or Dad's punishing me, but my killing the little ducks became a part of our family's nighttime storytelling. I can only guess what might have caused my rampage. A childish viciousness inspired by boredom? A tantrum because the little ducks wouldn't let me cuddle them as I cuddled little kittens? Primal human evil? Or making war against birth, which had brought a competitor, my baby sister, into the family? No way to know. At age sixteen, speeding to the beauty of a lake and the beauty of my girlfriend, I failed to see a duck waddling into the road, but I have not become a habitual killer of ducks and not a habitual killer of—excepting flies and mosquitoes—anything else. To protect my home, I fired a shotgun at humans, and, inspired by war-time propaganda, I volunteered to kill the evil enemies depicted in movies, but now killing others of my own species seems to me a horrible last resort, not, as some politicians seem to feel, an acceptable means for gaining wealth.

In school I learned the names of wars but not, as in Health Science, ways to prevent them. At home I learned to kill animals to keep from starving.

Each winter Dad would select a fat hog and shoot it between its bleary, terrified eyes. Then began the butchering, its start stabbing the fat throat and letting blood pour out into pigpen straw. Next came cleansing. The cookstove's north end was an enamel-lined reservoir, in which approximately three gallons of water were warmed for daily face washing and weekly baths, but to make sufficient water hot enough to scald the bodies of butchered pigs—so that bristles could be scraped from skin—an oblong five-gallon copper boiler was placed on top of the stove.

I vaguely remember helping to scrape pig bristles, and maybe I added a little weight and helped—or was allowed to feel that I had—in pulling on the rope to raise the dead pig high enough to be lowered into the scalding water. After scalding and scraping, the pig's skin was as smooth as my own, and the steel tub, into which the pig's intestines fell from its split body, was the same tub into which our family had to scrunch to take baths.

Seeing the pig split and its intestines slithering, like huge, glistening snakes, is a vivid memory, as are the two tales a salesman told Dad in my presence. One tale was of African tribesmen's splitting a living human by tying his legs to two saplings, which had been pulled low by many men's weight and then allowed to spring back up. The other tale was of a white American mob's tying a black man's legs to two wagons and whipping the horses to pull the wagons in opposite directions. I remember being paralyzed with horror, and I remember Dad's speaking sharply to get me to leave and spare myself. Later I'd learn that Dad had seen a black man disemboweled by whites and had seen another black man tied to the bumper of a car and dragged until his body was as lifeless as his bloody clothes.

After butchering a pig, my family would eat the liver first, because it could be cooked quickly, and we would have been hungry for weeks. I remember judging little bites of meat so they would flavor the largest possible mouthful of potatoes or bread, to make my stomach less empty. I remember waking up early because I was hungry. I remember the weather's getting colder and colder until, finally, it was cold enough so a hog could be butchered without the meat's spoiling. I remember the good smell of frying liver and, then, the delicious taste.

Four circular plates in the top of the cookstove could be levered open so that a soot-blackened metal poker could level coals for even heating. Mother or Aunt Jennie would lift one of the circular plates, make a high blaze with a newspaper, and singe pinfeathers off plucked pheasants' pitifully bare, shotgun-pellet-pierced flesh.

Sometimes, Mother or Aunt Jennie would open one of the circular stove covers and let us children hold slices of buttered bread over coals. With sugar frugally dusted onto melted butter, the smoke-tasting brown slices of thick homemade bread were one of my favorite treats—only excelled by the twisty, sticky, sweet cinnamon rolls, which mother sometimes made if she could afford to buy sugar and cinnamon. In wild raspberry season scraps trimmed from piecrusts and flavored by red jam were another treat.

My job on baking day was to take the measuring cup into the pantry and bring flour back to the kitchen. The flour was kept in a tall, maybe ten-gallon tin barrel, and I had to stand on a thick last year's catalog to reach inside. A story with a moral told that a child fell into a pioneer family's flour bin and smothered. At school a big boy told a story about a boy playing a trick on his parents by bringing white salt instead of white sugar, and I did this once, with no awareness that I was wasting our impoverished family's precious food.

Mother and Aunt Jennie worked hard to preserve vegetables for winter. Tomatoes, peas, and green beans were boiled and vacuum-sealed inside glass jars, which were then stored on shelves in our cellar, the cellar in which we huddled when storms threatened.

Once her family was in the basement, Ma extinguished our kerosene lantern, perhaps to conserve expensive fuel, perhaps to lessen the danger of fire should our house crash down on us. Huddled in darkness, we'd see lightning blazing through narrow cellar windows and flickering in glass jars crammed with food we'd eat after tornados had given way to blizzards.

Twice tornadoes twisted through our farm. Ironically, one tornado leaped over two old buildings Pa had intended to tear down. Then, the swirling cloud slammed into our new garage and dislodged it from its foundations. Next our huge corncrib collapsed onto a new, unused, and uninsured threshing machine, parked between sections of the crib.

# 2

White Lightning was our community's name for homemade whiskey, and when drinking, my father was as dangerous as any electric storm.

Drunk and getting out of his system whatever had to come out, he staggered across a room, firing his pistol into the floor. Nine bullets splintered wood up to and then around my bare feet. A circle of white splinters held me, numb and terrified. My four-year-old body's only injuries were scratches, but the man triggering bullets was the one who'd fathered me, and my mind suffered wounds that have not healed in all of these years, wounds with which one learns to live, knowing they'll never be healed.

From the north bedroom, the room in which their five children were born, my parents moved to a somewhat larger room, beyond the living room and beyond the combined dining room and kitchen, at the south end of the house. My younger brother, Rex, and I then slept in the bed in which we'd been born, and my sister, Ruth, slept in a child-size bed at the opposite end of the room.

In shadows and darkness I awoke and heard singing. There was no electricity in our house, and an inherited, battery-driven radio, the size of a garbage can, had been silent for years. The voices were those of angels, I knew, though I was not being raised as a Christian. Seventy some years later I think of what I believe was a spiritual experience, a moment of tranquility and beauty in the troubled life of the child I was. A dream? Perhaps. But a spiritual experience.

As an eighteen-year-old soldier I would remember my childhood experience one night when I heard women's voices singing inside an air-base chapel, near Laredo, Texas, on the Mexican border. I was alone, and I stood for a long time, surrounded by darkness and hearing the singing from the small, lighted chapel.

A few years ago one of my editors, a self-proclaimed atheist, suggested that I touch a large stone inside the cathedral in Padova, Italy. I touched the stone and felt the rhythms of centuries of voices, maybe yearning, maybe sad, as if each rock crystal throbbed with the feelings of hundreds of generations of lives. The feelings were like music, and I felt a calm sense of acceptance, of inclusion. The memory takes me to my center, even as the Padova stone is a center in a cathedral so vast the focus is not only upward toward God but horizontal, as one goes from painting to painting, statue to statue, altar to altar, breathing molecule after molecule of precious incense-fragrant air.

Awakening one dawn I saw a lone man walking north on the road past our house. Later that day there was some grownup discussion about the recent theft of chickens from our henhouse and maybe some mention of a man we'd hired from time to time to help with fieldwork. I said that I'd seen our hired man walking up the road. Why I said that I don't know. A childish trick to get some attention from grownups, maybe. Anyway, my testimony increased suspicion of an innocent man, who'd always been kind to me and my brothers and sister, a man I'd always liked, and our family never hired him again.

The same year in which I bore false witness I started a fight with a fellow grade school boy, and then, when he was about to pin me to the ground, I punched him in the face. I remember, as clearly as I remember some of my adult guilts, the unreasonable dislike I felt for the other boy. I remember that the yellow snot strings from each of his nostrils justified, to my third-grade mind, cruelty.

I struck hard, and my victim's lip spurted blood. He let out sissy baby sobs and told our teacher, who made me work at my desk and miss the rest of recess playtime.

In the year in which I committed a playground aggression, Adolf Hitler was orating about revenge. From the depths of humiliation and near-starvation imposed by England, France, and the United States, Germany, united under Hitler's dictatorship, emerged prosperous and proud. Ceaselessly propagandized, the German population felt moved to be led on and on, to greater victories, greater glory.

While the world was gathering itself for the satisfaction it felt it would find in more slaughter, I achieved a new wrestling technique and, for weeks, slammed my older brother Ray onto the black earth of our Iowa farm. The image of myself as the conqueror of my two-years-older brother persisted until he timed his fists to meet my lunges and knocked me flat. I jumped up, enraged, and, abandoning all of the new-learned skills that had served and then betrayed me, I charged. Ray knocked me onto my back again. Courage, grit, anger, sibling rivalry—male stupidity—I charged several times, while Nazi, Fascist, and Falangist soldiers were overthrowing the elected government in Spain, and I was knocked down several times before I accepted defeat.

I'm a little bit mad at you, many Americans timidly say today. I'm a little bit hungry, little bit tired. It's a little bit dangerous. He/she's a little bit selfish, little bit irresponsible, little bit crazy. That girl's a pretty little thing. And after marriage—traditionally, old-fashionedly, or retro—the little woman. The Unites States loves the word "little."

Damned little fool.

Where I grew up, "little" was not a compliment when applied to males. I wanted to be big.

Some neighbors had dasher churns, wooden vessels into which a wooden paddle was rapidly moved up and down to transform cream into butter. My mother's churn was a gallon-size glass jar with a screw-on lid, atop which a geared mechanism was soldered or bolted. Turning a crank made the gears spin two metal paddles inside the glass jar. Turning the crank was sometimes my job, and I'd proudly turn and turn, feeling that I was big, feeling that I was a worthy human being.

My father taught me to strike one ear of corn against a second ear of corn and create a gap in its rows of yellow, white, red, or blue kernels. Rubbing the striker ear back and forth in the gap would dislodge more and more kernels to fall into a pail, the patter of hard kernels against steel like that of sleet against glass at first, then softer as kernels fell onto kernels, the sounds like those of rain on a mossy roof. As the gap in an ear of corn got bigger, it was easier to pry loose remaining kernels. Divide and conquer, that was the stratagem—divide the Cherokee from the Shawnee, the Blackfeet from the Crow—and—Manifest Destiny, civilization of "the savages"—seizure of homelands, genocide.

Pa would do many ears while I'd do a few, but I felt proud. Pa let me carry a lightly loaded bucket to feed the little pigs. As the pigs grew, so did I, and I carried heavier and heavier loads of corn kernels—bright yellow or bright white, with a scattering of red, blue, and mottled kernels, from ears that our Caucasian neighbors, and we, called "Indian corn," unaware that all corn was Indian corn, unknown to Europeans until they'd invaded the New World.

The piglets I fed were as cute as kittens, but I didn't try to pet them because, Dad warned, the enormous mother pig, the sow, would clamp corn-crunching teeth around my little arm and pull me into the pen and eat me. A neighbor had been eaten by his own pigs after he'd had a heart attack and fallen inside the pig pen.

A friend, a woman, a musician, mentioned yesterday the singers known by their Italian name, *castrati*, males who were castrated in childhood so they could continue singing as sopranos, with "the voice of a child but with the awareness of a grown man."

Dad cut off piglets' little testicles, not to preserve the quality of their squeals but to keep their flesh from tasting "strong" after they were grown up and butchered.

What Mom called "my shame" had to be hidden from girls, and my hairless little scrotum and penis were omitted from the almanac's Signs-of-the-Zodiac man, "the secrets" written where nuts and pisser would have been.

Castration left blood-crusted slits and eventual scars on little pigs. The piglets grew and were butchered at home or sold, to be butchered elsewhere. Boys grew, and their play was shaped by the understanding that every twenty years there'd be a war.

Skeletons show that my Cherokee ancestors carried weights while still young, bones not fully formed, joints therefore somewhat deformed. Those ancestors were unearthed from where they had been interred, bodies in fetal curl, under the dirt floors of their families' homes.

Gravestones were scattered around the home of my Cherokee-Shawnee-Caucasian grandmother and around those of her many sons. My exhumed bones may one day show that I bore heavier and heavier pails of corn to feed my family's pigs and bore heavier and heavier armloads of the wood that cooked the flesh of pigs fattened by the corn I'd carried.

Thus, this, my brother and sister mortals, is my hopefully not-too-soon-to-end Cherokee-Shawnee Death Song. This, you literary critics, is my fame. I am the Shakespeare of pig-food bearers. One who labored to turn, a pailful at a time, tons of Indian corn into pork for Americans' dinner plates, I have turned myself into a post-Elizabethan word magician, who turns glacier-deposited cornfields' megatons into air so insubstantial he can bear it on his tongue and fit it into others' brains. I am one who makes horses, as huge as elephants, haul the weight of an abundant harvest into those tiny tunnels inside your heads, your ears. The deer I carry across my shoulders I turn into eons of megatons of earth's creation of centuries of leafy browse, become venison, become memory of hungry flesh weary from bearing a dead creature's accumulation of years, mind carrying the greater weight of having killed and thus having assumed the burden that all living—and therefore dying—creatures must bear.

My each day older and weaker flesh will become earth. More enduring, my bones will be monuments to a small human's laboring to be worthy of life—a small human's laboring to lift heavier and heavier burdens to feed animals, who'd themselves become food.

# 3

One morning, in my fourth autumn, my big brothers off to school — no games to win or lose, no fights — I savored a tiny yellow-blossomed sheep's clover and waited, my back against the big corner post of the woven-wire fence, which protected Mom's garden from any loose cow or sheep. I'd helped a hired man construct the fence. I'd helped by listening to his stories and letting that childless married man know the joy his wife had not yet given him, the joy of being pestered by a small child. He'd introduced me to the interestingly sour flavor of sheep's clover, which grew wild where one stretch of fence stopped short of meeting another stretch of fence, the gap between the two just big enough to let me through.

Beyond the fence and across the road were a schoolhouse and teeter-totter and swings. At morning recess the children, including my two brothers, were let out for a while to play — maybe hide and seek; maybe red rover, red rover, cross over, cross over; maybe pum pum pullaway, if you don't run, I'll pull you away; maybe gender-integrated baseball. Lonely and wanting to play, too, I slipped through the fence and crossed the road. The teacher was probably using recess for grading papers. She didn't know about her extra pupil, and by scampering back across the road when the end-of-recess bell rang, I contrived to enjoy many play times before I got caught — caught because someone tattled or because I didn't leave my fun fast enough.

My mother was working hard to empty the garden into canning jars for the coming winter. Probably feeling that my little sister was providing her with enough pestering, she yielded to my wish and, kindergarten not yet heard of, let me enter first grade at age four.

During school recess times I'd enjoyed the playground's wooden teeter-totter, its rope-strung rubber-tire swing, and its dozen or so playmates, and the big kids had been delighted to have a little one to baby for the fifteen minutes of recess. I had thought that first grade would be an all-day playtime. My first day of being an actual pupil, I joined in a game of hide and seek before school started and hid in a lilac bush. When the teacher pulled a rope to ring a bell, high up in a little belfry atop the shingled roof, all of my playmates ran to stand in the shadow of a wind-whipped flag and make a murmuring like that I'd heard when shushed and guided past a church.

The teacher and the line of pupils went indoors, but no one had chanted, "Allee-all-out in free," and I stayed in the lilac bush. The teacher sent my big brother Ray out, but he did not find me. Although she'd never joined in the games at recess, the teacher herself came out and looked around, calling my name. She checked the woodshed, a windowless, dark, and scary place. She checked the boys' toilet, a wooden cubicle with a dark, smelly pit dug under a wooden seat, into which two holes had been sawed. She checked the girls' toilet. She made a final check of the deep road ditch and looked toward the gap in the garden fence. Then, hearing increasing noise from inside the school, she went back in.

At first it was pleasant being alone and free to daydream and exult in having hidden so well. It was pleasant, breathing the fragrance of lilac leaves and the faint, lingering fragrance of a few blossoms, which had wilted and turned as brown as Dad's pipe tobacco but had not fallen.

It was pleasant, but I began to miss my interesting play group. After a short while I went to the door, through which all of my big playmates had disappeared. The door was heavy, but carrying bucketfuls of shelled corn had given me strength. I got the door opened wide enough to admit my scrawny little body. The hallway was shadowy and quiet and empty and scary, but a lone window lighted an enamel water dispenser inside a small alcove, and the reflected light showed two doors. I chose the door at the darker end of the hall, pushed, and, entering a room with many windows, I saw my playmates, seated in rows as straight as those in which they'd stood beneath the flag. Everyone was grinning and holding fingers to lips, to shush me, and pointing toward the second hall door, which was still swinging from the teacher's having gone out for a second try at finding me.

I was the school bad boy. I was a hero.

When, finally, the teacher came back in, she found her new pupil, in the smallest seat available to him.

A pencil drawing she made and gave to my mother shows that my feet dangle, unable to reach the floor, and on my desk is one of the books into whose knowledge I'd have to grow.

Starting school early added two years of joyful playground experience to my life, and it may have given my social skills a jumpstart, but in fifth grade I encountered arithmetic with the shocked puzzlement of a child happening into the parents' marital chamber at an inopportune moment. Only the after-school tutoring of a kind teacher enabled me to minimally coexist with arithmetic and not be kept back a year. My younger brother, Rex, would graduate from college cum laude in mathematics, but I still have moments of aphasia when trying to balance the checkbook or cope with income tax.

My father, my mother, and Aunt Jennie told bedtime stories, stories that let me and my brothers and my sister know who we had come from, who we were. My mother and my aunt also read from books. I remember the story of a Russian family's throwing their baby to wolves pursuing their sled. The older family members escaped while the wolves contented themselves with the morsel sacrificed to them. Of poems I remember a boy who stood on the burning deck, "whence"—a word as lovely as old crockery—"whence all but he had fled." The boy refused rescue because his father had told him to wait, and, a praiseworthy example to other boys, he would not disobey his father.

Books as few as flowers in my family's survival-level existence, my father's, my mother's, and my Aunt Jennie's stories were my only literature, until, in Putnam Township School Number Five, I began to learn to read—to read what was available, at home and on the school's four shelves. I'd skim, skip, and daydream, with varying degrees of understanding and enjoyment, through *Ivanhoe*, *Oliver Twist*, *Huckleberry Finn*, *The World Book Encyclopedia*, *Girl of the Limberlost*, *Trail of the Lonesome Pine*, and maybe half a dozen others.

Kind, highly motivated teachers encouraged my urge to make pencil drawings and crayon colorings. They also encouraged my urge to put stories of family experiences into words. Thus, at age four I began what's called the life of the mind.

An almost vanished Vanishing American, gray-eyed though black-haired, high-cheek-boned and tomahawk-blade-nosed, I did not feel like an outsider among mostly German American children, except for being younger and smaller and maybe somewhat more creative, maybe somewhat more intelligent.

The life of the mind was, at age four, a lot of fun. I "read" *The World Book Encyclopedia* from "A" to "Z." That is to say that I looked again and again at photos, from aardvarks to Zebras, and understood the few words I recognized from watching while hearing my mother and aunt read bedtime stories. My teacher also read stories to me, her only first-grader. She praised me for tracing the outline of my left hand, as she'd instructed, and also penciling fingernails and thumbnails without being told.

From *National Geographic*, years later, I'd learn that in tracing the outline of my hand, I'd joined my life with the lives of prehistoric humans, who'd blown mineral dust around hands pressed against the moist walls of their homes in caves, creating the oldest surviving form of human art. In addition to praising my adding fingernails to a penciled outline of my hand, my teacher smelled like flowers, and I would have penciled nails on all of the world's hands—clasped and raised in prayer or slapping each other in applause or clenched to strike—if she'd asked.

Once, while I was seated in front of her to go through my reading lesson, the heavy book slipped, struck the leg I had crossed over the other leg, and made my foot jump up, accidentally lifting my teacher's red skirt several inches up her thighs. I hadn't intended to be naughty, and the teacher simply smoothed her hem back down without reproving me, but that was one of the first of unintended harms I've done to women I've loved, and, philosophical as I may be about the inevitability of unintended harms, I remember continuing to read aloud, stammering out word after strangely meaningless word.

Not all of my naughtiness was unintentional. Big boys put me up to what they were scared to do themselves, running after big girls and lifting their skirts. For this outrageous assault on feminine virtue the teacher threatened, "I'll use this ruler across your rear if you don't behave." Uncharacteristically defiant after the big boys' flattery, I mumbled, a pencil in my hand, "I can use my pencil just as good," and was sent to stand in the corner at the front of the room, while big kids, including the big boys who'd egged me on, laughed.

With no intention of disparaging the official, Caucasian version of Thanksgiving, I gained what was probably my first literary celebrity with a story that highlighted eating turkey, even the feathers, and experiencing considerable, graphically told gastronomic distress. My peer audience was delighted, but my teacher imposed censorship. Still, she and other teachers encouraged my precocious talent as an artist and my talent with words. I am grateful to the teachers stud horse. He preferred his black Percherons, but the only available stud was a Belgian, the draft horse most farmers chose because it was the biggest and the strongest. The Belgian stud was roan, a mottled grayish purple, but the colts our Percherons produced were usually black. The stud's owner would drive into our yard, his car pulling a trailer. Mother would herd us into the house, decreeing that we had to play inside until the animal was gone. A lady, she never used the words "stud" or "stallion" but always said "the animal." Our herd bull, too. Always it was "the animal."

Though I'd chanced to see our gelding with a presumably futile approximate erection—the dangling phallus blunt-ended and as long as Mom's rolling pin—horse sex was, to me, thanks to Mom's moral stance, the banging of huge hoofs against the wooden trailer, the whinnying of two equally eager mates, the distant, wood-muffled screams of orgiastic fulfillment, the sight of the stud horse's huge butt and ribbon-tied tail disappearing in road dust—and then cute little colts.

The stud owner told Dad of being bitten, his arm seized between huge teeth, his body lifted off the floor of the cargo hold of a ship that transported horses from Europe.

Because of their natural combativeness male colts destined for fieldwork were castrated. Veterinarians crushed the testicles with specially designed pliers, but Dad had no such pliers, and his surgical tool was the same pocket knife with which he fashioned his children's toy whistles. He'd cut a length of willow twig and slowly work the bark from the slippery wood. He'd cut a flat air passage along the top, make a notch near the end, and patiently work the bark back into place to complete the whistle. His knife was always sharpened on a small whenstone and then on the leather sole of his shoe, but he'd whet the blade again before beginning castration.

The kick from a horse-sized colt could break bones and had been known to kill a man. To distract the colt and keep it from kicking, Dad twisted a ball of soft nose in a rope noose at the end of a wooden handle, a device he called a gnout. Dark, beautiful eyes told me that the pain was awful, and if the colt tried to swing its head and get free, Dad twisted harder and increased the pain. The pain at the front end would distract the suffering animal from what would soon be done between its hind legs. When torture and the consequences of trying to escape made the colt hold its head still, Dad turned the job over to my big brother Ray, while big brother Bob helped to hobble the colt's hind legs. The strain too much for Ray, he'd get me to help twist the poor colt's soft nose. There'd be a jolt, a desperate attempt to get free when each of the colt's testicles was cut off. A swab of disinfectant, probably creosote or iodine, would complete the operation, and the rambunctious young stallion was on its way to becoming a docile gelding, more controllable and less dangerous than any stallion and less splendid.

My father's rough surgery reminds me of my medical doctor cousin's being invited in to consult with an older doctor about how they might relieve a patient's brain from soon to be fatal pressure, caused when a mule kick left an arc of skull collapsed, like the dynamited roof of a coal mine. My cousin's technique, just learned at medical school, was to drill tiny and shallow holes either side of the fracture, then to slip hooks under the damaged section of skull and delicately lift.

"Naw, I'll take a rubber hammer, and when I hit good bone, beside the break, the jolt will cause the collapsed piece to bounce back up," the more experienced doctor decided. My cousin was already packing to leave when, as he'd foreseen, the patient galvanized into the throes of death the instant the hammer struck.

For children breaking horses to work was a frightening event. Colts were frisky, little, and cute. Young horses were still called colts, and they might still be frisky, but they were not little, and they were not cute. Terrified, they'd kick and rear back onto their hind legs and paw the air and try to run away rather than endure having hinged steel, called a bit, thrust between their teeth. They'd been contentedly opening their mouths to munch an unexpected treat, and, too late, they learned the price of oats. The bit hurt their tongues and gums unless they moved in the direction leather lines, attached to the bits, insisted that they go. Don't panic, don't try to fight this, get used to it, as I have, the gentle, old, already broken horse would suggest, and slowly, slowly, like pupils in school, colts learned to tolerate being harnessed, learned to tolerate having to help the old horse pull heavy loads.

Even after they were workhorses, colts could be dangerous. Our huge steel disk stuck in mud, the tractor tires spinning, unable to get traction, Ray harnessed four horses, old Flory, old Topsy, and two colts. I was, I suppose, fourteen or fifteen, and my job was to hold on to the bridles of the two middle horses, while Ray finished hitching the two outside horses to the disk. One skittish colt, its bridle too far for me to reach, lunged forward, and the other three horses instinctively started too. I was trapped in the middle, this right hand, with which I write, gripping one horse's bridle, left hand gripping the other. The out-of-control horses tossed their huge heads, trying to rid themselves of my weight, and I was dragged, terrified of falling beneath hoofs and then disk blades, which would cut me into bloody bacon strips.

Jolted so hard I lost consciousness, I still held on, until the enormous weight of the machine and the force of Ray's adolescent arms on the reins made the four horses stop.

Years later I'd read the small Bible the army issued and visualize the Four Horses of the Apocalypse, not as warhorses being ridden to rid the world of evil but as four black Percherons plunging out of control, about to trample and disk my bloody teenage body into the black, glaciated earth.

# 5

In my earliest years I loved kittens, because my cuddling and petting made them purr and made me feel what a parent feels, giving love to a child. I loved our two big dogs because they would lie, absorbing sun on the porch, and I could take naps with them, my little body stretched across their big, soft, warm, and rhythmically snoring bodies.

Disney TV and the manufacturers of pet foods make dogs seem as nice as humans, maybe nicer, but like humans, dogs are carnivores.

The dog across the road from our farm would bark at children as they walked on the road to school. The dog was black, and to make me stop whining for one more story, just one more, my parents would threaten, "You'd better go right to bed, or the black dog will get you."

Sometimes farm dogs would gather into packs and kill sheep, not for food but for the joy of killing — like tourists slaughtering Indian Territory buffalo to near extinction — like train passengers shooting Indians. I've seen years and years of news stories about packs of dogs killing children, and I recall that, near our farm, a small girl waiting by the road for her bus to school was seriously injured by a vicious dog.

When I was five or six, one of our own dogs attacked me. I was seated in a rubber tire swing and pushing a baby carriage back and forth to try to get my baby brother to sleep. It was autumn or spring, cold enough so that Mom had made me wear a warm jacket, and the thick cloth protected my throat. Summoned by my screams, my father ran up and kicked the dog. He must have been cussing it also, because a part of my escape-from-death story included my little brother's parroting, "Dod, damn you, dit off Ralph," that night, in his sleep.

The sleek, wolf-like German shepherd disappeared from our lives. I suppose Dad leashed the dog, led it out into our slough, far from the house, and shot it. He never acquired another German shepherd.

In cities men, women, and children were freezing to death, while sheltering as best they could under bridges. Police had driven them from their homes, for nonpayment of rent, and the homes then sheltered those slightly less impoverished or stood empty, landlords holding on to them and waiting for the nation's economy to improve. Many could not wait. They starved to death or were so nearly starved they could not fight off disease, and disease killed them.

By whining and whining that I was a big boy I got to stumble through grass taller than I was and frighten pheasants into flight, for Dad and Bob to shoot. When snow was deep, I stamped through the roof of a rabbit tunnel and kept on crumbling crusted snow until the rabbit ran out, to be met by a rifle bullet.

Although feeling big because I'd helped to hunt meat, I also felt exhausted, from slogging for miles through snow. I'd whine for a horsey-back ride, and my weight would be added to that of the dead rabbit. Finally back home I crouched as close as I could get to the kitchen stove and rested while my mother skinned and gutted and cooked the rabbit and put dinner on the table.

Rabbits' flesh kept my family and me alive through many harsh winters, and rabbits were just meat. In warm weather sometimes we'd find a nest exposed by the hay mower blades, and we would try to make pets of the little rabbits. We never succeeded. No matter that we offered carrots and stroked the warm, delicate fur of the little heads, sooner or later we'd look in the cardboard box and find the small bodies limp, the round eyes lifeless.

With a possum, captured by Dad in our oat field, our luck was better. Imprisoned in a steel barrel, which possum claws could not climb, the possum ate greedily all the kitchen scraps four little children could provide. Of all our wild pets it was the most durable, but it was not so appealing as fluffy baby bunnies. The possum's tail resembled that of a very big rat, and its white head looked like a skull. We never squabbled over who would give it a loving name, and we never petted it. It slept most of the time when we were awake, though maybe while we dreamed, it raged for lost freedom, teeth gnashing steel sides of a barrel roofed by clouds. Dad said that someday we should turn it loose, but we kept it and kept it, and finally a heavy rain came in the night and filled the steel barrel deep enough to drown our pet. We buried it, just as we'd buried the little rabbits, and our pet's skull-like head became an actual skull, while all the carrot and cabbage trimmings bestowed by well-intentioned children slowly recycled into the earth from which they had come.

Little calves were always our pets. We'd straddle their necks and push their muzzles into pails, to wean them from nursing and teach them to drink the skim milk left after butter fat was separated from what their mothers produced. We gave the calves names, and we'd stroke the soft hair covering future horns and talk lovingly. When the calves were hauled away in a truck, the one syllable word "veal" was the only answer to the mother cow's pitiful mooing and to my anguished questioning.

Animal life—and death—was always a part of my life.

In the hog house an opera of roars, growls, grumbles, and squeals tell an ugly history of which herd member will eat first and most. Glossy-coated calves scatter like spatters from pooled water as a bull plunges, a roaring cataract, into the barn, torrential muscles surging, to gorge a seemingly insatiable appetite—or to mate. A tomcat, scenting another tom's lineage among a purring litter, bites to death a pitifully mewing kitten as if it were a mouse. Black remember, said that we were Indian—and never said that we were not. From Dad's brother, my uncle George, I learned that we were Indian. From older cousins I learned that my grandmother's mother was considered to be the last full-blood, Chicabob her name, her long hair worn in braids. Chicabob is not a Cherokee name but an Algonquin name, I've recently learned from my brother Cherokee Geary Hobsen. His linguistic knowledge supports what I only remember as family assertion, that we were Shawnee as well as Cherokee-English-Irish.

My paternal grandfather was, according to family, a Cherokee. A photo shows him wearing neither the traditional Cherokee turban nor the many-feather war bonnet of movie tradition, but, somewhat rakishly tilted to one side, a cloth cap. A black bandage of shadow from the cap beak obscures one eye, and deep shadows underscore the prominent cheekbones said to indicate Indian blood. My grandfather's suit coat seems to be buttoned to the point where the breastbone joins together ribs, the point at which I now bear a red scar as long as some neckties—the scar a reminder that I would not be writing this had not science developed a surgical technique for stripping a vein from my leg and transplanting it to serve as an artery for my heart. Between suit coat lapels my grandfather's necktie, his "sisal," is slightly skewed to one side, and I, who once made a living as a portrait photographer, cannot straighten the tie. My Cherokee medicine man grandfather resembles his son, my uncle George, who resembles the Cherokee medicine man known as Jukiah, the one I've been said to resemble.

When Grandfather Salisbury was asked if he'd like to take what might be his only chance to meet me, his Iowa grandson, then playing with other kids in the nearby backyard, his reported response was, "Naw, I don't think I keer to."

From stories I somewhat know my absentee Grandfather Parm, and I know him from his medicines, which my father copied. Sassafrass tea, made with shavings from a sassafrass root, helped to suppress coughs. Pipe smoke blown into the ears helped earache. Grandfather Salisbury was "a courting-man," his "courting" leading to his abandoning twelve children and my grandmother "Mary Turner Salisbury," after swindling her out of land that contained a little coal. Survivor of the usual male love-breakup disasters, including one divorce, I hope that I have an open mind about Grandfather Salisbury, but if the case of Parm Salisbury vs. Mary Salisbury, nee Mary Turner, were on the docket, I'd be prepared to issue a judgment in favor of my loving, self-sacrificing grandmother.

I visited her when I was six, when I was twelve, and when I was seventeen, and I remember her as always old and always beautiful, her beauty formed by kindness, courage, and indomitable determination.

Today one hears often that a father has abandoned his wife and children, and the reason given is the desperation a man feels when he works hard only to be laid off by an employer seeking profit by shifting production to a cheap-labor country abroad. That is certainly not the only reason for the much-lamented destruction of the American family, but in this world it seems good to fix what you can fix, and trying to create an economy and a society conducive to supporting families seems better than creating a jobless society and then complaining about a child-welfare system.

# 6

It is over five hundred years since the genocide against American Indians began, and human mating is, generation after generation, turning the phrase Vanishing American into mixed-up melting-pot reality.

I am beyond the one-quarter blood the U.S. government sets as defining a legal Native American, but I'm too old to have gained any equal-opportunity advantages from being U.S. government certified. To me being Indian is important, because I grew up following my Indian people's tradition of living in harmony with nature and keeping an openness to visions from the Spirit World.

While my childhood life strengthened my Native American heritage, school was preparing me for European American society, and I dreamed a disadvantaged, mixed-blood farm boy's dreams, of being a big league baseball player, a football player, a jockey, a boxer, a pilot. Inspired by *World Book* pictures, I drew lance-wielding knights and elephant-mounted cavalry. I created a world, in my pulp-paper school tablet, on the backs of sale bills and in the white spaces between newspaper ads and news stories. While German and Italian warplanes battled Russian warplanes over Spain, and enabled Generalissimo Franco's rebels to overthrow the elected government, I dreamed of flying in an American warplane, a dream destined to become real.

My first travels among the human populations of this world were the travels of my amazed eyes, over picture after picture in the one-room school's *World Book Encyclopedia*. Aardvarks, with noses as long as my teacher's arms, Zebras, with stripes like cartoon convicts' clothes — and all in between — the world inside the *World Book* was as interesting and as neatly arranged as my rich aunt Em's parlor, whose glass-paned folding doors were closed during little niece and nephews' visits. To enter the world inside the *World Books*, at school, I had to ask permission from the teacher, who would, if I'd been good, let me choose from among volumes, all jacketed red and in rows like those of British soldiers in stories the teacher read aloud. In her soft, patient voice brightly dressed bad bad British lined up like shooting-gallery ducks for good good scruffily dressed Americans to shoot from behind trees, where they hid, like bad bad Indians, like me, and started the Fourth of July.

Words made the British redcoats' coats red, and I could make colored pictures with the crayons and pages the teacher passed out to pupils at certain times, but the world in *World Book* pictures was black and white. The only picture on the school's four walls was of George Washington, and he was tinted, by design or by time's altering of chemistry, as green as an unripe apple. The flag on its pole was red-and-white striped, like the foot-long candy cane Dad squandered food money for, and pounded off pieces for his children, one Christmas. The school's flag's stars were as white as frosted cookies, and when wind made stripes coil themselves up, like John Paul Jones's rattlesnake, then strike and strike, their crackling was rich kids' Independence Day firecrackers in the echoing streets of town.

Stars and stripes glowed against the sun, and the maple leaves glowed when a big girl swung so hard and so high the big boys sang, "I see London, I see France, I see somebody's underpants." The next thing I knew, it was winter, and all the trees were bare, except for our pine, from which Dad sawed one branch to be the school's Christmas tree, and the world would be black and white again till spring.

As I gradually learned to read the words under and between

encyclopedia pictures, I discovered that what looked like a sausage I'd seen in a butcher shop went by a name I could not pronounce, dirigible, and that it could fly, just as fat, sausage-shape caterpillars could fly once they'd grown up and gotten wings, just like fat rich men jumping from New York skyscraper office windows and turning into angels.

For my pictorial travels from wild-animal-populated Africa to wild-animal-populated Zoo, I had to walk for five minutes from my home, past the barking black dog, to school, but actual geography proved daunting. When I got to ride along to town, four miles from the farm, I'd desperately try to remember names on mailboxes the car blurred past and try counting and remembering crossroads and turns, and I'd be scared, knowing that I'd have to find my own way to groceries and Popeye and cowboy-and-Indian movies when I got big. I was already big enough to know that I shouldn't tell my fears to anyone or I'd be laughed at as a scaredy-cat.

Wanting to grow up and be able to drive to town, even at the risk of getting lost, I whined for my turn at the wheel of our secondhand 1929 Chevy truck right after Ray had had his turn. At whatever age I was then, I could barely see over the dashboard to try to stay in the cow-pasture lane, and when a scattering of boulders as big as Dad's head appeared, and he yelled, "Whoa!" my foot wouldn't reach the brake pedal, and, barely moving to begin with, the truck bumped to a stop.

Arlington and Aurora were the two nearby towns, where my family shopped, but they were so little they weren't at the front of the *World Books*, and I was so little I'd never learn to drive and get lost. How could I know that I'd grow and find my way to Atlanta and Zagreb?

I think now of my aunt Jennie's growing old and poring over the *Lamont Leader*, the weekly newspaper of the town where she'd been a girl. She'd read accounts of weddings, births, and deaths, and the family names would occupy her mind. Today many people know the names of movie stars and revel in stories of mansions, limousines, love, marriage, and divorce.

I've read of a psychology experiment in which New Guinea natives were shown films of pigs, chickens, birds, and other creatures they'd seen from birth in their daily lives. They did not see on screen the creatures they knew, they saw only light and dark. I remember my mother's mother's brother's son, Bill Harkin, who'd been committed to an insane asylum because he'd said that he must kill his parents to spare them from family disgrace having something to do with buried treasure and the War Between the States. Sometime after the natural deaths of both of his parents he was declared harmless and was released to live with our family. He'd been trained as an engineer and was said to have had a brilliant mind until a farm accident damaged his skull and possibly created a pressure that caused his personality disorder. After television was implemented, to condition human minds from childhood to death, my sister, remembering Bill's background in science, asked him what he thought of news clips he'd seen of men landing on the moon. To Bill it was just another television show, not real, and he replied, applying the idiom of our community to a world-changing event, "It's not all it's cracked up to be."

One time my seat companion on a flight from Ireland to Montreal was a very old Dubliner. Possibly on the basis that some of my people had migrated to Canada from a place near Dublin, the elderly man finally trusted me enough to ask the question that had been troubling him, "What is that I see out this window?"

What we had been seeing was the North Atlantic twenty or thirty thousand feet below our weight-compressed hip pockets, but by the time he became trusting enough to ask his question, we were over Nova Scotia. When I told him exactly the same thing a flight attendant's audio announcement had tried to tell him, he did not believe me. He could not accept that he was higher above earth than any mountain in Ireland or elsewhere, higher than thousands of feet of clouds below us. He could not imagine it. It was not real. The aging body, which was taking him to reunion with a son born of his body and another body, his aging body, with all its aches and pains from years of life and from hours of sitting, was real. I, with my forebears from Dublin and Doneghal—and never mind the red Indians—was real, real, but I was not able to convince another human of what most twentieth-century humans take for granted. We bumped onto earth, and the countryman of some of my people became a memory to me, and I probably became, to him, a part of his years of unimportant, forgotten things.

"You are only as old as you feel," the comforting cliché tries to reassure those of us whose various medical problems eloquently make the case that how old one feels is not entirely a matter of choice. I feel more alive when I realize that, four medically measured minutes from the end of a breath, I could be dead, a fact that seems as unreal as the earth of Nova Scotia thirty thousand feet below an old Irishman's shoe soles, nervously shifting on an airliner's carpeted aluminum floor.

Movies and television enable most of the world's humans to live in a state of illusion. My experience of screen images began in my early childhood, when our family, like other impoverished families, attended the outdoor showings of the free silent movies sponsored by Aurora, Iowa, merchants to lure possible customers. Once a week Buck Jones, Tom Mix, Ken Maynard, and other cowboy actors in white hats shot Indians off graceful ponies, while pretty women in wind-whipped sunbonnets drove teams of horses at frantic speed or wept and tended wounded men within rings of burning Conestoga covered wagons.

Before the start of one movie a big boy started bullying smaller boys in the front row. I heard Dad whisper to my brother Ray, "Go teach that kid a lesson." Without hesitation Ray went up to the big kid and made his warrior challenge. The big kid was so amazed or so intrigued by meeting a kid who wasn't afraid of him he struck up a friendship.

The kids' cartoon short subject, Popeye, was my favorite show. Popeye always smoked a pipe, as Dad did, and Popeye was a full-grown man, but he was little, like me, and after gulping down a tin can's worth of a magic potion, spinach, he would make his huge fists spin like Mom's egg beaters against the black-whiskered chin of a giant five times his size and then, with a final punch, locally known as a haymaker, he'd knock—all those years before rocketry—the thousand-pound bully into the sky, a constellation of five-pointed stars surrounding a black-whiskered sun.

After the cowboy had killed all the Indians the merchants' budget would let him kill, American doughboys, bayonets fixed, went over the top, leaving the Frenchmen they'd come to save huddled deep in their trenches. The Huns ran away, except for ones lying in mud, and a week or so later cowboys would kill Indians again and doughboys would kill Huns again, and everyone felt good, including the world's smallest doughboy and the world' smallest cowboy.

# 7

In a letter my sister, Ruth, wrote me her memory of one of our mother's many kindnesses, helping an elderly neighbor woman who had walked two miles across the fields in blistering midday sun—fleeing domestic violence or only loneliness—and vomited on our doorstep. The woman was generally despised by our neighbors, and the essence of my sister's story was our mother's transcending conformity to neighborhood opinion and treating the woman as a human in need.

A son with memories of a kind, self-sacrificing mother's caring for him, through illness after illness, winter after winter, I received sympathetically the story my sister wrote, but inevitably, my mind went to its own memory of the family from which the elderly neighbor woman had come.

The son had one eye, and the other eye was stitched shut. He was perhaps the age of my brother Bob, eight years older than myself.

Dad drunk and shooting dangerously near his children to terrorize his wife and rule the roost, my sister and brothers and I would try to find hiding places. Mine was the little galvanized steel chicken coop, around which I'd chased cute, fluffy little ducklings only a year or two before and hit them with a stick.

Our father's favorite son, Ray, had climbed into the hayloft, to hide from our father's rage. Too young and too confused to follow Ray, I was my mother's only hope. She gave me an apple for my brother Bob and told me to tell him not to come home from plowing or my father would kill him. I remember running a long way across the fields, my small feet encumbered by rubber boots, hand-me-downs from my brother Ray and still too big for me.

"Pa's going to kill you." That was my message, that was what Mom had sent me on my long run to sob to my brother. "Pa's going to kill you." Not "whip you" or "shoot to scare you" but "kill you," that was what I'd been told to say, and "God's going to kill you," I say to myself today—my brother poet Stanley Kunitz just reported dead—"God's going to kill you"—the simple truth, and the springtime sun becomes brighter, warmer, friendlier, knowing that it too will be—in time, in time, in obedience to laws of physics—doomed.

The tractor's rear wheels were each about five feet in diameter, and their lugs were shaped like ax blades to dig into slippery earth and provide traction. Lifting me up to crouch behind the steel fender, which shielded us from a steel wheel, my big brother patted my sniffling head and hugged my shivering little shoulders to comfort me and to keep me from being jolted off the tractor and under the plow. The plow's circular blade, its colter, sliced brown cornstalks, and two dinosaur-beak blades buried the stalks under glistening black earth. Pink worms squirmed unwillingly into sun and into the bright yellow eyes of birds following the plow. The birds were grackles, and their black feathers glistened, as shiny as the new-plowed earth.

Dead cornstalks, glued by mud to the lugs, slapped against the steel wheel shield and made it quiver against my shoulder. This was early spring, and the wind still had winter in it. I was cold and miserable. I was crying. Bob, more compassionate and loving than most twelve-year-old boys would have been, patted my back and helped me to eat his apple.

"Pa's going to kill you!" I'd said what Ma had sent me to say. My twelve-year-old brother Bob went on plowing, his sniveling, cold, shivering little four-year-old brother held against one warm leg,

# 8

WordsWordsWords. My father convinced a no-doubt-patriotic local banker that Bob's small war orphan's stipend should be exempt from the bank failure that was costing most people all over America most of their hard-earned savings.

Dad's ingenuity in presenting a plausible basis for saving his stepson's education money was one of many indications of resourcefulness and intelligence. My father dead these many years and some of his less admirable qualities in this manuscript, I hope that I can praise my father, the man, without presuming to praise him as one source of whatever intelligence I have. He had, I remember his saying, only two years of schooling before the school was closed, eliminating any further formal education.

Childhood memories usually a mingling of fact and imagination, I am not sure if the school closed because of no financing or if it closed because of vigilante actions' terrorizing the teacher and ending further schooling—the teacher a young woman who considered herself too good for local drunks or a man suspected of being "queer," a suspicion arrogant illiterates often direct at educated men in the United States.

Dad told a story of men, possibly Indian-hating racists, breaking into the school at night and nailing, above the blackboard, the tails of cattle—cut after a normal butchering? or while the animals were still alive? and from whose herd? For answers I have only memory of story, a confusion of horror surrounded by the uncertainties and speculations of Dad's own childhood memories of the deed and of the stories told about it.

With no public libraries or other sources of books available, Dad seemingly pretty much educated himself by reading more affluent people's discarded newspapers, labor union and farmers' union newsletters, barber shop magazines—whatever interested him from the little available. With townspeople and farmer neighbors Dad would discuss social issues, quoting from articles he'd read in *Wallace's Farmer*, the *Des Moines Tribune,* and the *Farmers Union Newsletter,* which printed the opinions of union president Milo Reno and faithfully reported the dedicated, selfless statesmanship of senators Borah and LaFollette, New Deal "socialists" before there was anything but the same old bad deal for farmers.

In my own, mostly taken for granted, education I found that I could get teachers' respect by using Dad's large vocabulary, even though I pronounced words as he did without having heard them pronounced aloud correctly. Often, for no discernible reason, I'd use the English pronunciation, not the American. My using noticeably large words caused my schoolmates to consider me a teacher's pet, and the teacher's correcting my mispronunciations cut me, as the saying went, down to size.

"Orientated," I parroted, trying to explain why Europeans took for granted the names "the Near East" and "the Far East."

"Oriented," the teacher corrected me, to the pleased tittering of classmates.

What's in a name? Last year the president of my university was forced to apologize because he'd said "Oriental" instead of "Asian."

"Confisticated," I named the way Hitler was stealing Jewish citizens' properties, the way white Americans had gotten the property of Indians, including my family's two-thousand-acre plantation—the way white Americans would soon get the homes of Japanese Americans.

"Confisticated."

"Confiscated."

And—a rose thorn by any other name, the pain the same—whites still have the land.

Although Dad believed strongly in the schooling he had never had, he also believed that humans, able to read or not, needed to eat, and when Lamont High School put his stepson Bob to work helping build a brick walkway as a manual training project, Dad took Bob out of school, declaring that if he was only going to work, not study, he'd be better off working at home helping with harvest. School authorities intervening, Bob continued the education that would extend through one year of engineering study at Iowa State College, completed successfully before the peacetime draft and World War II ended further study.

I remember Jonathan Williams, publisher of Jargon Books, saying that he took walking trips from his home in North Carolina, his purpose to record old stories. I remember his making the point that the minds of people with little or no formal education in reading are more mentally retentive. Ironically, he had rejected a long poem called "Howl," written by that proponent and practicioner of declamatory oral tradition poetry, Allen Ginsberg.

Memory. This is the Age of TV, and TV presentation is made to fade as soon as the advertised product or politician is sold. During my growing up TV was not invented, and, our home without electricity, we only heard radios while shopping in nearby towns.

My dad told his and our family's stories. At an early age he had worked at mining coal for big companies, as did his brothers, but Dad suffered from claustrophobia and had to quit the mines. He worked for a lumber mill, slamming a sledgehammer to dent the company name into the ends of huge logs before they were floated downstream. He worked on farms in several states of the United States. For years he made his living as a traveling banjo player and singer of old British, Scotch, and Irish ballads.

Some sense of my father's life as a traveling musician came with the appearance of a blind fiddle player and his wife. They were walking through the countryside, seeking food and shelter. Dad took them into our home, gave them food, and arranged for the husband to present a concert in the one-room school, where I was maybe in third grade. I suppose a little collection of money helped the blind musician and his wife on their way.

Dad, Mom, Aunt Jennie, Bob, Ray, Ruth, Rex, and I were blessed by northeastern Iowa's black earth, bestowed by a great glacier's relentless urge to melt itself in seeking to reach the equator's eternal summer, and we were blessed by abundant rain out of clouds' relentless surge toward rejoining eternal polar snows. For half of each year, the growing season, we were well fed. For half of each year we were hungry. Vegetables, fruit, and meat, which Mom and Aunt Jennie had sealed in glass jars, were carried up, day after day, from the musty, rat-infested cellar's shelves and cooked in pans whose bottoms were blackened by soot from our wood-burning cookstove's comforting heat. We ate less and less as glass jars' numbers became, day after day, smaller.

Blizzard after blizzard, snow drifted higher in fields and sloughs and made hunting for rabbits and pheasants difficult. Blizzard after blizzard, snow rose on straw and manure banked around our house to keep wind from driving between walls and foundation and to insulate food in the cellar from freezing. This insulation not enough one winter night, pork or beef sealed in its own cooking juices froze, shattering glass jars, and the rats had an unexpected food increase while we humans had less. Meal after smaller and smaller meal, snow rose higher and higher, and the mound of potatoes in a wooden bin in the cellar dwindled. I would blow against a window's magic ice-crystal castle walls and melt a peephole, hoping to see my dad, his game bag heavy with rabbit for dinner, but often I'd see only snow writhing like giant white snakes over snow.

Mornings I would wake, my own breath as gray as dandelion

puffs. Warm between my big brothers under thick blankets and quilts, I would scent pancakes being cooked in pork fat, the smell rising through holes dark in the gleaming metal ring nailed around a hole in the floor. The hole let a black stove pipe thrust up to join the brick chimney on the roof, and the stove pipe was our bedroom's only source of heat.

I would distract myself from hunger by daydreaming cowboys shooting Indians or knights fighting knights, until my brothers were awakened by the smell of food, and we would, all three, huddle as close as we could get to the stove pipe while pulling clothes over the long winter underwear in which we'd slept, pajamas unthinkable when the clothes we had were patched and patched to make them last and lard was our only memory of meat.

My parents and Aunt Jennie rationing themselves and working hard—feeding and milking cows, chopping and carrying wood to keep all of us alive—I sought loving attention by declaring that I didn't like dumb old fritters, not even though they were sweetened by sparse dribbles of molasses. Sensing the power of threatened suicide, I went on a hunger strike for several minutes. Ma's threat of a "darned good whipping" did not prevail against my new sense of power, and neither did Pa's time-tested trick of mixing butter into molasses. He called this concoction "gray horsie," maybe because molasses without butter was the lustrous color of a bay horse's glossy hide, and the butter made it look gray. I had to eat fritters or nothing, but when I surrendered, I still rebelled by picking out the kernels of home-canned sweet corn that Ma had added to batter for a little extra food value.

My worked-to-exhaustion family struggling against economic oppression, I made things worse by being picky about what little food we had. That's my guilty memory.

"No, I understand. Being fussy about food is about the only power a little kid has," responded my friend the well-known poet William Stafford. Although politically as powerless as a small child, he had declared himself a conscientious objector and had resisted the might of a nation maddened by war.

A real hunger strike is a slow suicide, more noble than defeated Romans falling on their swords or a Japanese warrior's carving his own entrails. My small hunger strike may be understandable and forgivable, but noble it was not, aimed as it was against my parents and my aunt Jennie, who had often gone without food so that I and my sister and brothers might eat.

Some of my friends are tender about wild animals, and I value their sensitivity, but due to who I am and what I've lived, I have different feelings. To kill for food, whether it's to kill a carrot or a rabbit, seems preferable to starvation, seems natural, and seems spiritually right.

Generations back, northern Iowa's hard maple forests had virtually disappeared into the furniture of the well-to-do, and deer had been hunted to near extinction. I only recall my father's killing two deer—one of which, because I had mumps, I could not enjoy eating. However, in addition to cottontail rabbits and, less often, fast-running jackrabbits, we fed on squirrels, pheasants, wild ducks, and geese.

We hunted a variety of prairie chicken, easily killed because it could scarcely fly. Its meat was dark, tough, and stringy, but it kept me and many others alive while, bird by bird, it became, like the Celts, like the Romans, like so many Vanishing American tribes, extinct.

As a teenager I'd head west across the fields, right after school, and a friend would head east from his farm home a mile from mine. If one of us roused a flock of wild ducks and killed one or more or missed, the flock would fly over the other one of us, and there'd be a second chance. Ducks were incredibly durable. Once, hunting with only a rifle, I was able to hit a lone duck as it rose, slowly in strong wind. Three rifle bullets parted chest feathers, but the duck flew on. I have killed and eaten many wild ducks, but wild geese are extremely wary, and I've never successfully hunted one.

My father, always a better hunter than I'll ever be, got several geese. They were huge, and they fed our family for many meals. Once my father shot a goose, with no apparent effect, but it flew, following the mile of sloughs that led to a neighbor's farm, and dropped in the yard right in front of the neighbor. Laughing, he thanked my father a week or so later, or we'd never have known.

That neighbor had a good sense of humor, and his humor sometimes had a witty bite to it. "Ralph doesn't mind a hard day's work. He can lie right down beside it and go to sleep," he said once and liked it so much he repeated it, like a poet repeating a favorite poem in reading after reading. He made his mild insult a part of my legend, a part of others' image of me and my image of myself.

There were hunting laws and seasons, but out of conformity to a law greater than that fashioned to regulate sportsmen, the law of survival, we hunted according to our need, except in the breeding season, which would provide some of next winter's food and the next and the next and on and on.

A spiteful, possibly racist neighbor had done some talking, and a state game warden threatened my father, "If I hear of you shooting a pheasant out of season again, you are going to find me on your doorstep."

My father told him, "If you show up on my doorstep again, there'll be one dead game warden." The game warden must have been bluffing. He never came back. My father wasn't bluffing. He had children to feed.

To harvest crops before they were lost to rains, winds, or winter was crucial. Farmers hired temporary help, and the hired men slept and ate in the houses of the farms for which they worked. One night one hired man was awakened by frightening sounds from the first story of his employer's house. Arming himself with a small rifle he had either brought with him or had borrowed from his employer, he slipped down the dark stairs, eased the stair door slightly open, and saw the farmer and his wife tied to chairs. Two armed criminals were beating them and demanding to know where rumored money was hidden. The farmer and his wife either had no hidden money or would not tell, and hearing one of the criminals threatening to kill the wife, the hired man aimed his small weapon at the threatener's forehead and squeezed the trigger. Quickly shifting aim, he killed the second criminal also.

Most hired men were reliable, hardworking laborers, but some were not.

Returning from hunting one day, I saw our temporary hired man putting my brother Rex on his back and spreading his legs. I was twelve, Rex eight, and neither of us had heard about sex crimes against children. All the same, I knew something was wrong, and I ran, alert to aim my rifle and shoot. The hired man saw the way I was holding the gun and pretended that he'd only been playing.

Shy, easily embarrassed children, Rex and I said nothing of the incident. The hired man's temporary work ended, but some months later he reappeared at our door, accompanied by a larger man who claimed to be a Sioux Indian.

Dad was suspicious, and though his visitors seemed to be friendly, he came back into our house, with some excuse or other, and slipped his pistol into his coat pocket. Later, when the supposed Sioux started to pull a gun, Dad whipped his pistol out and into aim. Our former hired man and his companion said they'd only intended to show Dad their pistol, and they left, walking up the road toward town.

Dad would next see the men when he was asked to identify them in court. They were convicted of kidnapping an elderly neighbor, taking his money, and stealing his automobile, leaving him naked and bound with barbed wire.

A letter came from our former hired man; it was addressed to my

Drinking water for us and for our horses, cows, and pigs was pumped from a two-hundred-foot-deep well in one of two ways. One was hard work. Thin gloves protecting your hands from freezing, you grasped the steel pump handle, a three-and-a-half-foot steel lever, and worked it up and down—not easy for a growing boy, but the job had to be done. The second way of pumping water was easy. A vaned wheel atop a seventy-foot steel tower turned in the wind and, by means of a series of gears, powered the up-and-down motion of a rickety wood-and-steel shaft to draw the water up into a spigot, for humans, and into a pipe that filled a rowboat-size steel tank, for horses and cows. Water for the pigs had to be carried in huge steel buckets and poured into nailed-tight wooden troughs. Our drinking pail was pumped full by our windmill or by one of us and carried into our kitchen.

Our well was the only one that did not go dry during the terrible drought of 1934. I still have pictures in my mind of cattle tethered in the roadside ditches, to get a little grass, and cattle eating dry straw because there was nothing else to eat. Some cows ceased giving milk, and that made things hard for humans, especially for children. Our neighbors drove horses and wagons for miles and filled five-gallon milk cans from our well to provide water for themselves and for their animals.

Our well had been drilled deep because the water in the earth beneath our farmstead was between two rock formations, and water flowed mysteriously from somewhere maybe hundreds of miles to the north, maybe from a glacier melting near the North Pole or at least from Canada—Canada, from which our great-grandfather McAllister had come, after emigrating from Ireland, to escape either Ireland's potato famine and/or British oppression and/or, as family legend put it, revenge after a man-killing.

Potato famine, oppression, man-killing, whatever, I was not in Ireland or in Canada but in Fayette County, Iowa, and having survived depression, hunger, and illness, I was eight years old during the drought of 1934, and I remember the first hummingbird I've ever seen. The tiny bird seemed as brilliant as a fairy tale emerald, and there was a fairy tale ruby at the throat. The bird was also as inert as the gems it called to mind. Wings would never whirr through hot summer air again, and beak would never again sip nectar from flowers. The bird had flown into my life from who knew how many miles away, toward the scent of water, and ironically, it had fallen maybe only seventy feet short of the animals' drinking tank. The bright, glossy feathers of the bird and its tiny size were vivid in the mind of an eight-year-old, and they are vivid in the mind of an old man.

Today, having to carry water into the kitchen from the one of our two bathrooms still functioning, I think that conveniences like running water become a part of our lives and free us from having to think about humble things, releasing minds for loftier quests. But I think that our society takes convenience for granted and, without thought, slips into the slavery of reassuring routine, while routinely voting for the candidates with the most money to spend on TV, politicos whose greed is destroying the earth.

# 9

In my early memories corn had to be harvested one ear at a time. A sharp steel claw riveted to the leather palm of a canvas glove split tough husks so they could be stripped off and left for fertilizer in the field. Bob not yet old enough, tall enough, and strong enough to work at picking corn, Mom, her gentle hand transformed by a steel animal claw, worked beside Dad, day after day, to harvest the crop before snow made it impossible for our horses to pull the corn wagon.

Years after we had a tractor-powered corn picker Dad still used a horse-drawn wagon in low-lying parts of our farm where mud made the use to the tractor difficult. One day, when I was fourteen and helping my brother Ray glean corn from a muddy field, the two horses hitched to the wagon started to run away. Ray ran, grabbed the reins, and was jerked under a huge, steel-rimmed wheel. The wagon only lightly loaded and the earth softened by autumn rains, Ray was not crushed. Getting his bruised body upright, he jerked the reins to make steel bits bite into soft mouths and forced the runaway horses to stop. Mastering our team with reins and voice, he drove them back to where I stood transfixed by fear of the danger that Ray had already survived. We picked corn, loaded the wagon, and drove home, where we took turns at mounting the five-foot-wide wagon's tailgate and hurling shovel-fuls of corn onto the pile growing higher and higher in the crib.

Ray's close call when the wagon ran over him was but one of our family's many close calls. Once, while learning how to unload hay, Bob set the fork too deep. It caught between wagon boards, and when our tractor lunged ahead to drag the hay rope through pulleys and raise a huge bundle of hay up and into the loft, the wagon itself was jerked up. Before it reached a dangerous height, Dad grabbed his teenage stepson in his arms and leaped to the ground, saving himself and Bob but fracturing his heel against a rock.

Public heroes come and go, but every family has or needs to have heroes, for pride, for each generation of children's daydreams, for role models.

Though not immediately discernible as enviably heroic individuals, my mother and father and Aunt Jennie were an awesome triumvirate, all working hard to feed, clothe, house, teach, and make happy five normally ornery and too often ungrateful children.

Because of a hernia my father had been able to stay out of the war in which Bob's father had died — the Great War, the War to End All Wars, finally blithely, cynically renamed World War I, but always to my father "the rich feller's war."

"Sure I stayed home, to take care of the soldier boys' women and give them a little loving," I once heard Dad taunting Mom, who'd possibly taunted Dad with not being the patriot her first husband had been.

Dad's courage was not an officially sanctioned military courage. He had killed a man, but he had killed to save his own life, not to save a ruling cabal's position of power in the world.

My mother's heroism includes giving birth to six children, enduring the loss of an idealistic, patriotic young husband and one child, and living as a single mother. As I write, the woven image of an owl is tacked on the door behind me. Weaving helped Mom to ease the loneliness of old age and to ease the day after day, night after night dread of death.

I gratefully remember my mother's devoted care of me and my sister and brothers. I have dim memories of being cuddled and read to and of being comforted in illness — homemade dumplings drifting like clouds in a sunshine yellow chicken-soup sky.

I smell turpentine in a house painter's recently cleaned brush, and I am, in memory, coughing and struggling to live through a winter's night in a cold, drafty room. Mom would get out of bed, after her long hard day's work, and walk the cold house in her white flannel nightgown, gray robe, and threadbare slippers and heat turpentine and lard in a tin can held over the flame of a kerosene lamp. Then, she'd soak a flannel rag in melted lard and safety-pin the rag inside my winter underwear, to warm my scrawny little cough-racked chest and keep me from dying. I was, I've no doubt, sleepy and grouchy and whiny under the itchy, bad-smelling warm cloth, but Mom's cuddling and crooning soothed me into life-sustaining sleep.

By the light of a kerosene lamp — whose chimney sooted black if you tried to make the light more bright — my family would play checkers, old maid (with no sensitivity for my maiden aunt's feelings), hearts, and a few other card games. Using the backs of "Vote for Dial Salisbury for Sheriff" cards, someone in our family penciled, inked, or crayoned the emblems for a game called Cordettes. I remember nothing of the game, but I remember its name, which I've never heard outside my family, and I remember the joy of being a family, warm and loving, all together. One learned to add, subtract, compete, and have fun. There were bendings of the rules to accommodate players of our several ages. It was winter. Snow was higher than grownups' heads. There was wood or coal in the stove. Sometimes there was popcorn, and sometimes molasses glued popcorn into balls.

In winter we had to pitch hay for ten to thirty cows and for four or five big workhorses. We had to feed pailfuls of shelled corn to little pigs. Big pigs' sharp tusks could chomp and grind whole ears of corn, cobs and all, and we had to be careful to keep our arms out of reach of those tusks. We squeezed teats the size of weiners and squirted cows' milk to fill pails. We put clean-towel-strained milk through a hand-cranked centrifuge called a cream separator. A creamery bought the cream for making butter and cheese, daily dispatching a truck to pick up our five-gallon cans and those of other farmers on the route.

We kept enough cream to make our own butter. Ignorant about heart-threatening cholesterol, we drank whole milk. We fed twenty or thirty rat-killing cats a little skimmed milk, and with most of the skimmed milk we "swilled" the pigs to make them fat to butcher for pork or to sell. We combed the manes of horses and curried and brushed black hides smooth. With the ax for chopping wood, we chopped ice and made drinking holes for horses and cows. If snow was so deep cattle could not wade to the drinking tank without freezing the milk in their udders and splitting flesh, we pumped and carried dozens of pailfuls of water through snowdrifts to the warm barn.

I think of this while reading in *The Book of Lapland*, Johan Turi's compassionate account of women whose breasts would freeze while they tried to nurse their babies without halting the family's hours-long trek through blizzard to shelter.

My mother was wary of letting her children out of doors to play in the snow. Every winter we were ill several times from lack of vitamins.

I think of my brother Leland, who'd only survive as my parents' and my aunt's loving words. I remember my own winter illnesses, colds, chicken pox, both kinds of measles, mumps, and whooping cough—which had killed our doctor's child. My mother had reason to want to keep us indoors, but often—perhaps when she'd have gone with Dad to town for groceries—her children would play for hours, having snowball fights, making snowmen, snow forts, and snow castles. The broad-bladed grain shovel, which doubled as snow shovel to clear paths to barn, hog house, and chicken house and the lane from garage to the snow-plow-cleared road, was also a great shovel for cutting stiff snow blocks to build igloos. Aiming sticks straight as rifle barrels, we'd hunt walruses, seals, and polar bears, right out of our one-room country school's *World Book Encyclopedia*.

Still quite small, I'd tag along with my brother Bob or my brother Ray when they "ran trap-lines," baiting with intestines of rabbit, chicken, or pheasant steel-jawed traps and camouflaging steel with dried grass near to where the dens or the tracks of weasels, minks, civet cats, and skunks had been located.

If the trapped weasels and minks were still alive, they could be clubbed to death, carefully, not to damage the fur. With skunks and civet cats, however, a carefully placed .22 rifle bullet to the head was necessary, not to wind up smelling too bad to go to school.

At some point or other the trap lines became mine, my brothers maybe more concerned with smell-sensitive, perfumed girls than with trapping animals to get money to be able to afford to go on dates. As my brothers had, I'd skin my catches with a sharp knife, scrape away clinging flesh, then rub salt into the pelts and stretch them on boards for the weeks of drying before they could be sold. This was my first success in making money—only a little, because there was a large difference between the price of a mink pelt and the price of a mink coat, but a little was more than nothing. I was growing up. I was living as my people lived and had lived for a long time. I was becoming a man.

# 10

I guess my father was a celebrity, traveling to many states and being applauded and paid for strumming banjo and singing. He married a widow destined to inherit a farm, and in marrying, he elected to limit the audience for his music and stories to us, his family. Since he owned a suit, a necktie, a diamond stickpin, and black patent-leather shoes, I guess he was as respectable as a former prison inmate could be, and he almost always changed to dress-up clothes before going to town.

An exception was his interrupting work, during a snowstorm, and driving while still wearing warm work clothes to bring a forgotten school lunch pail to his snobbish, timid, and ungrateful fifteen-year-old son, me. I can see, through the falling rubble of my fragile adolescent pretensions, his eyes, red from cold wind searching rows of clean-clothed town kids—including pretty girls—looking for the carefully combed, Indian-black hair of his forgetful son. Dad was dressed in not particularly clean rubber chore boots, a chore jacket frayed, patched, and stained with tractor grease, and a scruffy work cap, whose ear flaps dangled over ears still red with cold.

The study hall teacher, a middle-aged woman, saw him and took, from his work-stained hands, my shamefully beat-up tin lunch bucket, smiling amiably and respectfully all the while.

Fitting in and being acceptable were community imperatives. As Caucasians our across-the-fields neighbors were unnoticeably foreigners. They had migrated from Canada, as my mother's people had. They were the first foreigners I had known, though there'd been, briefly, another family of neighbors, referred to as "some kind of Bulgarians or something." The family of "Bulgarians or something" were "as dark as niggers." The area's one black family lived a few miles beyond my actual notice, but I remember my third-grade teacher, who'd grown up near them, speaking well of them and making a point about having been a childhood friend of the children. Other people speaking of them sounded worried and disapproving.

Our English name was not advantageous, whether our German American neighbors knew we were Indian or did not. During World War II a group of drunks threatened my father in a tavern, not as an Indian but as "a goddamned Englishman." An older German American present restrained the would-be attackers by telling them, "Charley is a good Englishman."

Not a parent but, yes, a parent, my aunt Jennie worked hard, getting meals alongside my mom or by herself when Mom was away.

Not parent but more than playmate, awesomely older brother Bob was a hero and role model for his four little half siblings.

Bob had a hernia operation and thus made himself able-bodied and subject to the peacetime draft. He was among the first soldiers to land overseas in World War II. He was captured in the first large—and failed—American offensive in North Africa. He survived bomb, cannon-shell, and land-mine explosions. He survived the vengeful intentions of a German soldier whose dead buddy Bob and another American had been ordered to carry. The intervention of a disciplined, principled German officer saved my brother. Bob survived a tank driver's trying to crush him and other prisoners who were being transported to prisoner-of-war camp. He survived an American bombing attack on Palermo, Sicily's railroad station. He survived Italian rifle bullets fired into the ranks of prisoners, some of whom had cheered the bombardiers. He survived hunger, cold, illness, and other rigors of prisoner-of-war camps. He survived guards' gunfire and escaped. For nine months he survived as an escaped prisoner, working for Italian farm families in exchange for food.

After prolonged malnutrition and jaundice Bob weighed only ninety pounds when he was liberated by a Polish tank brigade, weighed only a little over one hundred pounds when he and Ray came to see me in Laredo, Texas, where I was training to be an aerial gunner.

"When you were a soldier, did you kill anyone?" a girl asked my brother Bob, who'd been invited to talk with her class, and he was, he told me, deeply disturbed. How did he answer a girl the age of one of his daughters? He told her that he'd never aimed at anyone, only joined others in triggering bullets into the terrain from which enemy bullets had come.

World War II and Vietnam — the eldest and the youngest, Bob and Rex were our family's military heroes. I was no hero, only a soldier.

Almost always the hero, the cowboy, in cowboys-and-Indians play, Ray was denied the role of military hero because our father refused to sign for him to join the navy, sparing his favorite son the dangers of combat but ironically dooming him to suffer, at age fifty, the heart attack that proper medical care in the navy might have prevented.

For nearly two and one half years I endured dangers in bomber training and did okay. As a man who believes that war is as outmoded as the practice of draining sick people's blood as a medical remedy, the heroism I choose to claim is for having refused to carpet-bomb civilians during my country's attempt to subdue North Korea.

"To protest the Korean War, I resigned from my post as a United Nations translator," Dan Levin, a novelist, scholar, editor, and veteran of World War II, told me, "but was that war the lesser of two evils? I still don't know."

And I still don't know if my farewell to arms was the least of many evils, still don't know if a massive human effort to replace war with peaceful alternatives would be effective. The United Nations is a hope, small nations banding together to oppose or at least modulate the direct or indirect imperialism of larger nations is a hope, but I still don't know if there is any alternative to nuclear extermination of the human race. Hope. Optimism. I dream, as I move toward my individual extermination, one day, one beautiful day, at a time.

"You stop vilifying those little ones," my mother would say to me, and I regretfully suspect that I was sometimes a bully while playing games with my sister, Ruth, two years younger than me, and my little brother, Rex, four years younger.

Ruth did not take age-and-sex-discrimination lightly. Once, considering me to be too rough in a game, she picked up an empty medicine bottle or one of Dad's empty whiskey bottles and bopped me on my daydream-addled head. In some other child-size disagreement Ruth threw a knife—not an impressive butchering blade but a dull, butter-spreading table knife—and the knife missed my gleefully fleeing body but did not miss the window, past which I fled, a window Dad would have to replace before the season of cold and snow, and replacement would cost dollars we'd need for coal and food.

The only girl in our family, Ruth jumped from a high platform into cushioning hay, to prove herself to be like her brothers, brave.

Daddy's girl, a favored child most of the time, Ruth sassed Dad one time too many instead of doing whatever work he'd told her to do, and he whipped her, as he often whipped her rough brothers, with a razor strop. Enduring pain, she remained heroically defiant and either prevailed or at least impressed me so deeply I've remembered her as prevailing.

In a family dominated by males, my sister Ruth could only declare herself by rebellion. Visiting our father's mother, she refused to sleep with the old lady. Dad threatened his only daughter, "If you don't behave, I'm going to get rid of you and get me a little nigger girl."

Ruth, probably four years old at this time and innocent of any racist implications, declared, "I don't care if you get one as black as the ace of spades."

Granny, Dad's mother, cried, delighted, "I never saw anyone stand up to Charley before."

After persuasion or coercion Ruth—destined to become vice president of a bank, despite her liberal politics—obeyed, but rebellious still, she wet the bed.

She was raised to be a lady, not working in the fields, but outnumbered four to one by unchivalric male playmates, she learned to be strong.

"I was so mad that, at one point, I almost tripped him and gave him a shove into the vault, even if he did have a gun," Ruth told me, referring to the man who'd robbed the bank where she was at work. She'd already toed the hidden switch to bring the highway patrol, and following bank guidelines not to resist and endanger herself and a bank customer, my sister controlled her temper. She helped the customer, an elderly lady, to lie down on the floor, as the thief had commanded. The thief drove away, switched cars, and escaped.

What my family called "the East Road" was a favorite lovers lane because no farmhouses, only fields, lined the two-mile-straight stretch of roadway, which dead-ended against our farm. Late one winter's night a carload of high school students, intent on beer and each other, made the youthful assumption that roads lead on forever. At a speed calculated to impress, the driver plowed through a snow-filled ditch and crashed against one of our fence posts.

Ruth saw bloody faces inside the crashed car, and the sight of blood had always caused her to faint, but after her husband, Bob Walker, a veteran of World War II and the Korean War, had thrown snow onto an engine fire and prevented the fuel tank from exploding, my queasy sister helped to extricate hysterical boys and girls from their carful of shattered glass, helped the young people into the warmth of our family's house, and helped to staunch more blood than a thousand nosebleeds would have caused. Conquering a weakness in herself so that she could ease the suffering and possibly save the lives of others may have been my sister's most heroic moment.

A hero to all of the elderly, whom she has helped throughout her years of work in a small-town bank, my sister Ruth is also a hero to me. I celebrate her loving compassion in caring for our aged mother. I celebrate her mothering Rex's children after his divorce, and I celebrate her mothering all of her brothers' children, including my own.

Rex's thirty years of service spanned the Cold War, the Korean War, and the War in Vietnam, and he retired as a full colonel. During the Cuban Missile Crisis he was taking off from the St. Louis Municipal Airport, his mission to nuclear bomb a part of Russia, when a small private plane nearly crashed into his bomber. The civilian pilot realized his error in time and avoided killing himself and my brother's crew — and avoided dropping a nuclear bomb onto St. Louis, where my youngest son, Brian, now lives.

From the concealment of darkness and trees a machine-gunner sends bullets, which ricochet off the runway ahead of a huge American plane. The pilot, my baby brother, hits the brakes, slows some, then eases off, letting the wheels surge faster, repeating the sequence erratically, to confuse the sniper's aim, and my brother saves his crew, his cargo of American supplies or wounded, and himself.

Bullets puncture the skin of his plane as he flies low, to drop ammunition, food, and medicines for surrounded U.S. troops.

A crewmate's home video shows Rex piloting a plane hurtling between rows of palm trees toward a barrier of palm trees, crewmates' faces expressing terror of the expected crash, terror of death, but the plane, heavily loaded with—equipment and troops being evacuated? American wounded? American dead?—lifts amid cheers, loud on the silent film, my brother's eloquent, skilled right hand leaving the controls to lift to signal that it's just his usual, no sweaty-dah, no problem—and he lives to fly through exploding rockets' red glares, to give proof through the night that one of our family's heroes was flying planeload after planeload of Americans to hospitals in a former Asian imperialist enemy of American imperialists, Japan, my brother saving lives at the risk of his own life, while our Red-Indian-Irish-English-American family's middle sibling was home, trying to save lives by writing pacifist poems and writing an essay about his volunteering for World War II and then refusing to fight in Korea, that essay written to support his son Brian's refusing to fight in Vietnam.

# 11

Dad had one of the first cars to be seen in my mother's part of the world, one of the very first cars put into mass production to replace horses and buggies, a Model T Ford, a "tin Lizzie"—which had brought Dad to Iowa as a traveling musician.

He was also a bootlegger, a not uncommon career combination, so I've been told. Prohibition and his travels as a singer and five-string-banjo player provided his opportunity. Shortage of alcohol during World War II and big dance bands' travels in big buses provided the same opportunity in my own time. Dad's bootlegging seems to have been a family-owned and -conducted enterprise. Some of the numerous brothers set up stills hidden along creeks in Kentucky. Dad was the family's traveling salesman.

At some point his activities included carrying two suitcases filled with bottles and traveling by train to Minneapolis. In what was either an attempted hijacking by a big-city competitor or a revenuer's attempted arrest, Dad felt a gun muzzle against the back of his neck and was told to set his two suitcases down on the sidewalk. Dad's companion? accomplice? moved up behind the gunman, put a pistol to the back of his neck, and told him to drop his weapon and go away.

Sometimes Dad strummed his banjo and sang, "God bless those bootleggers, I wish them all well, and those United States marshals I wish them in—" Strum! Strum! Strum! Strum!

Accompanying Dad to a tavern, Ray and I would some-times be given interestingly twisty pretzels, whose salt crystals crackled between our milk teeth. Occasionally, we'd be given mouth-puckering sips when Dad was testing the readiness of his bubbly crock of home brew, and I have a vague memory that Mother objected once—or maybe that was when I was given a puff on a cigarette. In any case, I remember that I took the sip or the puff, wanting to feel big and to be loved by my father, but I also knew that he was taunting my mother, and that made me feel bad.

Once, in the spirit of scouting adulthood for eventual invasion and colonization, my big brother Ray put me up to stealing one of Dad's fruit jars filled with home brew and stored in our scary, rat-infested cellar. Motivation? Probably an urge to win something from the tyrannical—albeit usually benign—adults, an urge to venture into a forbidden and forbidding land, plant our proud little flag for the future, and then skedaddle back to the motherland. In any case, the exploit was a total success. I got the jar of beer without dropping it, and Ray and I bore the plunder out to our skeletal wigwam, mostly walled with air and hidden among weeds. And we drank some cool bubbly liquid and were, not yet in our teens, quite drunk on beer, and drunk on our secret power of rebellion. And we were not caught.

I grew big, and wanting to be big and then bigger, bigger than any human is meant to be, I drank too much and drove, imperiling others, and was not caught. And luckier than I deserved to be, I did not drive drunkenly into anything. Or over anyone.

It is supposedly scientifically proven that Indians have less tolerance for alcohol than do whites. One of my two sons does not drink alcohol, one drinks a beer now and again with friends. My daughter drinks wine with dinner. All three have seen my bad example a few times, and I would ask their forgiveness.

"We're tripping," I've heard people say after taking drugs at parties.

"I had a bad trip," a friend said, ruefully labeling a nightmarish drug vision, like someone lamenting a foolish purchase.

One of those opposing the War in Vietnam and not wanting to give officials an excuse to arrest me, I stuck to alcohol, which was legal for white people and okay for me so long as I passed as white. Iowa still had an old law that made it illegal for an Indian to buy alcohol, and I remember an Indian's being jailed in my hometown, West Des Moines, Iowa, for trying to buy whiskey.

Like drinking, smoking was a male ritual. A traditional Cherokee smoker, Dad would surround himself with blue pipe smoke for hours and hours, every night after work. Cuddled in a creaking rocking chair to hear his stories, all of his children became heavy inhalers of secondhand smoke at an early age.

At ages eight and six or nine and seven, Ray and I found the bowl and partial stem of a pipe buried in the barnyard. We cleaned it in the horse tank and, after drying it in the sun, did what we'd read about in a book, smoked corn silks. The pipe tasted awful, and not long after our triumphal entry into the order of grownup smokers, we vomited—puked the word we always used—puked, and if we didn't like someone we'd call him a little puke.

Traditionally, Cherokee men smoked together crowded into a small sweat house and experienced visions, possibly due to the lack of oxygen, a phenomenon I've only seen in an air force training demonstration, in which one airman was ordered to remove his oxygen mask. In a short time he seemed extraordinarily happy, as if drunk—or as if having a very good trip on marijuana. Somewhere short of brain damage and eventual death, the training demonstration ended but went on and on in memory and intensified when a gunner—ironically, the nose gunner—in another bomber in my squadron accidentally pinched his oxygen mask hose shut in his gun-turret mechanism and, in full view of myself and others, in our own glass turrets, died.

A close friend told me that in a navy poison-gas familiarization chamber, he fumbled his mask, dropped it, panicked, and ran through the entire chamber until he found the exit door and lived to escape his burning oil tanker in the invasion of North Africa and died, after years of Alzheimer's. Lewisite, faint smell of burning rubber; cyanide, odor of almonds; mustard gas, the reek of thousands of smearings on hot dogs—I passed through air porce poisongas training chambers, took the few sniffs demanded, put my mask back on, and survived to escape death in a few dangerous situations and am now gratefully breathing the air of this good world.

I can't remember when I began to dream of exploring Earth by flying over it, but I do recall the excitement of seeing a silvery biplane taking off and landing in a cow pasture at the edge of the Aurora fairgrounds. Rides were offered, but our family had no money to spare—no money to throw away, Mother would have said—and Dad, who'd once been offered a free ride somewhere and kept his feet on the ground, did not yield to my pleading.

While a beautiful airplane flew around and around over the fairgrounds, splendid domestic animals were being judged for prizes—horses, cattle, hogs, and sheep—and some new farm machines were on display, including tractors, whose engines' horsepower would outdo many workhorses, and you didn't have to feed tractors when they were not in use—no mention in the sales talks of the cost of gasoline and oil—no mention, and probably no thought, of the Arab world's someday rebelling against foreign domination, just as American Indians had, just as America's colonial forefathers had.

Some seemingly splendid humans were also on display at the Aurora fair. Actors' impassioned voices made tent fabric and my heart quiver, and drawn to the sales pitch of a tough-looking barker and intimate glimpses of possible future matings, some big boys, including my big brother Ray, let me join them in sneaking around to the darkness in back of a tent, where we pressed our whiskerless cheeks into glowing grass and peeked under the edge of canvas to see, for free, what grown men had to pay to see, a woman whose purple silk swirled as she danced herself all but bare and offered a "Louisiana belly rub" to any man willing to drop more money into the barker's hat.

One of us, still only dreaming of being a man, shoved under the uplifted tent edge a St. Bernard dog. Too big to mate with town bitches, the hapless dog would dry-hump anything on all fours, including kids down on the playground playing leap frog. Men who'd paid to enjoy a girlie show resented the canine intrusion, but the town constable was too late to catch the gang of which I was a part. We quickly became part of the larger gang thronging the dusty midway.

Before we let our parents' voices catch us, to end our fun, we got to see the dismantling of the fruits and vegetables display. None of the actors I'd seen in silent movies had ever displayed hunger, but hungry vaudeville actors, some still wearing makeup, gorged themselves on sun-softened tomatoes. One of the troupe assured onlookers, and himself, that the tomatoes might not have won prizes, but they weren't quite spoiled.

The actors' naked hunger made me feel that soon winter would come blizzarding down from the North Pole again, and rich men would reelect a rich man for president again, and spring would be as unreal as electric light on makeup and lipstick on faces on stage or on merchants' make-do movie screen, a white-painted storage-building wall. No electricity would ever ever ever reach from the shining wires in town to illuminate and warm our farm. Unlike us wild geese would fly thousands of wintry *World Book* miles to nest in Louisiana, where it was always summer — where pretty women in swirling purple would rub their bellies against your empty belly and make you feel good — and where my brother Bob would, one day only a decade away, train, among rattlesnakes and alligators, for war. At the south end of Iowa's Mississippi River, and at the edge of the Gulf of Mexico, Louisiana would never — it seemed to my adolescent mind — never be more than pictures — never be more than words words words in my frostbitten ears.

Before New Deal electricity and New Deal prosperity for farmers brought a radio into our lives, my sister and brothers and I would sometimes listen to baseball games on an electric radio in a grocery store, where we were allowed to wait while Mom and Dad did business elsewhere, like borrowing money from the bank to be able to buy groceries until hogs, calves, or oats and corn were sold. The grocer was a Chicago Cubs fan, and the games were broadcast by Ronald "Dutch" Reagan, who would, years later, find other employment.

Strung on tall poles, electric lines glittered like strings of a giant banjo and powered radios, but lines would not be strung along dusty or muddy or snow-blocked farm roads to reach farmhouses like ours until I was in high school.

When our family got electricity, Dad, frugal from a lifetime of habit, installed the minimum of nearly everything. The electric bulbs, one in the ceiling of each room, were the smallest then available, about the size of a spool of thread. Still, they cast more light than kerosene lamps, and I was better able to study and to read the novels I could bring home from the high school's traveling library. Dad's one extravagance was a little radio, and after the nightly news of new war in Europe, and reports of what was being paid for wool, pork, and beef, our family could listen to popular music and other entertainment.

I remember the green light of the radio dial. It shone like the one traffic light in the town of Oelwein, twelve miles from my home. The green light shone in the tears of a gruff road-crew foreman, who'd appeared in the dusk to ask if he could listen to his son, an Irish tenor, who was trying to find fame on *Major Bowes Amateur Hour*. Whether the foreman's tears were from joy when his son won an opportunity to go on and upward in show business or from disappointment when the young singer was jolted out of his dream by the crowd's chanting "Give him the hook!" — this I cannot recall, only the green light's glow when my father as a young musician came alive.

# 12

Weakened by hunger and sickness, my brother Leland became a name on a small stone.

Weakened by hunger and shivering when blizzard winds sent drafts and a powdering of snow into our house, my family was often ill, and drinking from the same water dipper, the water so cold it made teeth ache, we passed germs around. Someone may have known about vitamins somewhere. We didn't, and even if we had, there'd have been few in what food we could afford. I was five or six when I saw—and ate—my first orange, brought by a distant cousin from Florida, a generous, middle-aged lady who tried to hug me and Ray when we came home from school but only succeeded in sending us bashfully scurrying under a table.

In the Depression's winter months our milk herd was our salvation, and hay stored in the barn loft was the milk herd's salvation.

I remember being cautioned, while carrying a kerosene lantern into the straw and hay of the barn. I remember Dad or Mom carefully suspending the lantern from a nail driven into one of the enormous ceiling beams. My lantern-cast shadow would stretch, as big as a black picture-show ape, from my black rubber boots, as I stood beside Mom or Dad, who were milking cows while balancing on one-legged milk stools. I'd play hide and seek with my sister and brothers and dart to hide in mangers among fragrant mounds of hay beneath the glistening, contentedly chewing muzzles of cattle, and when someone else was being caught, I'd scamper to reach base and be what all humans want to be, in free.

Finally there were no more soothing sounds of milk being squirted into steel pails, and I was sleepy and ready to be found and carried by my mother or my father out into the cold and into the warm, kerosene-lamp-lit house and upstairs, to a cold but soon to be warm bed.

My aunt Jennie did not join my mother and father at milking, nor did she work in the fields. She did housework and chores around the house and did her share of looking after five children. When Ma and Pa were busy at bedtime, Aunt Jennie would read to Ray, Ruth, Rex, and myself, two of us piled onto her lap, the others perched on the rocking chair's wooden arms. If our parents were gone for the evening, maybe visiting a neighbor, Aunt Jennie would sometimes make us a one-layer chocolate cake, topped with cream and sugar frosting, which the handheld beater had spun into airy smoothness. Another of her specialties, in which she took pride, was what people now call cottage cheese, what she called Dutch cheese, "Dutch" the approximation of the German word for Germans, *Deutsch*.

Usually, my mother was amiable with her sister, but there was some friction, and Jennie seemed to know the extent to which she could make our home her own and make her sister's children the children she would never have.

I grew to keep my wobbly perch on a one-legged milk stool, a bucket clamped between my knees as I squeezed milk from teats the size of sweet-corn ears, all the while hearing the bawling of calves, deprived of their comforting nursing and just beginning to learn what it might mean to grow and be big. The girl calves would soon be heifers and stagger under the weight of our enormous bull to be "freshened" — my family's word — and give birth and begin to give milk to humans. The boy calves would soon have their little tails twisted to make them clamber up a ramp and into a truck, in which they'd travel to a city—named Waterloo, after the one where Napoleon had been defeated, in our one-room school—and be butchered into tender meat called veal.

When sap surged inside our maple trees, Dad would cut elderberry twigs into short lengths and hollow them by thrusting a stiff wire into the narrowest end and pushing white pith out the broader end.

Ray and I would stand at Dad's elbows as he worked, and he would make two of the hollowed-out elderberry twigs into popguns. We'd wad paper into the narrow end of the popgun. Then we'd wad paper into the broader end and push against this with a stick. Air between the two wads compressed and shot the small-end wad out to kill the Hun or Indian or masked bandit one of us had become.

Dad took most of the hollowed-out elderberry twigs and forced them into holes he'd bored into the maples at a height his two little sons could reach. The hollow twig became a spigot, from which maple sap would slowly drip into a pail. The pail would gradually fill, while all of us slept and dreamed and worked and played, and once a day Ray and I would empty small pails into one big pail, which we'd bring to Mom. A grimy little finger thrust into the maple sap tasted sweet, but the sap became much sweeter after Mom boiled it and thickened it into syrup. Once she boiled and boiled until she'd made maple sugar, which her little ones could nibble like candy, but boiling took time and chunk after chunk of wood, and Mom had housekeeping and planting and hoeing to do, and also firewood would be needed to keep us from freezing to death in winter.

Our breakfasts were usually pancakes and eggs and, after we'd butchered a hog, bacon strips, unsmoked and mostly fat but meat. When we ran out of maple syrup, we'd be given, sparingly, syrup made by mixing hot water with white sugar.

Ordinary field corn was normally fed to fatten hogs, but while kernels were still in their soft stage, Mom boiled them for us to eat. One winter, with food money scarce, Mom parched field-corn kernels in the oven, and we ate them with a little salt. The kernels would not explode into soft white puffs like popcorn, but heating in the oven made them split, and pig fat made them soften enough to eat.

Chronology eludes memory, but one year corn prices were so ruinously low that Dad stored the entire crop, burning ears of corn to heat our living quarters after the firewood was gone. Not selling — "not giving away" — our corn made our suffering worse, but Dad's gamble paid off. Prices finally rose, and we were better off than farmers who had sold low out of desperation.

Guarded by big brother Bob, six years older than Ray, eight years older than me, ten years older than Ruth, and twelve years older than Rex, we little kids are little squirrels, excitedly waiting to feed ourselves what our Kentucky-born Dad calls "hazelnuts," what people call "filberts" in Oregon, my present home. Bob has used pliers and fingernails to remove thin shells, and the nuts are heating against the side of our big steel barrel-shaped woodstove. The narrow air space between the glowing stove and its nickel-plated safety shield is just right for keeping nuts from rolling off onto the splintery living room floor.

The brown hazelnuts resemble little brown marbles. A nut warmed, big brother Bob gives it to one of us little ones, and we lick the nut, then dip the wet nut into a little salt cupped in one hard-scrubbed hand.

We little Native American–European American kids are enjoying eating salty hazelnuts or filberts, and we are enjoying hearing the only music we know, Dad's singing and banjo playing, though, let's say, he is singing not for us but to Mom, singing "Little Birdie," the song with which he'd courted her. "Tell me, little yellow bird, why do you fly so high," a rare song, seldom played professionally because it requires so many on-stage resettings of the banjo, a banjo player from New York City told me.

My father had grown up working the earth with a hand-guided plow pulled by a calf. My sister now has a calf yoke on display above her fireplace. Our family used horses for farm work, but while I was still a small child, my father invested in a tractor. My father was light skinned and tried to pass as white. He followed Cherokee traditions in hunting and farming and storytelling, but most of my knowledge about our Cherokee heritage has come from my father's mother and from his brothers. In the United States of my father's time it was an enormous disadvantage to be thought Indian and especially so in Southern or border states, like Kentucky. In my own time race discrimination was the dominant American practice. Black troops were segregated during my twenty-nine months of military life in World War II. During my basic training I slept in a windowless hut, as drafty as an Iowa hog house. Black troops slept in tents at the muddy bottom of a gully. Whistles blew, and black troops were rousted from their beds, to answer roll call and begin a day's hard labor. An hour later whistles blew outside of my hut, and I rushed from bed in darkness, pulled on clothes, and stood in the snow to answer roll call.

Cowboys and Indians. My brother Ray was older, bigger, and stronger. He got to be the cowboy. Cowboys and Indians. Thirty-four years old, I learned, from a historian, that most cowboys were either African Americans or Native Americans, whose low social status forced them to accept hard work and a hard life. I grew up hearing some old stories of hunting and battle. I hunted for food; I trapped animals, whose pelts I sold; and I have lived to write, as well as I can, for as long as I can, about my life's prolongation of my Native American heritage and European American heritage.

"Let's be cops and robbers . . . Doughboys and Huns . . . cowboys and Indians . . ."

A worn-out straw chore hat his sombrero, my brother Ray, two years older than me, four years older than Ruth, and six years older than Rex, was destined to snap our cap pistol, and — boy soprano voice imitating sound of the caps we could not afford to buy — "BANG" another pesky redskin bit the dust or bit the green or brown grass or fell to the Sir Walter Raleigh tobacco-tin-patched linoleum floor, which was flowered — flowered, as was wallpaper stained by decades-ago-dried rain — flowered, as were garden borders — flowered, as were sloughs and roadside ditches — flowered, as were graves.

Newspaper cartoons and silent movies made Ray want to be a cowboy, not an Indian, and his preference doomed Ruth, Rex, and me to rubber-band war bonnets around our shaggy little black-haired heads. Our poor kids' imitations of splendid movie head-dresses were the feathers of pheasants, which Pa hunted so that we could eat meat. Pa's hunting weapon was not a bow and arrow. It was Ma's dead Irish American father's old double-barreled shotgun, the two hammers curled like a daddy sheep's horns.

Like millions of kids — Scandinavian American, Spanish American, English American, French American or any-other American — my little Irish-English-Shawnee-Cherokee-American sister and brothers and I played and played what we'd been taught to play, cowboys and Indians, and once, as if our gleeful "Bang! You're dead!" had disturbed the millions and millions of cowboys gone into earth, a real Wild West six-shooter washed up after a storm. Although its rusty shape was barely recognizable as that of a pistol, I felt an awed sense that play could be real.

This sense came again when, right out of the movies and out of the unpopulated, tree-and-weed-bordered East Road, a ten-gallon-hatted horseback rider galloped.

Dust risen from hoofs kept us from seeing whether the cowboy's belt held a six-shooter or not, but while he stood guard against any oncoming cars, an immense ghost nimbus of dust appeared, in it a herd of a hundred or so steers, driven by another cowboy, who cracked and cracked his bullwhip over the backs of future steaks until the herd ambled past our yard gate and disappeared.

"Be good or the gypsies will carry you away!" our mother warned, and gypsies sometimes passed, in gaily colored, horse-drawn wagons, and we were good sometimes and naughty sometimes, and the gypsies did not carry us away.

Pa, Ma, Aunt Jennie, and big brother Bob all preoccupied with laboring for most of each day to feed the animals whose eggs, milk, and meat would feed our family, I discovered a way to get the sense that I was loved—loved better than Bob, even though he could work like a man; loved better than Ray, Dad's eldest son, who got automatically the share of love Leland had forfeited early by dying; loved better than Ruth, who was one of a kind in our shared childhood, a girl; and loved better than Rex, the baby of the family.

My way of overcoming the competition and being the most loved was simple: get sick.

Blizzard winds and dietary deficiency made my act convincing by making it real, and I was successful in persuading my mother and Aunt Jennie to cuddle and coddle and entertain me, far into the night, though they had to work at hard farm chores all day and got little sleep.

Advertisers' copywriters have, I was told in journalism class, two ways of inveigling potential customers: please them or irritate them—whatever gets attention.

To advertise my little self, to get the attention of overworked parents and aunt, I'd throw tantrums, threatening suicide by holding my breath while lying on my back on the warm or cold earth and pounding it with my heels.

To get attention and to punish everyone for not loving me enough, never, never enough, never, never, I'd hide. Once I hid in a warm, clover-fragrant manger and petted and petted little new kittens, which had been asleep on soon-to-be-eaten hay. Once I scrunched into an apple crate, straw softened to make a chicken nest, and while calls outside became ever more gratifyingly anxious, I slept.

Sleep was, and may always be, the most secret, best, and sometimes scariest hiding place. Once I trudged a long way through the long grass of the hog pasture, and so snakes wouldn't bite me, I hid on a half-buried rock, as big as our kitchen table, its flat top warmed by sun. Wanting to be found, always, always, wanting to be found, I'd left the pasture gate open. Afraid I'd been eaten by pigs, my parents frantically searched and called until I awoke and, rested, scared, and lonely, answered.

One night when the free outdoor silent movies were to be shown, my mother said that she'd had more than she wanted of cartoon fist fights and cowboy-movie shooting and old nearly worn-out newsreels' battles, and she declared that her three youngest children had had more than they wanted as well. It did no good to protest that I'd not fidget impatiently all the way through the war in which Mom's first husband had died. Mom's decision was firm, and my bawling my eyes out and yamping my head off would not get me into town to see Popeye the sailor and Felix the cat. Yamping was my family's word for sobbing. I yamped and yamped and fell flat on my little back and pounded my heels against one of the solar system's smaller planets and held my breath, but Mom only yanked me up by the arm and gave my backside a dust-cloud-creating swat.

None of my usual arguments persuasive, I decided to hide in the back of our truck. After we'd parked in town, where films were to be projected, as usual, against a white wall, I would, I thought, pound against the back window of the truck cab, and by that time Dad couldn't take me home without missing the exciting cowboy-Indian shootout himself.

Not wanting to miss the movie by falling asleep after I'd gotten there, I decided to take a nap, from which I'd awaken when the truck began to move. Unfortunately, my sleep was deep, and also unfortunately, my habit of hiding when I didn't get my way was very well known. By dusk, and well past time to leave for the movie, my parents had been searching for over an hour in all of my old hiding places. They'd searched the chicken house, where I'd once fallen asleep while hiding in one of the boxes that held nests. They'd checked the hay manger but found only kittens. They'd checked the bed-size flat rock, far out in the hog pasture.

Finally, I was hungry enough to wake up and yamp for supper. It was many days before disappointment at missing the movie gave way to merriment, and I became the little hero of a family comedy, no longer the little villain.

Red Dog was my father's name for an iron-oxide-dyed gravel, which was good for surfacing farm driveways, because it packed hard enough to keep rain from turning it into mud. Allowed along on the trip to get the Red Dog gravel, I played beside a creek and became so enthralled with the beauty of wet stones, glistening in sundown, I dawdled and dawdled, pretending not to hear my father's more and more urgent calls. I heard the truck engine start, and belatedly answering Dad's summons by yelling and yamping, I ran back to where I could climb the steep creek bank. The truckload of glistening, red-gold gravel was just disappearing among willow trees yellow with autumn, Dad teaching his naughty bullheaded middle son "a damned good lesson."

I ran and ran, jumping over cowpies the neighbor's herd had plopped onto green-grass-covered earth — ran and ran, hopelessly trying to catch up to ever more faint sounds of the ever faster twentieth-century engine, until my century-straddling, mixed-blood Indian father finally decided that it was time to turn the truck around, to take his sniveling and no longer rebellious little son home.

The world was constantly teaching me things. My main rival sibling, big brother Ray, taught me how to fight by knocking me flat when we had a disagreement. We wrestled, and, bare-knuckled, we punched like the prize fighters we'd seen, their pillowy black mittens shining in the bright lights of a carnival in a nearby town.

Our family name the name of an English lord, who had probably been our ancestors' master, Ray and I dueled, like knights we'd seen in a film, shown after Popeye the fist-fighting sailor man and after the Indian-shooting cowboy Buck Jones. Our knightly swords were sticks that wind had blown off trees in our maple grove. The chargers we rode to attack one another were also sticks, from which we'd snap twigs and peel bark, then straddle while holding the thick end as horse head, letting the thinner tail end stir up dust behind our onslaughts. Knightly jousting had to take place in the grove, hidden from Mom, who'd have feared that our swords might put our eyes out.

While waiting for Dad and Bob to return with a grain wagon and put us back to work, Ray and I were bored and wanted to sword fight. Since there were no sticks, Ray armed himself and, chivalrously, armed me with the stalks of bull thistles, and these became our favorite weapons.

Their thorns jack-knife-scraped to be sword hafts, we'd thrust, parry, and whack and wound one another's legs with the thorns at the striking end and be entertained until it was time to help load a wagon again. Then one summer we inflicted a few ritualistic wounds, and feeling that jousting wasn't fun and would never be fun again and why the heck had we ever thought that it was fun, we entertained ourselves by throwing clods of dirt at posts, keeping score each time a clod burst into what looked like black cannon-shell smoke against the gray wood post.

Saying my morning prayers and calling up, as well as I can, my loved ones gone into the Spirit Land, I sometimes see Ray as an eight-year-old standing in a photo, which includes me. We are in front of our grandmother's house in Kentucky. Both of us are squinting against the sun reflected off Turkey Creek, flowing behind the camera. These are hard times. Ray and I look like children in Prevent World Hunger posters, not near death from starvation but emaciated from hunger. And yet, as Nikki Giovanni has written of her own hard childhood, "What people forget is we were happy all the time."

In school I made use of the fighting skills I'd learned from Ray, and I won peer-group respect by fighting and defeating any boy who was of my size or at least not so much smaller as to make the shame of victory worse than the shame of defeat. I probably kept my self-proclaimed champion status by not picking fights with opponents who were stronger.

When I was nine or ten, my drunken father shot at or near my defiant mother, who had started to walk up the road in front of our house, threatening to go to a neighbor's telephone and call the sheriff. With me sniffling and tagging along beside her, she had not quite gotten parallel with the school. Bullets were kicking up dust from the road just ahead of us, Dad's wobbling hand triggering off shot after shot.

Terrified, I left my mother to continue her solitary trek toward what she hoped might be salvation. Mind nearly numbed from terror, I walked down into the road ditch, climbed back up the other side, onto our front lawn, and continued walking, while bullets made the angry sound of a boiling teakettle past my head. I walked right up to the porch, where Dad was teetering and sporadically shooting.

I do not recall what I said to my father. I only know that I pleaded with him not to kill my mother. I do not remember if he said anything in answer. I do remember that he stopped shooting, and I remember that my mother, more fearful for me than she'd been for herself, came back and persuaded Dad to let sleep straighten out whatever alcohol had made unbearably wrong inside his head.

I guess I should feel some pride in having tried to save my mother instead of simply running away, and perhaps I do feel pride, but it all happened a long time ago. Whether my long-forgotten words had any lasting effect after Dad's sobriety returned I have no idea. For whatever reason the incident I speak of was, I believe, Dad's final shooting spree. Unlike his own father he worked long hours, day after day, year after year, and suffered hardship to raise his children. Of course I am grateful. Of course I've forgiven my usually loving father for his insane times. And of course I love him and pray for his ongoing life, of happiness and beauty, in the Spirit Land.

# 13

Where does childhood end and youth begin? Memory and dream what they are, maybe no age ever ends, but confronting my drunken father's gun to beg for my mother's life was maybe, for me, the turning point in the unending childhood all of us bear in us, on our way to—and, I hope, beyond—the grave. I did something. I tried to change my life, to change the deadly fear of submitting to overwhelming violence, overwhelming force. Today I do not expect immediate results, in the world around me or in the formation of what people call my character, but by act or by word I try to change what seems to need changing.

Eleven years old in 1937, and in my opinion no longer a child, I no longer walked a few hundred feet up the road to a one-room school but instead rode on a bus to a school that had many rooms, including a basketball court and indoor toilets.

At age twelve my mother had lost her mother. Needed for work at home, she had had to leave high school after two years and lose her dream of becoming a teacher. She wanted her five living children educated. Dad agreed with Mom about education. He had had to endure the tyranny of being intelligent far beyond his two years of education and had had to educate himself. Some good genes were evidenced by Dad's natural musical ability, his powers of logic, and his large vocabulary. Aristocrat-venerating authors of my English people's past would have believed that Lord Salisbury or one of his noble friends had left a brainy bastard in the working population bearing his name.

A bookworm but certainly not a highly motivated scholar, I only wanted to go to town school so that I could play basketball, a pitiful ambition for a scrawny kid, who would always be short. In the one-room school I had taught myself to dribble a worn leather basketball by bouncing the ball up and down the aisles between study desks before school, during recesses, and for a while after school. In winter the school was cold, and the ball was too flaccid to bounce. Maybe informed by my brother Bob, who would have been studying high school physics, I learned that heat expanded air, and by putting the ball on top of the school's wood-burning heating stove until the dusty leather smelled scorched, I could bring the ball back to its round shape and resume practicing. Up and down the aisle between pupil desks I dribbled the ball until baseball season extinguished the stove and divided the school into two softball teams, anywhere from half a dozen to nine on each. A teacher-imposed quota system divided eighth-graders and first-graders evenly, no matter whose best friend might be on the other team.

No student of architecture, only a mixed-race, mixed-up farm kid with dreams, I was awed by big buildings. Before my enrollment in the Aurora Public School I'd gone there, with my family, to watch my brother Bob play basketball, his uniform black shorts and an orange shirt with a black number on it.

Before going to games to see my brother shoot baskets and to hear him win tumultuous, echoing cheers, I'd only been in two brick buildings. One was a jail, where Dad had briefly visited a relative or a friend, while Mom had tried to keep three little kids quiet, her tense face telling the world that she did not belong in this jail and that she was more than ready to resume traveling to visit her mother-in-law in Kentucky, where she didn't belong and didn't want to be either. The second brick building of my pre-adolescence experience was the Fayette Country Courthouse, where Dad paid something called taxes.

On the lawn there was a cannon, a real, big cannon — in those days a Weapon of Mass Destruction.

Inside the courthouse stairs were made of white stone, and my little feet, in their hard-soled Buster Brown shoes, made big echoes. The most amazing thing about the courthouse was a huge room where Dad and I could pee indoors, not in a rusty gallon can but in a gleaming metal trough, made, surely, of gold.

My third brick building was the Aurora Public School. When I started eighth grade, the two-story building seemed so huge I was scared I'd get lost, but by doing what I was told and by watching students who'd been in the school for seven years of their lives, I found my way into the seventh-and-eighth-grade room, found the boys' lavatory, and found the echoing war whoops and the stop-and-go whistle of the basketball court.

I imitated most boys by pretending boredom with studies, even when interested. I did my study hall assignments hurriedly and then read novels from the lending library. Reading books about World War I heroism and patriotism and seeing my brother Bob's father's uniformed photo, I dreamed of fulfillment as a soldier, killing and dying for Uncle Sam. I dreamed of becoming a pilot, like those who recklessly flew speedy Spads and maneuverable Nieuports across dime magazines' colorful covers and pulp pages, and I shot down in flames the Kaiser's Fokkers and Pfalz, in the War to End All Wars, the World War, the Great War. My role model father was Captain Eddie Rickenbacker, America's top combat ace, and in my time I wanted to battle German Messerschmidts over Spain, and battle whatever Count Ciano flew for Mussolini in Spain and in Ethiopia and Albania and Greece, and high school girls as pretty as movie starlets would gratefully and lovingly look up and give me, give me, give me, me, me their applause. I read an earlier generation's novel titled *The Crimson Tide* and daydreamed that I, a poverty-stricken one-hundred-pound farm boy, might win football glory at Harvard.

The last time I saw the school that had so awed a twelve-year-old farm boy, the building was empty, its windows starred by stone-throwers, who'd maybe not yet graduated to shooting holes in rural mailboxes. Now the building has been torn down to make a town recreation center, to accommodate the bored children of an affluent society, a society that is rapidly being torn down, to be replaced by one consisting of many have-nots and a few haves. The still quite serviceable Aurora school building was abandoned so that pupils could be sent to a recently constructed—at the expense of taxpayers—consolidated school, which included underpaid teachers, a full-size basketball court, and seating for many spectators.

To provide a fraction of the cost of the new recreation center, the town of Aurora sold bricks from the old school building, with a ghostly image of the structure white stenciled onto each brick. My kind, public-spirited sister bought me a brick, and the brick, with its image of the building where I studied rapidly and then read book after book from the lending library, is now a bookend propping up one of my rows of books.

There'd been a dusty old organ in Putnam Township School Number Five, but none of my teachers had been able to play it. In the Aurora town school I had to try to sing in what was called the Glee Club. One of my friends and I were ridiculed before the entire group of junior high boys and girls because we were too shy to raise our voices. "Chair-warmers," the white-shirted, neck-tied, contemptuous man at the head of the room proclaimed. "In every group there are what I call chair-warmers, because all they do is warm the chairs they are sitting in and do not sing," and he pointed straight at my friend and me. While warming a chair in the back row, where someone alphabetized as "S" had to sit, I learned some lyrics exotic for a kid who lived among Iowa cornfields—"Red sails in the sunset / far out o'er the sea / please carry my loved one / home safely to me."

Dragooned into singing, or pretending to sing, in the chorus of the all-school operetta, I had to attend night practices. At one of these a big fellow three or four years older than his classmates began sexually groping girls. They were immature, inexperienced, and embarrassed, and what amounted to child molestation went unreported.

One of the majority of immature, inept, and bashful juvenile males, I joined with others in bouncing rubberized-string-attached rubber balls off the butt of a high school girl who was waiting to sing and scarcely noticed our transgressions. A year or so after my participation in group sex she accepted too many free drinks at the local tavern and was gang-banged by middle-aged drunks on the pool table where I'd won some and lost some at rotation and crazy eight.

January 24, 1938, in the midst of a harsh winter, I reached age twelve, the traditional Cherokee age for the rites of manhood. I was interested in girls, of fourteen, fifteen, sixteen, but if they were interested in a scrawny twelve-year-old, their interest was more motherly than loverly.

One late fall day Dad, Ray, and Bob were involved in some heavy work, and, probably with no thought for Cherokee manhood tradition, Dad told me to take his shotgun and bring home some meat. It was practical to send the son who was not quite five feet tall and weighed less than a hundred pounds and was not fit for heavy farm work. I didn't think of that. I only thought of being trusted, of being well trained, of being, at last, almost, a man.

Boot buckles jingled, frozen snow crunched underfoot, and as ice particles abraded rubber free of manure, black chore boots shone in pale sunlight. Gripped in my dirty-white-cotton-chore-glove-protected right hand, the shotgun's varnished walnut stock gleamed, and lightly resting in my dirty-white-cotton-chore-glove-warmed left hand, the well-oiled gun barrel glistened, blue-black, except for its brass-bead front sight.

Our dog Shep quarried back and forth, searching brown grass and the frosted stems of thick weeds, his nose black in a white cloud of breath, catching the scents of hidden pheasants.

From snow-capped tops of fence posts, their cries clear in cold morning air, crows warned other crows of a danger that was not theirs, and from across frozen miles the commanding whistle of a train engine, bound for inconceivably distant cities, seemed closer than the scolding crows.

Because of yesterday's brief melt and last night's hard freeze, a field fence glittered, little silvery icicles lengthening every rusty barb. On all fours I followed my ever more anxious, ever more eager dog under the bottom strand of barbed wire and stood among cornstalks as tall as a man, above the snow, which had kept them from being harvested.

Dried stalks clattered as my dog plunged between them, and knowing that tonight's dinner would be scurrying ahead of the pursuing dog, I walked fast and slipped off the glove of my trigger-finger hand.

Frantic wings battering brown corn blades to raise a multicolor body into pale sun, I aimed, squeezed the trigger, and the splendor and beauty of the first pheasant I'd ever hunted became the thud of meat onto frozen earth.

A second pheasant flew, and firing too hastily, I missed.

A third pheasant flew, half hidden, only rising slightly, bronze belly skimming its own shadow on tan tassel tips.

I swung brass-bead front sight into aim, and, gun bucking back against my shoulder, explosion echoing, the bird hurtled on, then crumpled and plunged. Rattling stiff stalks, Shep led me first to the second pheasant, its jungle-camouflaged body vivid against frost.

My cold trigger-finger hand clenched around the pheasant's warm neck, I spun, as my father and brothers had always done, today's dinner so fast and so hard I was left holding a bloody, deep-blue, white-masked, red-wattled head to toss to reward my dog, the morsel disappearing into cloudy breath and crunching teeth. Locating the other bird, I repeated the beheading, the gift.

Adrenaline still high, I felt proud, but knowing that I'd missed the second shot, I also felt a humility, which merged with a larger humility, the humility of knowing that I had taken a life to sustain my life and the lives of my family. My family's Cherokee prayers for the life taken had vanished as Cherokee lives had been taken, generation after generation, but the feeling, the awareness, would live in me and would live in other humans as long as there was human life to sustain itself by feeding on other life.

Shep bumped against my thigh again and again, ravenous for the pheasant innards, which would be a second reward after we'd reached home, where Mom would gut, pluck, and, over a newspaper blazing in her stove, singe pin feathers off the bird, before cutting it into pieces for cooking.

In youth I lived two lives, the life of the town, during my hours in school, and the life of nature, in which I labored hard to get food, hunted to get food, and a few times had to take rifle or shotgun and deal with criminals, who wanted to take our food or our meager possessions.

Not all invaders were human. To save a few bushels of corn, and to practice our hunting skills, my brothers and I would shoot rats. Where rats were concerned, our pride of somewhere up to thirty cats were the real hunters. The mother cats were as heroic as Plains Indians riding into a herd of stampeding buffalos to kill a winter's worth of meat. One small mother cat dragged back to her kittens a rat as large as herself, a three-inch slash in her side covered by crusted blood.

Once when my only weapons were my strong, callused, hard-worked teenager's hands, I saw the tail of a huge, fat-butted rat dangling from the space between two corncrib boards. Hoping that one of my brothers might come and run to get a sharp-tined pitchfork to thrust between the crib slats and into the rat, I grabbed the tail and pulled down hard. The rat tried to turn to attack, but trapped by the width of its fat butt, held hard against wood, it could only squeal with insane ferocity, until, needing to get on with whatever my father had told me to do, I let go.

Dad heard an unusually frantic barking one night, and arming himself and turning on the yard light, he went out to find a rabid skunk pursuing our barking dog around and around our farmyard, while the dog, knowing that this was no ordinary skunk, kept on wisely retreating, his barking summoning Dad to honor canines' and humans' treaty for mutual aid and defense. Like any victor in a life-or-death situation, Dad got to tell the tale. "Soon as I got a good bead on that white-striped black head, with all them little teeth glistening with hydrophobia, worser than any rattlesnake bite, I squeezed the trigger, then got me a long-handled shovel and moved around upwind and buried the bloody mess so's old Shep wouldn't roll in it, now it was dead."

Both witness and participant, Dad had to be the bard for old Shep, and the story could only became mine and my brother Bob's with the telling, for we were away from home, caught up in our own species' madness. Call it hydrophobia, call it rabies, call it war. A madness by any other name still kills.

# 14

I'd read Putnam Township School Number Five's copy of *Huckleberry Finn*, and, at age twelve I stood, in darkness, on the bank of an Ohio river and heard, as Huck Finn had heard, distant voices that seemed as close to me as my father was, and he was standing right beside me.

I felt close to my father in more than a physical sense. His favorite son, Ray, fourteen, had had to stay home and help our brother Bob, then twenty, with farm work, and, my mother a lady and therefore, by her choice, a non-driver, Dad was trusting me to help him drive back to his boyhood home to visit my grandmother. I was four years away from reaching sixteen, which was then the legal age for becoming a licensed driver. I was small for my age and had to drive while perched on my rectangular tin lunch bucket, driving only at night so highway police would not notice that my eyes were scarcely able to see over the steering wheel, while my right leg stretched to toe the accelerator and maintain highway speed and, when the situation demanded it, to stamp on the brake.

During daylight I'd seen huge stern-paddle steamboats and side-paddle steamboats, moving under clouds of their own making through the water of a river as wide, between tree-lined banks, as our farm's hog pasture was between fences. Huge wheels steadily turning smooth brown water into torrential white foam, the boats, as big as houses, had awed me, but standing with my father beside the night river, lights as small as fireflies on the opposite shore, it was a raft and Huck Finn and Jim that came to mind.

After a few moments of nostalgia, for Dad, and dreaming, for me, I had to resume driving so that Dad could get some sleep in the back seat, wedged between my ten-year-old sister Ruth and my eight-year-old brother Rex.

Somewhere I passed a burning farmhouse, its roof still on though shingled by glowing coals, all four walls still standing but all ablaze, flames leaping, like terrified survivors, out of windows and then drawing back into a family of fire. No vehicles and no people were in the brightly illuminated yard.

My foot, numbed by miles of pressing accelerator pedal, had just touched the brake when Mom decreed, "Drive on! There's no hope!" her words saving all that could be saved, time on the road and her daughter and sons' innocence of horror, an innocence still alive to save, despite black-and-white newsreels' glimpses of London homes torched by German incendiary bombs.

Tired from his hours of driving in daylight and in darkness, while I'd slept, Dad stayed asleep longer, and I drove longer, than had been intended, my mother dozing beside me and sporadically waking to tell me family stories, to try to keep me awake. The two of us saw what seemed to be the lights of a large city and almost awakened my dad to take the steering wheel through traffic before Mom decided that the still-distant swarms of dim glows were those of fireflies, or, as we called them, lightning bugs.

When the flickering glows were finally in the roadside ditches and hills alongside, Mom knew she'd been right to let my father sleep and to let me continue steering, mile after mile, between long stretches of unlighted farms and between the dim burglar lights of stores, in sleeping towns.

Too drowsy to be apprehensive, I was driving through the dimly lighted outskirts of Cincinnati—named for a Roman forerunner of America's George Washington in civics class—before I'd foreseen entering the city. So late at night, or so early in the darkness of not yet dawn, the driving seemed no more frightening than what I had been doing, and I felt very accomplished, very skilled, very grown. My mother, not an experienced navigator and doubtless as sleepy as myself, directed us around and around, block after block after block, until I noticed that we were passing the same advertising signs again and again. More alert, I finally saw a road sign directing us toward our destination, Kentucky.

The last of my previous times in Dad's boyhood home I'd been eight, and I'd been tired and cranky at being crowded in the back seat with my no doubt equally tired and cranky sister and brothers, Ray and Rex. Needing a bowel movement, I was sent under the bottom rail of a fence and up a hill to squat behind a bush. A horse-drawn wagon full of black people—maybe the first I'd ever seen—appeared on the road that intersected the road where our car waited for me. Afraid of black people, who might be gypsy kidnappers for all I knew, I hastily made use of the newspaper Mom had provided, then ran down the little hill, stumbled, fell, and rolled until I bumped against a fence post.

Four years beyond the humiliations of my previous travel I had driven through long stretches of the night, through Cincinnati, across a long bridge, and into Kentucky. When Dad woke up and praised me, I felt very manly, felt proud.

Dad drove us south into the land of his birth and his growing, in hardship, to turbulent young manhood. We were on the Old Ground, "Kentucky, Dark and Bloody," its hills and hollows so crowded with the spirits of slain Cherokees and Seneca the two tribes had made a treaty to fight there no more. This was the land where Cherokees first entered written history, "Cherokee" probably the Anglicization of a Spanish military historian's word, "Chalaque," the Spanishization of the Choctaw word for my people, "Tsaragi," meaning, scholars say, "ground hogs" or "cave men," a name bestowed because a horde of armed and dangerous strangers first wintered in Kentucky caves after entering the

Choctaws' homeland, as refugees—refugees from some presumed battle, with other factions of our common Iroquois population or with some other faction of our common ancestry in the human population. Our true name, Yunwiya—meaning approximately "we the people"—had been, long before my birth, overwhelmed, even as our warriors had been, and "Cherokee" was the only name I knew for my people.

At some point while Dad was driving us, we encountered a road-repair gang, guarded by a single man, a shotgun resting on his shoulder. I knew that Dad had been in prison, but I didn't know if he'd ever had to work with pick and shovel to fix bumpy roads. I didn't ask.

"Oh, send me a letter. Send it by mail. Send it in care of the Birmingham jail."

"You had to be ready to fight for yourself. There were men in that prison who'd misuse other men the same way they'd been misusing women," Dad told my mother, who told my sister, who last year, overcoming shyness, told me.

"I seen one convict swing a razor and leave another's guts all hanging down."

As Dad's own might have done had he not warned, backed away around the room three times, and, when cornered, shot dead a drunk about to attack with a knife.

I remember Dad's story.

"There was a feller who'd cut other men in fights and had got everybody scared of him. He didn't like me dancing with this girl he was sweet on, and, after doing some drinking, he came at me with a knife. I kept on backing away from him, and he kept on chasing me, probably enjoying himself like a cat playing with a mouse. My third time of backing around the room, one of my cousins saw what was going on and put a gun in my hand. I warned that drunk feller to drop his knife and get the hell away from me, but he kept coming even after I'd throwed down on him with the pistol, and he kept on coming even after I'd shot him the once. He kept on coming after me, and I kept on shooting, and finally he dropped dead."

That's my approximation of what Dad told me.

The drunk was not a mixed-blood Indian but the son of influential whites, who were able to influence the prosecutor and judge, and Dad was sentenced to prison.

"Birmingham jail, Love, Birmingham jail, send it in care of the Birmingham jail."

After a year, the family finally able to afford a better lawyer, the governor reviewed the sworn testimony of witnesses and granted a pardon.

I read in this morning's paper that, after suffering fifteen years of a twenty-year sentence for a rape committed a few blocks from where he was at work, a father of two children was proven innocent by DNA testing and released to rejoin his family. In the *New Yorker*, in the doctor's waiting room last month, I read that scientists have developed a new system for improving the accuracy of eyewitness identification and thus for reducing the numbers of the dozens? hundreds? thousands? of citizens sent to prison or executed each year for crimes they did not commit. I read that prosecutors have shown no interest in preventing the imprisonment and execution of innocent citizens.

# 15

To reach my father's birthplace and visit my grandmother, my family had to leave our car a few miles outside of Maytown, named for some of our kinfolk, the Mays—one of whom was then a U.S. senator—and we had to walk along, and in, Turkey Creek. My grandmother lived on a small farm in what, years later, my university geology class map would designate as Salisbury Gulch.

At the edge of my grandmother's front yard, and right at the edge of Turkey Creek, the first poplar I'd ever seen stood twenty-some feet tall. I can't remember if it was alive during my previous visits, but by the time I was twelve, it was dead, and its gray branches flared like the quills of a threatened porcupine.

In memory my grandmother is always working, her fingers ceaselessly mending clothes or peeling and slicing apples even when chatting with her daughter-in-law, my mother, who would be "chipping in," that is, helping with the work.

I'd loved my grandmother ever since our first visit, when she'd given me sweet slices of apples, which she'd been drying for winter, but at twelve my main interest was exploring a strange new world. My twelve-year-old cousin Harold, nicknamed Hood, was my mischief-loving guide. We were the same age, but he was tall, like his mother, my aunt Beck, and he looked fat, but he was strong. I remember a cow's trying to kick him while he was milking her. He shoved his shoulder deep into her hind-leg socket to prevent a kick, shoved her against the wall, and held her like that until he had finished milking.

Small for my age and scrawny, I wasn't up to manhandling a

full-grown cow, but again and again I tried to prove myself in other ways. With Harold and some of his friends I climbed posts up to a huge Bull Durham tobacco sign along the highway and walked ten feet of four-inch board to prove that I was not afraid of falling fifteen feet into traffic. To impress the other striplings—none of our voices immune from slipping back into a childish falsetto—I opened my jackknife and, cutting and peeling poster paper, turned the fierce Bull Durham bull into a steer, thus winning the tittering approval of my gang—my gang.

Walking along the highway, back to my aunt and uncle's place, I heard the roar and felt the wind as a car passed, and, a farm kid who was accustomed to living on a dirt road with little traffic, I started to step back onto the highway, but Harold grabbed my arm and pulled me sideways, as a second speeding car hurtled past. He saved my life, and wherever he is in the Spirit Land, I bless him and thank him and pray that he is well.

Since my family's last visit Harold's father, my uncle Dial, had been elected sheriff. The salary was small, but the payoffs from, for instance, illegal nightclubs, locally known as roadhouses, were lucrative. My uncle had bought a house large enough for his family of twelve, and he drove a big black car, but even more impressive, he owned a paintless wooden rowboat. The creek below my uncle's house was deep and fast flowing, but Harold knew a stretch that was calm and not deep enough to drown his not quite five-foot-tall cousin. Harold could swim, but he was no lifeguard. Once I stepped too close to the edge of our safe zone, and, the creek bottom melting under my feet, I nearly slipped into the current but paddled frantically and managed to get back to safety.

Treacherous as the creek was for swimming, even more deadly were the typhoid germs carried in sewage from miles upstream, and we weren't supposed to swim, but out of sight, beyond a bend in the creek and hidden by trees, we swam nearly every day.

My father and Uncle Dial came down to the creek to call us for dinner one time, but we were already rowing back to the landing, our hair drying in the afternoon sun.

One time my little cousin Billy was playing in the sand too close to the edge, and my uncle was distracted by talking with the brother he hadn't seen for years, my father. Before anyone noticed, white torrents were carrying Billy's small body away. My uncle, dressed in his best suit, sheriff's star gleaming on his lapel, ran into waist-deep water, grabbed his little son's ankle, and saved his life.

Cursed by our family's genetic problem with cholesterol, Billy would die of a heart attack, still in his early twenties.

Once, while rowing the family boat to town to pick up groceries, Harold and I docked beside a house that belonged to a relative. Her son, also named Ralph, was home on leave from the navy. It seemed very special that he bore my same name and was in uniform.

After a brief visit with Cousin Ralph and his mother, Harold and I walked into a section of town where we would have been forbidden to go if Harold's fervently Baptist mother had had the slightest idea that we might go there. On the sidewalk in front of a colorfully lighted tavern a huge bouncer was again and again absorbing hard punches and again and again knocking down an equally huge drunk, who kept getting up and trying to reenter the door, out of which he'd just been thrown. It was exciting, it was scary, it was better than newsreels' Brown Bomber, Joe Louis's battering pale-bodied losers, it was real.

Hearing my light and Harold's heavy footfalls passing on the sidewalk, bare-breasted women leaned from upstairs windows and laughed, amused at what might have been the dimly illuminated sight of a hefty father bringing his spindly son for an introduction to carnal sin.

As ignorant about venereal disease—and lung cancer—as we were about typhoid fever, Harold and I ended our exploration in the red-light district by gleefully taking puffs off a nearly full-length cigarette, which some fumbling drunk had dropped. The only consequence was our mistakenly feeling that we had been very manly. Stars and the lights of Maytown families shimmered on black ripples and typhoid germs as Harold and I finally, dutifully, rowed, with his mother's groceries, home.

"Squat over the toilet in gas stations. Don't sit on the seat, or you'll get the bad disease," my mother had warned before the start of our journey to Kentucky. One of my uncle's deputies had — or my aunt and my mother feared that he might have — a venereal disease, and after some late-night crime investigation he had slept on one side of a double bed, while I'd slept on the other. When itchy pimples appeared on my groin, I bashfully asked Harold if I'd got the bad disease just from being in the same bed. He laughed and laughed and finally told me that I'd picked up chiggers while blundering through bushes near the barn. His suggested remedy, the application of salty bacon grease on vigorously scratched pimples, gave him a good horse-laugh at my expense, but it also resulted in a cure, because it made the itching so unbearable I overcame bashfulness and asked my mother. She embarrassed me further by asking my aunt Beck. Aunt Beck's prescription was the same cornstarch she used to ease her baby daughter's diaper rash. This humiliated me, but it eased the itch, and eventually the chiggers were gone.

# 16

As older brother to Rex, I suppose that I passed on some of the bullying, the toughening, Ray had inflicted on me, but the fact that I was four years older than Rex encouraged me to somewhat imitate the fatherly care that Bob had bestowed on all of his, years younger, siblings. Afflicted with diarrhea from green apples, and too shy to use the hole-in-the-ground toilet at our grandmother's place, Rex was desperate enough to ask me what he should do. I tore off some green leaves to serve as toilet paper and agreed to stand watch along the trail while a future war hero and commandant of the American military mission in Morocco rushed uphill into some bushes.

With my fatherly best self in charge, Rex and I walked from our grandmother's place for about an eighth of a mile along Turkey Creek and waited for our parents at our uncle George and aunt May's place. One of their sons, Dempsey, was my age and fun to be with, but when Rex and I arrived at dusk, Uncle George was alone in the house. Seated under the pale, flickering of a gaslight, he greeted us in his usual quiet, friendly manner, and then he resumed reading his Bible, his expression beatific.

Looking deeply into my eyes as we stood beside my dead father, my uncle George would sternly say, "We all come to this."

One time Uncle George let Dempsey and me go along on his hike through the hills as a gas-line troubleshooter, a job I'd only known from the little bottles of mercury my uncle carried to replenish what leaked from whatever instrument required mercury. As innocent about mercury poisoning as we were about a science that would, in eight years, atom-bomb two cities, Dempsey and I immersed pennies in mercury, thrilled when we'd succeeded in making the copper disks as silvery as dimes. The magic of alchemy was what we sought, not the 900 percent profit, which we never tried to realize.

While Dempsey and I aimed straight sticks, pretending that they were the muskets with which our Redcoat ancestors had killed our Redskin ancestors, Uncle George scribbled mercury-regulated pressure-gauge numbers into a logbook, to be able to give early warning of any gas-line leaks and their locations. One time gas had exploded and hurled Uncle George's wife, Aunt May, out of her kitchen and into the fire-quelling water of Turkey Creek. I knew this, and when I wasn't too busy at not falling downhill, I stared apprehensively at the black metal meter boxes as if they were newsreels' bombs.

Coming down off the hill and walking along a stream, we stopped to greet a dozen men who were operating a steam-engine-powered buzz saw, turning felled trees into boards and loading them onto a truck.

"Gyppo loggers," my uncle explained to me, after we'd gone past the men, "up here stealing timber from an owner who lives way off in New York."

I didn't ask why my uncle George didn't report the theft to the sheriff, his brother Dial, but even at twelve I probably guessed that my religious, moral uncle George probably felt what may have been true, that the New York owner was one of those outsiders who gained wealth from Indian land as if it had always been theirs. The gyppo loggers weren't discernibly Indian, but they were of a tribe, locals.

I got to see the first log cabin I'd ever seen outside of a book, and I got to meet some more cousins briefly and to meet another aunt. I'd heard that she was the best singer anyone had ever heard, but she did not sing for us. She was pitifully emaciated, in her sewn-together flour-sack dress, and she looked ill. I knew that if she had sung for us, it would have been sad singing, whatever she sang.

All of my uncles still living near my grandmother grew tobacco. Not the mild stuff Harold and I had puffed in the form of a drunk's dropped cigarette, the tobacco my uncles grew was Indian tobacco, locally known as old-twist, probably because a tobacco plant was hand-twisted to get the moisture out of it before it was hung to dry in the smokehouse, where meat was being smoked for preservation and flavor. I only smoked a pipeful of my Cherokee people's sacred medicine once, and it was so strong it made my tongue shrivel.

At age twelve I was fascinated by the symbols of warriorhood and war. My uncle Dial's Luger pistol had impressed me, but I was even more impressed by an empty 75 mm. cannon shell that my uncle Lee had brought home as a battle souvenir. I think now of my lightly armed Cherokee people slaughtered by the Weapons of Mass Destruction of those days, Spanish, British, and American cannon. I think of the many tribes massacred when European American armies employed germ warfare, using smallpox-infected blankets.

One of my cousins gave me an arrowhead, which he'd pried from a tree. I remember that it was beautiful, a shiny black with a band of red, which I associated with blood. The gift was not to me alone but to my brothers as well. Back in Iowa it survived in our family for months, but children are heedless and also wise enough to value living more than they value possessions, and one of us lost the arrowhead while playing and having fun.

Once, on our way to visit our grandmother, Harold showed me a barn-size corrugated steel building, a hole in its side. A man had been walking beside that building, and just as he'd gotten to the spot where I was standing, a piece of machinery exploded through corrugated steel and smashed the man's head. The unpatched hole in the wall was a memorial of his death, somewhat like roadside crosses planted to show where people have died in car wrecks.

Visiting our grandmother was not merely family love or family duty; Harold and I also had swimming in mind. I usually made the journey to Granny's house, and to the swimming hole, by walking and then wading with Harold and two of his younger brothers, Tom and Beezie, short for Beelzabub, a good-natured, likeable kid whose actual name was so outshone by his nickname I've forgotten it. At least once we were allowed to ride a Morgan mare and a mule as huge as our Percheron horses in Iowa. The Morgan had been trained to single-foot, that is, to put forward simultaneously both feet on the same side, and the result was a smooth journey for the lucky rider. The mare had a saddle, but the mule was too big for any saddle. Mounting by standing on a steep hillside and swinging a leg over the mule's saw-tooth backbone, I rode Indian fashion, bareback, and I had to sit slightly to one side of the backbone to avoid being bounced high and dropped onto the tenderest body part known to a person of my gender.

Fortunately for me and for my children and grandchildren-to-be, I arrived sexually intact and heard some of my grandmother's stories. Then I swam in the clear, typhoid-free water, which Harold had dammed with head-size stones to make a pool twelve feet wide. It was deep enough to swim in, without barking knees on the pebbly bottom, and it also smelled as nice as any encyclopedia's Roman bath, due to the overhanging branches of a tree, possibly a linden, whose shade also prevented sunburn. I learned the human world's most basic swim stroke, the dog-paddle, a humble distant relation of the Olympic games' Australian crawl but effective in keeping me—and, in three years, two other people—from drowning.

Courage. Pride. Cowardice? Does honesty really require self-condemnation? Oh well, briefly, humiliatingly: my two-years-younger cousin pelted me with pebbles. Feeling hopelessly outnumbered by cousins and disoriented by being hundreds of miles from home, I pursued but not determinedly enough to catch up and inflict the elder's correction of a younger required for membership in an orderly family.

As county sheriff my uncle Dial was the center of a natural vortex for violence, and in fact an assassin had been hired to kill him. Someone informed my uncle, and he sent two deputies to intercept the hired killer when he got off the train. They disarmed him and made sure that he caught the next train back to West Virginia. Rumor had it that he was a McCoy, his family half of the bloody Hatfield and McCoy feud. I'm sure that my uncle didn't want to start a McCoy-Salisbury feud, but also he was being consistent with advice he'd gotten from Theodore Roosevelt, "Tread softly and carry a big stick." My uncle's big stick was the Luger automatic pistol, which he wore out of sight in a shoulder holster under his suit coat. That weapon emerged into potentially deadly aim when a political opponent pulled a gun. Some talk followed, and there was no bloodshed. I envied Harold that he had been beside his father all during the encounter.

A TV interviewer was surprised — and maybe distressed — at some of my books' accounts of violence, and, yes, I've heard stories of some violence, seen some and experienced some.

After being pardoned and released from prison, my father moved out of state so as not to be killed by the family of the man he'd killed. The revenge ethic was an uninterrupted tradition in the hills of Kentucky, where my father had grown to manhood, and it is an uninterrupted tradition elsewhere. The United States remembered the sinking of the *Maine* and invaded Cuba. The United States remembered the sinking of the *Lusitania* and went to war against the Germans in France. "Remember Pearl Harbor" were the words of a popular song. Some U.S. politicians made damned sure that the electorate did not forget the World Trade Center and the Pentagon attacks. Should we try remembering that the Soviet Union committed national economic suicide by invading Afghanistan? that Iraq is one of the graveyards of British imperialism?

In Floyd County, Kentucky, two men met on a one-way footbridge and fired pistols at each other until there was only one.

A man sneaked up behind someone he hated for some reason or other, pinned his victim's arms with one of his own arms, and emptied his pistol into the pinned man's chest. The dying man fell but was able to draw his pistol and kill his killer.

Television, with its preponderance of violence, had not been invented yet, but hey, who needed it.

Twelve years old, survivor of a bullet through a window and glass falling onto my baby bed, survivor of malnutrition and disease, I daydreamed of being a movie soldier, a movie cowboy, a silver-star-wearing killer sheriff, winner of dramatic gunfights, not like my uncle, conciliatory, careful, and judicious about the use of force.

His peacemaker's abilities were put to a hard test when one of my habitually drunken cousins decided to wreak belated revenge on the grandfather who had forsaken his wife and twelve children.

The only grandfather to live while I was alive maybe about to be killed, I rocked with my cousin Harold on a small suspension bridge and listened to a loud-voiced old preacher talk about everlasting life. We watched while he waded, his suit-coat tails afloat, and turned to receive his first convert, an attractive young woman.

Arms pressed tight to control her sinfully buoyant skirt, she let herself be rocked backward against the old preacher's black-suited, white-shirt-cuffed arm. While he prayed, she sent bubbles heavenward and was finally brought upright, sputtering, her errant skirt a diaphanous water lily spread on the sky-reflecting surface of brown water.

A few miles away my grandfather's sins were not being forgiven, but he was saved all the same, saved not by the words of a preacher but by my diplomatic sheriff uncle's words, heeded fortunately by my drunken cousin.

Near the end of my visit Harold and I were playing a game, imitating a movie heavyweight-boxing champion, John L. Sullivan, whose huge hand was so quick it could catch flies. Harold and I kept count, to see who could first catch and crush a hundred.

The game ended when we heard gunshots from the direction of Maytown, only a mile or two up the road. In early dusk a pickup truck sped toward us, a torrent of sparks streaming from its front bumper, which was broken and dragging on concrete.

A car was in fast pursuit of the damaged truck, one of my uncle's deputies leaning out a window and firing his pistol. Both vehicles were around a curve when a tire blew out, the explosion louder than those from the deputy's gun.

We heard the story after my uncle and my father came home. The driver of the pickup truck had gone mad and driven into a crowd lined up to buy movie tickets.

While my uncle's deputy had been in pursuit of the killer, a second madman, unrelated to the truck driver, walked up to the crowd of people who were trying to help the injured. "I'm Alley Oop, the cave-man," the lunatic was shouting. He was naked and armed with a baseball bat, his version of the cartoon caveman character's club, but he did not attack anyone.

A third incident occurred in the same week. A respected medical doctor began stopping cars and offering the startled drivers' handfuls of goose shit to eat.

"Moon madness," people were saying, and, the moon moving into its next natural phase, as it had been doing for eons and eons, the immediate moon-madness episodes ended at three, unremarkable to two boys, one of whom had just killed a hundred flies, the other almost that many. The world still had plenty of flies and plenty of people, and there was war in the news.

My father introduced me to a distant cousin, a politically powerful man, who was thought to have hired the supposed McCoy assassin. The distant cousin was all amiability, not a trace of viciousness. He shook my hand. He looked me in the eyes. He smiled. He made me feel that I was or could be important. At age twelve I didn't yet know that he'd offered to guarantee my sheriff uncle's reelection in exchange for my uncle's embezzling and sharing twenty thousand dollars, which my uncle had been given to spend on Wendell Wilkie's presidential campaign.

I'd only experienced a courthouse as a huge echoing building, with a shining room where one could pee indoors, but my father told me that politicians bought blank ballots from the county official in charge of distributing them, then created what was called "the chain." A political supporter would mark the illegally obtained ballots and wait with a sack of money and some already marked ballots in an alley near the polling place. A voter would slip an already marked ballot inside his shirt, get his legal ballot from the polling officials, and exchange the two inside the voting booth. After depositing the already marked ballot in the ballot box, the voter would take his unmarked legal ballot back to the alley and exchange it for money, thus completing his link in the chain. In spending Wendell Wilkie's twenty thousand dollars to buy votes, instead of pocketing half, my uncle lost his own bid for reelection. He had not killed anyone. He had survived World War I and attempted assassination, but he would die of cancer, after working in a nuclear plant during the U.S. arms race with the Soviet Union.

# 17

Having survived some of life's dangers, including my own immature driving, I returned from my Kentucky adventuring and family bonding. I returned to farm work and to the same brick school building where I'd completed eighth grade, but now, not yet thirteen, I was in high school. There teachers despaired of my ever learning algebra, encouraged my writing, and advised me to consider spending my adult life working for newspapers. A principal, as self-assured as some medieval religious leader, declared that there would be no mathematics after algebra because the parents of all in my class were too poor to send their children to college. He taught all of the boys in my class, even those from town, farming principles instead of geometry.

In a book I read how to do what I'd already done, pull a calf from the exhausted body of a young cow. The book did not say that little hoofs that had never touched earth would glisten like sea shells. It did not say that I'd have to use an empty gunnysack to keep my hands from slipping off the little forelegs when I pulled a living being—as I'd been pulled—into the world. The book did not say that tatters of birth sac would flutter like pale little surrender flags when my rough hands cleared nostrils and massaged slime-covered ribs to start breath.

From the agriculture class textbook I learned what my father's generation knew from experience, how to determine the age of a horse by looking at its teeth, and from the same book I learned how to measure the butterfat content of milk. However, when I joined the air force, I could not do the mathematics required for navigation. I could fly a plane out to fight an enemy pilot, but I could not do the mathematics required for finding my way home.

Our teacher's observation that my classmates and I were too poor to afford more than a high school education was valid, but ironically, World War II's G.I. Bill enabled nearly all of the boys in my class to graduate from college, and most became teachers.

Two years younger than my classmates, I felt shy and confused when a girl developed a crush on me and wanted to be with me every possible moment. Somewhat more mature two years later, I invited her to ride in a car crowded with other juvenile couples, all of us planning to go to a lovers' lane, but my first date's father strode up to the car and angrily ordered her to get out. Thus ended my first, but not my last, opportunity to experience something of romance with an older woman.

I recall now a sweet conversation with the first girl whose bare breasts I was blessed with seeing, when her uniform did something unexpected during a basketball game.

Both conversation and erotic awareness ended when our big principal backhanded a shy junior high boy at the far end of the study hall. Blood spurted from the boy's mouth as he tried to explain that he was late because he'd been ill and did not know the new time for being in his seat. My father's drunken brutality years back not forgotten, I felt, and whispered, intense hatred for the huge school administrator. The girl looked at me with respect, interest, even admiration. But I was fifteen, she sixteen and taller than me. She was intelligent. Pretty. What if we'd dated? What if she'd offered what basketball kinesthetics and untrustworthy buttons had revealed? Would having added touch to visual admiration have made me a different person?

Youth, yes, youth. Trying to write about sexual love, I remember the advice of an older and wiser writer, "Don't do it!" and I will not attempt to describe the beautiful shape of a breast emerging from a pink bra, for me to see and to feel, at age sixteen, in an empty high school auditorium in Independence, Iowa. Elsewhere in the building a basketball game, at which I was supposed to be cheering for friends, went on and on to its own climax.

Drunk and somewhere near my mother's first husband's portrait, at the top of the stairs, Dad became enraged about something, and, as he sometimes did when we children were naughty, he pulled the belt from his pants and lashed out.

"My breast!" the woman who'd nursed me and sustained my life cried. "You've hurt my breast!"

What followed I can only vaguely remember—a sobering up, a reconciliation, life going on—but my mother's cry of pain and outrage is vivid, deep in my mind.

To my shame I must confess that my second tactual exploration of what film ads call "frontal nudity" involved letting a more aggressive juvenile persuade me to join him in what was called "grab tit," these days euphemized as "inappropriate touching."

While I was committing a juvenile sex crime, older criminals were stealing farmers' chickens and tractor gasoline to sell in Chicago's World War II black market. Often I'd awake in darkness, hearing barking and deciding if some fox, skunk, or weasel was being driven away by our dog or if someone were robbing our henhouse or fuel barrel.

Cowardice. Courage.

Courage? Sometimes no, sometimes yes. One night I was awakened by my mother's trembling hands' shoving into my hands Dad's shotgun, still warm from air risen to where it had rested on nails above my parents' door. I was sixteen, the nearest approximation of a man in my home. Rex was only twelve and asleep. Ray and Dad were far off in the woods, hunting those little nocturnal animals with reportedly clean eating habits and with hands like human hands, the animals locally known — as were our only black neighbors — as coons.

"Chicken thieves," my mother's frightened, and frightening, words, I hurriedly dressed and followed her down into the kitchen's lingering odors of our hours-ago dinner.

"Count to one hundred," I ordered the woman whose orders I'd obeyed from the moment the doctor had prevented my killing her with my butt-first prenatal obstinacy and then had prevented me from garroting my newborn self with the umbilical cord. "Count to one hundred," I instructed the woman who could not fulfill her passion for becoming a teacher of strangers but had taught her children the first numbers they'd learn.

"Count to one hundred, and then turn on the light," commanded the war film hero whose acting debut had consisted of mooning his father, his aunt, and a doctor then squalling to beat hell when yanked on stage and prompted, with a swat on his little butt, to clear his throat.

"Count slowly to give me time" — time, oh, all the time I might have left to live in this blessed world — "time to get behind trees." And by then the invaders — maybe not local thieves but meat-thieving black marketeers, who'd killed a neighbor — would be silhouetted when Mom reached the count of one hundred and switched on the yard light.

Some months previously my seventeen-year-old brother Ray had shot and shattered the lantern that a thief had been holding up to dazzle a chicken and pluck it from its roost — to take home to eat or to sell to black marketeers. Ray had shot a local thief, as it turned out, and an amused and talkative local doctor cut a dozen shotgun pellets out of a disreputable neighbor's face, we'd later learn.

As resolute as my father, as resolute as my big brother Ray, and as resolute as my soldier brother Bob, I strode stealthily, on tennis shoes' rubber soles, toward dark trees, which would protect me from whatever pistol bullets might be fired by the men, two men I thought, hearing heavy footsteps on the chicken house floor.

Silhouetted in blinding light, I sought the earth — "hit the dirt" — as I'd seen newsreel infantrymen do. Frightened, my mother had counted twice as fast as I was counting and had turned on the yard light. Terrified, I aimed at shadows and shot three times, emptying the gun, and shadows, dark against darkness, ran away.

# 18

Yesterday the high school age daughter of good friends, who are Jewish, asked if, one day soon, she might interview me about World War II. What should I tell her? That I'd enlisted, at innocent, idealistic age seventeen, to save pretty newsreel Jews from Nazis and then had had to watch Jew-hating training sergeants mistreat Jews? Should I tell her that all of the two hundred Americans I saw asphyxiated, burned, and crushed to death were accidentally killed by hastily undertrained Americans, by the failure of hastily manufactured plane parts or by weather?

Here, the page making everything safely, blessedly unreal, I can tell a girl younger than my daughter that World War II was a part of my youth, sex surging into divine confusions with love, cosmic harmony, and other impossible-to-define dimensions of existence.

Yesterday's request from my friends' daughter reminds me that, only a few weeks back, my niece Evita Sikelianos — great-granddaughter of the great Greek poet — emailed and asked if I would help her with a high school project. She wanted to know my thoughts and feelings on the day when Japan made what's now called "a preemptive strike" against Pearl Harbor.

Fifteen that day, I heard about it from my parents. They'd been listening to the radio news and were very concerned that my brother Bob might be killed.

I milked cows, fed cows and pigs, ate breakfast, shaved, washed, and rode the school bus, now driven by my brother Ray. Everyone on the bus that morning was quiet, and from time to time I'd notice someone staring at me, knowing that my brother Bob was in the army and in danger.

I felt uneasy and scared for my brother, and I felt the generalized lynch-mob anger that the entire country had been feeling since a deluge of propaganda against Japan, Germany, and Italy had begun. For months I'd been clipping out newspaper pictures of warplanes and pictures of pinup girls and covering the walls of the bedroom, mine alone since my brother Bob had gone to the army. I'd heard that Canada was allowing sixteen-year-olds to enlist in the Royal Canadian Air Force, and I began daydreaming of following the shadows Lockheed Hudson bombers cast as they flew over our farm, bound for Canada, from which they'd be flown to Iceland and then Great Britain, lend-lease from the United States.

My brother would be shipped to finish training in Ireland, a nationally known newswoman reported, and I clipped the story and mailed it to my brother, who was already in Ireland when he finally received my letter, my mention of the destination he'd already reached censored, the newspaper clipping removed from the envelope.

To prepare my body for war, I chinned myself daily, trying for one more, just one more, until my exhausted, and strengthening, arms would no longer lift my hundred pounds of muscle and bone, and hyperactive glands, and some brain.

Like British newsreel commandos scaling the cliffs of Nazi-occupied France, I climbed a thick hay rope twenty feet to the roof peak of the hayloft, and then, dangling from the steel hay-conveyor track high above bone-breaking board floor, I went horizontally, hand over hand, thirty feet, to finally let go and plunge like a paratrooper onto a pile of cushiony hay.

To prepare my mind for battle, I dutifully read the propaganda incitements of newspapers, read *Model Airplane News'* descriptions of warplanes, and experienced orgasm-resembling release in seeing British Spitfires' gun-camera films of Nazi bombers bursting into flames in newsreels.

To pay my father back for the terror he had drunkenly inflicted some days of my childhood, I demanded that he stand up when the "Star-Spangled Banner" was being played on the radio. He muttered some objection to my fanatical patriotism, but he stood.

I scaled up model airplane blueprints for a primary glider to one-third the size of a real glider and started construction, reasoning that I was maybe only half as heavy as some grown pilots and might, if all went well, try a short flight into high wind, trusting to luck I'd land okay, since my plans did not include controls.

With a handsaw Dad had sharpened for his own purposes, I cut some old inch-boards into narrow strips and, with binder twine culled from straw stacks, fastened together the skeletal fuselage, from which I expected to dangle, quite as I did daily from the hay-conveyor track. Whenever I wasn't doing farm work or schoolwork, I devoted myself to my labor of love or, given my warrior motive, my labor of abstract hate.

For the first time my insane cousin Bill Harkin became interested in war and interested in me. He'd been trained as a mechanical engineer, and my effort to imitate the Wright brothers had made a bridge between his life and mine. I felt uneasy, the privacy of my creative dream disturbed by Cousin Bill's peering between the horizontal slats of the empty corncrib. "The Hobbs and Docket," he'd mutter angrily over and over, and similar phrases, which sounded like gibberish, whatever they may have meant in his inner world.

The corncrib slats were like the bars of an insane asylum, I can think, these decades later, and I see the irony of Cousin Bill's apparently harmless craziness connecting with my obsessive adolescent devotion to the far-from-harmless craziness of nations, which were daily slaughtering thousands of our own kind in war.

I'd only been afraid of my formerly murderous cousin once. He'd strode toward my brother Rex and me as if he were going to attack us. We'd stood absolutely still, probably paralyzed by fear, but finally he'd walked away, leaving us to resume throwing a baseball back and forth.

Feeling increasingly deranged from being spied upon while trying to enjoy the fulfillment of creating my glider, I summoned the courage to ask my mad cousin what he wanted. He did not answer. It was as if I had not spoken, but he went away and stopped coming to watch.

I'd read that real airplanes had been covered with strong and expensive linen, but I had no money for linen, and the tissue paper with which I'd covered small model airplanes would not have been either affordable or available in the size required. I made do with empty farm fertilizer bags. They were probably somewhat stronger than stores' wrapping paper, were somewhat waterproofed, and were a pleasingly metal-like, shiny black.

I weighed one of Mom's flat irons and calculated the point where it must be lashed into place to make the plane balance like a teeter-totter, its fulcrum point the wing's point of maximum lift, about a third of the way back from its front edge. Rex, who'd turned twelve in February, just after I'd turned sixteen at January's end, was my ground crew, and to increase the prospects of my glider's becoming airborne, I ordered him to climb with me to the top of the straw stack and hold the glider until I yelled "Contact," just like a pulp-paper-magazine, World War I, Lafayette Escadrille pilot. Then, running while pulling forty-some feet of tied-together lengths of discarded binder twine, I'd tow my glider into the air.

I descended from the straw stack, keeping my towline taut.

"Contact!" I yelled and ran as fast as I could go, into the strong wind.

I felt my glider take flight at the end of the twine, I risked a glance over my shoulder and saw the shining black glory of a dream realized, but for only a moment. My inexpertly tied knots slipping, Mom's flat iron bailed out of the pilot's seat and plunged, like a parachuteless jet-plane passenger of today, while my glider teeter-tottered nose-up, tail-down, stalled, side-slipped, and became broken lengths of kindling, crumpled paper, and a few words from Rex decades later, after he'd become a command pilot, still impressed that his impractical dreamer-poet brother had figured everything out correctly — except how to tie knots.

A few years ago my wife and children gave me a wonderful birthday present, the chance to pilot a glider — a real glider, as sleek and as beautiful as a rainbow trout.

I was swimming in air, effortlessly swimming in air — and silent, so silent that I came up alongside a golden eagle, who remained preoccupied with scrutinizing the earth hundreds of feet below for something to eat, until my wings' shadow changed fierce hunting intent to startled dive for survival.

Recalling my flight in a graceful, German-designed glider, I remember that my cousin Stacy was killed while piloting a glider carrying troops in the invasion of Normandy.

War still a teenager's dream, I studied the basic training manual Bob had brought home on his one furlough. Instructed by the manual, I marched Rex around and around our farmyard. I taught him commando fighting, learned from a book I'd bought. Once, when he applied a mugger's headlock from behind and surprised me, I automatically drove my elbow back into his solar plexus and knocked out his breath. I hadn't intended to hurt him, and I knew it was painful — how painful I learned later when he drove his elbow into my solar plexus and left me gasping on the ground.

"The next best thing to war is sport," Spartan King Menelaus told the world and has been quoted for over two thousand years.

Since the United States was not, at that moment in history, at war, since Aurora High School had only baseball and basketball teams, no football team, and since my five-foot height was not helping me to basketball stardom, I devoted myself to the United States' national sport, baseball.

Dad promised to buy linseed-oil-fragrant fielders gloves for Bob, Ray, and me as a reward for our working extra hard and extra long, and then he decided he couldn't afford the extravagance after all. Mom told him he couldn't break his promise, no matter what, and he came up with the necessary money somehow. Throwing rocks to hunt birds, squirrels, and rabbits was his closest experience to baseball playing, and the one time he'd tried a few minutes of batting practice with his sons, he'd missed the baseball more than he'd hit it. Talked into umpiring for the hometown team's game with the team of another town, he'd called balls strikes and called runners out when they'd already safely reached base. Only his impartiality in making the wrong calls prevented our opponents from charging a rigged game.

As a former singer and banjo player, Dad understood my wanting to gain celebrity as a baseball star, but despite my fanatic commitment, and despite hours of practicing, I did not win Dad's or anyone else's acclamation.

I labored hard, and pleasurably, at baseball, and I won a few glory moments, but I did not play well. Any chance at improvement ended when a 170-pound teammate did a high slide into second base during practice and broke my ankle.

Unconscious for a few seconds, I roused up and tried to get to my feet, but only the right leg obeyed my brain's command, and I flopped around in a circle until the coach ran over and grabbed my shoulders to hold me still. The baseball field was part of the fairgrounds, five or six blocks from the school. Instructed by Coach, two boys joined hands to forearms and formed a seat. I was carried, broken bones grating against each other, to a chest-high barbed-wire fence. Hoisted over to another pair of waiting arms, I was transported to the school, where nature's anesthetic took hold. I could hear people talking and asking me things, and I answered, but no one heard me.

The coach telephoned Dad, and he interrupted his farm work, changed to his town-going clothes, and drove four miles to pick me up. I was conscious by the time I was laid down on Dad's Studebaker Commander's back seat. I could hear the bones grating while I was driven sixteen miles to the family doctor. Finding that the ankle bones had been jolted back into place, the doctor mixed white powder with water and formed a cast.

While I was immobilized, my bruised heel began to fester inside the cast. Everyone except Aunt Jennie had gone somewhere, probably to visit friends, and there was little my aunt could do for me. She seldom rode in a car, let alone driving one, and anyway ours was gone. She gave me compassion, that was about all she could offer, while infected flesh swelled against a nerve, causing intense pain, which finally subsided after several hours when pus burst through bruised flesh, relieving the pressure.

Baseball eased the boredom of boys for one hour each school day, and my accident not only made life somewhat unusual, somewhat interesting, for the time of the emergency, but it continued to supply the sight of cast and crutches as a reminder. A scrawny fifteen-year-old bookworm usually, I became a celebrity. Fellow students, including nicely perfumed girls, leaned over me and signed their names. I was a hobbling one-boy roll call.

Bringing most of their large families with them, my father's brothers, Uncle George and Uncle Dial, drove from Kentucky to visit my dad, and unable to join my brothers in farm work, I was endlessly entertained. To see the movie *Gone With the Wind*, I had to sit at the back of the cinema house in a folding chair, separate from the rest of the audience, my uncompromisingly straight cast resting on another folding chair. I taught myself to rise up on my crutches and do what amounted to a one-legged Cherokee stomp dance, a proof of my courage and ingeniousness that pleased my uncles into complimenting me.

Best of all, I couldn't work and could read book after book from the lending library. When the toe-to-hip cast was removed, I was shocked that my sturdy leg had dwindled to a pale, flaccid, black-haired member no bigger around than a normal arm. A school friend whose family had moved to a farm on the Wapsipinicon River invited me to visit and swim and give my ankle the limbering-up exercise the doctor had ordered.

Swimming every day improved the awkward dog-paddle I'd taught myself while swimming with my cousins in Kentucky. Learning to swim enabled me to save two lives later that summer, and it almost ended my life.

The Wapsipinicon River's flooding had left several willow trees half rooted in the bank, half submerged in the turbulent river. I dived too deep too near one of these trees, and for a terrifying few minutes I was tangled in branches, my breath nearly gone. Finally, I struggled free, hot summer air more precious than any I'd ever shape into story or poem.

While swimming with my friend's older sisters and tussling with them for possession of a floating ball, I became fascinated with the disarrangement of a swimsuit top and persuaded myself that I could let fingers find what eyes had already touched. It would seem accidental, I imagined, but a stinging slap brought me out of imagination and into a real world.

Later that summer, my fifteenth, I rescued two young women from drowning. They'd been drinking with high school friends, partying in cars parked among bushes in that remote place. I was sitting on a log at the edge of the cold, clear swimming hole and possibly shyly thinking of bare skin glimpsed through auto windows, my thoughts frustrated by the pestering friendliness of a boy, bored at a family picnic and battening on to me.

Earlier that afternoon I'd encountered a young man and a young woman as they'd emerged from bushes onto the trail I was walking. True to my polite upbringing, I'd said, "Hi." The couple had not responded to the United States' taken-for-granted shortening of

"How are you?" and I was innocent enough to be puzzled at the seeming discourtesy.

A boy still, but nearly a man, I bashfully stared as two young women approached the swimming hole, swimming-suit-or-under-wear-clothed bodies parting the leaves of bushes.

"They're as drunk as skunks," was my pestering ten-year-old companion's interpretation of what I might have chosen to think a charming natural awkwardness, consequent to walking barefoot over rough ground's twig fragments and troublesome pebbles.

The first young woman dived, slender body briefly that of a pale white bird in flight, then that of movie mermaid garmenting bare beauty in the silken ripples of a lagoon. Pale foot soles, criss-crossed by red welts from twigs, vanished into the pool, in which vanished Vanishing Americans had probably swum, the pool Caucasians had known for generations as Joy Springs.

The second, and the prettier, young woman entered the cold water as her surreptitious admirer always did, timidly, halting after each splashing step, while flesh gradually accustomed to the shock of feeling winter in summer.

Slowly, slowly, deeply appreciated or shallowly lusted-for near nakedness vanished, gowned in a garment woven from underground ice's melting maybe hundreds of miles to the north.

"Don't come out any further. It's too deep," the swimmer cried, sounding, after her icy plunge, quite sober.

"It's not too deep," the prettier young woman objected, her voice drunkenly slurred and quarrelsome. "It's not too deep. I'm just too short." Pool bottom crumbling under the weight of flesh — so desirable in the dreams of a boy — words became incomprehensible bubbles.

The more sober young woman's pale arms flashed from cloud to cloud, through reflected sky, and her half-submerged face was made beautiful by courage.

The drunk seizing her friend's arms, I saw rescuer become victim, saw eyes as blue as the pool beseeching me, compelling me, as they sank. I was drawn, slowly, reluctantly, drawn to wade without, for the first time in my life, noticing cold. When I had to swim, I swam awkwardly, a dog-paddle stroke the only one I'd somewhat learned.

Panicky, I seized, as the drunken young woman had seized, an arm. That arm jerking itself out of my clutching fingers, I grabbed blindly into the tangle of two bodies I'd daydreamed of fondling. Long hair slipping through my fingers, I tightened my grip, frantically flailed water, one armed, and swam, until the three of us were able to wade thigh-deep water to pebbly, foot-sole-afflicting shore.

"You saved her life," the ten-year-old pesterer said in an awed voice as I resumed my seat on a log beside him, still sputtering water. "You saved her life, and now she's cussing you," the boy continued wonderingly, in shocked disapproval.

It was true. One of the two maidens in distress I'd saved from drowning was throwing drunken curses in my direction, some disarrangements of her scanty swimsuit the basis of her complaint, her malediction the first of several I've received from women—sometimes deservedly—in my life, in my long life. Ten then, the boy who—sixty years ago—admired what must have seemed to him my bravery, would be by now seventy—or dead—maybe killed in the Korean War, during which I'd almost gone to prison for refusing to fight.

To save or to help save the life of another person—by dog-paddling to the rescue or by refusing to fit finger to electronic gunnery trigger—should strengthen pride and maybe does, somewhat, but my fidelity must be to whatever I felt when blue eyes, wildly searching for succor, found me and compelled me. Whatever it may mean to the rest of my life and what may come after, I could not do other than to try to save another human from death. And still, in the best moments of my life, I'm drawn, inexorably drawn, to the wordless supplication of what compels me to write.

# 19

The son of a Cherokee who'd killed in self-defense, the brother of a soldier fighting Germans in Africa, I seized my first opportunity to be a Cherokee warrior, a movie-dream hero.

Since there was no indoor plumbing and a tin can had come to seem an embarrassment from childhood, all of us boys had formed the habit of urinating behind trees or behind the corners of buildings, where no one walked. Our corncrib had been reconstructed after being flattened by tornado, years back. The rebuilt crib was not far from our heated house but far enough to be out of kitchen windows' line of vision.

In a hurry one below-zero night, I slipped on ice while running full tilt, and lying, hoping I'd get my breath back before I froze to death or peed my pants, I heard footsteps moving over the floor of an oat bin located above the corncrib.

Self-pity and cautiousness replaced by fear, my breath came back fast, and, my need to pee somewhat abated, I got to my feet, careful not to slip and fall again, and grabbed with both cold hands the only weapon I could see in the dim moonlight, a piece of steel that had once eased the jolts of a wagon's bouncing from rut to rut and now braced a ten-foot-high sliding door to keep it from flapping in wind and slipping off its track. Shaped more or less like a broad-bladed sword, the spring made a resonant warning sound as I pounded the corncrib door. Overhead the footsteps stopped.

I could hear my brother Rex's radio music, turned up loud inside the house, and I knew that he would not hear me if I yelled for him to bring a gun. My mother had gone to visit the wife of my father's hunting companion while the two men and their hounds hunted raccoons in a nearby woods. My brother Ray would have been at a dance, hunting for love. My aunt Jennie would have been asleep in an upstairs room beside my sister. Cousin Bill Harkin would have been asleep in his downstairs room, and even awake, he'd have been living some nightmare memory and of no help.

No more footsteps sounding, I thought I'd maybe heard the stirring of rats over oats, but I also thought that whoever was in the bin overhead had moved quietly and might come charging through the ajar corncrib door, wielding a club of his own or shooting. Uncertain, I solved the simpler problem of easing the pressure in my bladder. Over the shrilling of winter wind against rafters and the spring-thaw sound of my giving moisture to the roots of the elm tree beside the corncrib, I again heard footfalls in the oat bin above my head, not those of scurrying rats but, I was almost certain, those of a heavy man, a man crossing the wooden floor and crunching the thin scattering of oats left after half a winter's feeding of animals. Someone was nearing a board ladder nailed into the wall closest to where I was hastily buttoning my pants, in that pre-zipper time.

The lighted house was only a three-hundred-foot run from where I stood, shivering and trembling in darkness, but instead of sensibly fleeing, I again banged the echoing corncrib door. A memory of crazy cousin Bill's watching me build my doomed glider in this corncrib may have raised the dread that whoever was in the oat bin was a lunatic, escaped from the nearby state insane asylum.

Crazy myself, maybe—as crazy as mass-murder-serial-killer nations—I acted a role for an audience not really there, my audience a vaguely imagined movie crowd, my role that of a fearless hero, banging steel against wood and hurling up into darkness a warrior challenge too profane for any movie of those days, "Come down and I'll kill you, you son of a bitch!" The heavy footsteps overhead ceased, then slowly moved, crunching oats, back from the ladder. A few more heavy blows against wood encouraged the retreat.

A window was set high in the oat bin's far wall, but with the bin so near empty, it was probably unreachable, and anyway, the fall to frozen ground would have been hard enough to break bones. Only a few feet above the top of the threshing machine, garaged between corncribs, the oat-chute hole in the oat-bin floor would be a tight fit for any man trying to descend, any man heavy enough to make the oat-crunching footfalls.

I listened silently, considered risking a hopefully stealthily silent run to arm myself with a rifle and then running back to capture the invader — grain thief or madman.

Footsteps again moving toward the ladder, I again banged steel against wood, vibrations hurting cold-numbed bare fingers and loosening my grip.

Car lights blazed on the snowy road. A car sped past our driveway, and the sound of its engine echoing, the footsteps overhead turned and moved away from the ladder.

I propped my steel weapon against my knee and felt that the knee was trembling, from cold or fear, as the unpropped door was trembling from wind. My hands only beginning to warm inside jacket pockets, I heard the footsteps become again louder, closer, overhead, the man maybe starting to rush down the ladder. I banged once again against the corncrib door, vibration of the steel club stinging my numb hands.

Again and again I threatened, with steel against wood and with my voice, against whatever the thief or madman intended and against my own fear. Each time the footsteps became silent, but there was no reassuring retreat. I stayed as silent as my enemy overhead and listened for the board ladder rungs to creak against nails, under great weight.

Again propping steel against thinly clothed knee while warming bare hands inside my pockets, I considered fleeing to end the impasse, which my warrior impulses, Dad's warrior stories, and movies' patriotic fervor had created.

A few minutes later lights blazed over snow again, and my father drove into the yard, a 12-gauge automatic shotgun in his car, a .32 automatic pistol in his pocket. I was relieved, but fear had left my mind, just as urine had left my adolescent body.

We couldn't just leave a possibly dangerous man loose in our farmstead, Dad agreed. The county sheriff was twenty-some miles away, and through years of incidents we'd gotten used to solving problems ourselves.

"I better climb up there and get him," Dad decided, but drastically overweight, he was no climber.

"Let me," I pleaded—a little boy again, begging, Let me go to town, go to the neighbor's farm-foreclosure sale, go hunting, go to work in the fields—and I justified my almost-grown-up supplication, not with any heroic movie jargon but with a boy's, a son's, plaintive, heartfelt logic, "I kept him up there with just this steel club all this time"—all that time of enduring cold and terror and trying to sustain a heroic dream of a self I hoped to be.

Let me—risk my life, prove my courage—let me be a man, a man a man can be proud to have fathered, let me, me, me, goddammit, let me, please, please, please.

My father regarded his middle son in the glow of the coon-hunting lantern. "All right," he decided, a father whose own father had deserted him. "All right. You take my pistol." The pistol with which he'd defended himself and defended our family several times. The pistol with which he'd shot a ring around my bare feet when I was three or four. The pistol that had sent bullet after bullet past my head when I was ten and moving, though terrified, to plead for my mother's life.

Pistol gripped in this hand in which I hold a pen, flashlight between these teeth from which words of rage and words of love have issued, I climbed the ladder, alert for any sound in the darkness above me. On the top rung, shifting flashlight from teeth to left hand, I leaped beyond the stairwell wall, behind which my opponent might be hiding. Body turning, midair, I aimed my father's pistol into shadows moving to flee or to attack, but when I landed, feet shifting on creaking floor, flashlight-encumbered arm swinging for balance to keep me upright, I saw only a mound of oats, as pale, almost, as a snowdrift, in the beam of the flashlight. Twenty feet from me the oat chute was maybe wide enough for a man's body to have dropped through it. Above me the open window showed only night.

Someone had somehow escaped my vigilance, or there had been no one, had been only the sounds of a rat, fattening himself on oats, or maybe only winter wind and the settling of boards, loosened years back by tornado. I'll never know the reality, but that time was a rite of passage into manhood. I'd measured up and won the respect of a father who'd often made me feel unvalued, unloved.

Three years later an atomic bomb turned my dreams of warrior manhood into shadows burned onto a concrete wall.

# 20

For Bernard Wessels, my brother Bob's father, the American army may have been a way of transcending his bearing a German name and being of a bloodline that had lost their last two wars. His was a sad and not unusual story, death from meningitis in a Texas training camp.

My nation, aided by radio, newspaper news, and newsreel, was living its dream of war, and, my dream my nation's dream, I enlisted at age seventeen in the army air corps. At that age I could enlist if my parents gave written permission and if Dad signed a form stating that my work was not essential in supplying food for the war effort. "I don't want to stand in the way of your career," Dad said, an unusually bookish speech for him, and even though he was getting older and certainly needed my help on the farm, he signed. Her eldest son a prisoner in Italy, Mom was reluctant, but, patriotism winning a silent war with motherly concern, she either signed or let Dad's signature allow me to enlist.

Dad and I went, I recall, to a young lawyer's office to have the release document notarized. The lawyer's attractive, pregnant wife was in the office, and, not having taken much notice of pregnant women before, I thought that she might be deformed.

When I went to find the air corps recruiting sergeant, the Veterans of Foreign Wars post commander, a veteran of World War I, noticed the notarizing signature on my consent document and said, "That lawyer has been helping cowards to get out of the draft, but we're going to fix him, we're going to find a way to draft him, even if his wife is pregnant."

Fat, gray haired, and balding, the man in charge of the Veterans of Foreign Wars post did not accord with my pristine movie dream of heroism, and his scheming against a young expectant father did not accord with my vision of a benign democracy. My mind was on dressing in a nifty uniform and wearing silver wings and winning the love of a girl as pretty as a movie star. The old veteran wore a blue overseas cap, idiomatically known as a Go to Hell cap, but except for the military hat, he was in ordinary town-man clothes.

Because the army air corps recruiter was not available that day, I decided to drive to a nearby town and take the naval aviation exam. I made the drive with the friend whose 170 pounds had broken my ankle in baseball. Both of us failed the navy pilot test. My ideal vision of myself wrecked like the glider I'd built, I pleaded with the tough sailor who'd administered and graded the exam. Wasn't there a second chance, a way to take the exam again? There was not. The Army Will Make a Man Out of You, an enlistment poster had promised, but the navy made the seventeen-year-old man I thought I was into the insecure seventeen-year-old boy I actually was.

A week later, I found the army air force recruiter and scored the highest exam score yet made at that enlistment station. My pride ascended on the Go-to-Hell-Hatted vfw man's praise.

To complete enlistment, I rode one of the trains that had, during my childhood, made buildings' reflections shake in quaking display windows and made car-seat springs quiver under little butts tense with fascination and fear.

A high school friend was traveling with me, and at the train's first stop we saw one of our former teachers, now a naval officer. Following him, intending to announce our enlistments, we blundered into his meeting with another former teacher. They were rumored to have had an affair even though he was married. Despite the facts that he was on his way to combat and that we'd just interrupted a complex, emotional moment, he was admirably friendly and poised. He joined my friend and me back on the train and stood in the aisle and talked with us for two hours, until we got to Des Moines, where he caught another train and where my friend and I were sworn in as flight cadets and given little silver wings.

For months I marched once a week with the civil air patrol and read government manuals and learned something about aerodynamics and used my being in town as an opportunity to date girls, until my eighteenth birthday, when I could legally be called to active duty and was.

"I need two volunteers to sweep the floor!" a corporal shouted.

"Never volunteer. It's a trick. I saw it in a movie," I heard the guy in line on my right whisper to a guy on his right.

"Let's volunteer. It's better than waiting and waiting and waiting in line," the little guy on my left whispered to me and held up his hand, like a teacher's pet offering to pound chalk dust out of erasers in school. The kid was dark skinned, a Hispanic, a "spik" someone had called him. He was the only fellow soldier who had offered friendship. Gray eyed but black haired, and still deeply tanned from summer after summer of working in the sun, I looked to be what I was, an Indian, and I might have seemed to be Hispanic. Maybe responding to friendship with friendship or maybe bored with waiting in line, I held up my hand and volunteered to sweep the cluttered room, although the only broom I'd used before was the one I'd pretended was my horse and straddled and ridden around the living room, while I'd sounded a falsetto "Hi, ho, Silver, away!"

"Okay. You two volunteers move up to head of the line, and you two guys at the head of the line, you get up and sweep.

In a uniform, smelling like what I did not know were mothballs, I was living my dream.

"Fresh meat! Fresh me-ee-eet!" seasoned soldiers taunted, lessons of playground bullying learned well enough to last for what might be a short lifetime.

"Forward march!" a guy with two stripes on his sleeve commanded, and we three dozen or so recruits, destined, we'd thought, to become glamorous pilots and officers and gentlemen, marched in our new uniforms through cold mud, my left ankle's bone scar aching.

The scar, which had welded my three broken ankle bones, was thin enough to allow the ankle full flexibility, and it was so strong I'd resumed doing the most demanding farm work and had passed the rigorous pilot-training physical, but the healing had left my left foot turned slightly out, and standing at attention, mud rigorously scrubbed from trousers, shoes cleaned and shined, I turned my ankle slightly to make my feet match and hide my defect from the officers, who required physical perfection.

I went through basic training at Jefferson Barracks, Missouri, and there were barracks for drill sergeants, but trainees were quartered in either tents or shacks. I slept in a shack, through whose board-covered, glassless windows blizzard winds blew and covered olive-drab army blankets with snow. Each morning the plank floor was white except for a dark circle melted around the small steel cone-shaped, coal-burning "monkey stove."

I'd wake when whistles sounded for black soldiers, quartered in tents at the bottom of a ravine, into which melting snow from my squadron drained.

I'd wake again an hour later, when my own area's whistles shrilled in the darkness, as white drill sergeants woke up white troops. Always trying to be a hero, I bounded barefoot from bed to snowy floor, jerked the dangling light-switch cord, and bounded back onto my bunk to pull wool shirt and pants over long wool underwear, wool socks over feet, whose melted snow I'd dried with the corner of a blanket, and soldier boots over socks. Last I donned a wool sweater, a wool cap, and a heavy greatcoat, only then taking time to tie my bootlaces. Once dressed, my four hut mates and I would rush into darkness outside our lighted hut, to stand in snow on the frozen mud street until it was time to respond, "Here!" —pronounced "Yoh!" —for roll call. The black troops' white sergeants were already marching them off to work.

I fired and dismantled and cleaned and put back together rifles and pistols and, once, a new automatic weapon called a "greasegun." Small, simply made, and capable of killing large numbers of enemies, it was being tested for use by guerilla fighters in occupied Europe. Two of us scored perfect scores while firing this weapon, our bullets all concentrated in cardboard targets shaped like men. My cowinner of firing-range honor said it was sad, because he could really shoot, but he'd failed a physical exam and would not be sent into combat.

Prone on my belly in snow, to fire an old World War I rifle at targets, I saw ice floating down the broad Mississippi, but it would be years before I'd learn that thousands of my Cherokee people had crossed this river in winter on the death march called the Trail of Tears.

After a day's training there was a short time to read, converse, and write letters. I'd written my girlfriend every day and had not heard back. Then I'd received a reply and realized that, without the tender rituals of our two warm bodies, she bored me.

At the end of a twenty-mile march I stood in the rain, in dim light, distinguished gleaming front sight from water beads glistening on pistol barrel, and aimed at the head of a man who'd just sped his truck past my guard gate. Following orders, I was squeezing the trigger when the truck's brake lights flared as red as the blood I'd later give for a transfusion — my pint of blood saving a life. The truck driver saved his own life when he looked in his rearview mirror, saw the pistol aimed at his head, and hastily got out of his truck to stand before me in the rain and show his pass.

Weeks later, guarding a secret-weapon airplane, I was under orders to let no one come near. No one tried until dawn, when a dozen coverall-clad men and women arrived to swarm over the gleaming silver plane they'd been hired to repair.

Both of these incidents happened at air bases in the United States.

In Northern Ireland my brother Bob nearly shot an old Irishman who was too stubborn to pay any attention to any young American with a gun. Hearing the command of "Halt!" an American officer stepped out of a door at the top of the stair and into the line of fire to rebuke my brother for following orders and damned near killing a janitor.

I'd live to read of German soldiers condemned to death at Nuremburg, their defense that they had been soldiers following orders to kill.

One night I was armed with a short-barreled riot gun, locked inside a steel-mesh fence, and ordered to shoot anyone who came out of a brightly lighted door. For four hours I heard all that mankind needs to know about war, the ferocious guilt-ridden voices of madmen reliving, in tortured nightmares, the killing of other human beings, the loss of friends.

One guy in our squadron considered himself tough and routinely called other men "shit." The first time he called me by that name, I challenged him to fight, and he backed down, looking crestfallen and worried. I was, I realize now, behaving like my father's little man, just as my brother had been when he challenged a bully at the outdoor movie.

A tough guy who was one of my hut mates yelled for two men talking outside to shut up and stop disturbing his sleep. One of them immediately stuck his head in the dark doorway and yelled, "Get your ass out here!" Fearing either a beating, possibly by two men, or punishment for having unwittingly yelled at noncommissioned officers, our hut's tough guy stayed silent, and after a few insults the challenger and his friend walked away, still talking loudly as they walked.

Though full of propaganda-and-youth-induced patriotism, I innocently committed two acts that could have sent me to prison as an enemy spy.

While still in basic training and braving the rigors of mud and cold familiar to infantry soldiers and while trying to fight off, unaided, the pneumonia that eventually almost killed me, I was standing with a buddy—the same one who later caught a burst of shrapnel in his abdomen when a machine-gun cartridge exploded in a jammed firing chamber. He'd worked for a time at the Boeing plant in Seattle, and he recognized a huge plane we could see as it flew over us—a B-17, I thought, until my companion put me wise that it was a top-secret bomber, the plane that would, two years later, bomb Hiroshima and Nagasaki, a B-29.

A few days later I saw a B-29 on the ground as I rode a troop train into Denver, and with a small camera I'd bought back home, I photographed the plane that enemies would have risked their lives to learn about. For weeks I kept the blurry snapshot in a small photo album I was planning to send to impress my girl back home. Naturally I showed the photo to buddies to impress them with my inside knowledge, and while I was learning to take machine guns apart and put them back together in the dark, someone unlocked my footlocker and removed one photo from my album and snipped one frame from my roll of negatives.

I was lucky not to have been court-martialed for the B-29 snapshot, but I pressed my luck once again, trying to send home a training manual marked "classified," wanting a souvenir. Packing to ship out for another air base, I couldn't find my carefully packaged and addressed souvenir, and when I asked another soldier if he'd seen it, he gave me a pitying look and advised me to forget that I'd ever had it.

My first distinction, as far as my squadron noncommissioned officers was concerned, was my having been assigned the bunk in which a celebrated heavyweight boxer, Lou Nova, the Man with the Cosmic Punch — and a gifted publicity agent — had slept when he'd undergone basic training. My second distinction was doing more chin-ups, sit-ups, and so on than army ratings called tops. My third distinction was coming down with pneumonia, a distinction that did not please the orderly room sergeant, who said, "I've got a training schedule, and don't you go goofing off on sick call, or I'll make you a hell of a lot sicker when you come back."

Sick for a week, I kept on coughing and marching and standing at outdoor tables, icicles gleaming like polar bear teeth under them, my fingers, numbed by cold, taking rifles and pistols apart and putting them back together. Then I saw, posted just under the orders of the day, "Disregard rumors. If you are sick, go on sick call," signed by a captain.

"Sure you can go," said the sergeant, who knew the difference between a captain and a sergeant. He also knew the difference between a sergeant and a private, like myself. "First, pack all your gear into barracks bags and deliver them to the squadron warehouse." Sweating from fever, coughing, head pounding from the worst headache I'd ever had, I carried my heavy load, checked in my bags at the warehouse, trudged back to the orderly room, and waited an hour until an ambulance made its scheduled stop and picked me up.

Finally under care in the base hospital, I overheard a doctor say, "My god, look at his temperature, it's a wonder he's not dead," and I felt as I'd felt when I was a little boy, coughing and waiting for my sleepy mother to come and comfort me.

A nurse sticking a needle into my arm and drawing a sample of blood, I thought it was another Wasserman test, the only blood test I'd ever had before, and I said to myself, I haven't even had a date for a month, and she's checking me for venereal disease.

I spat phlegm into paper cup after paper cup and took pills, not the sugar-coated aspirin with which I'd been treated for fever as a child but a new drug called sulfa, a "wonder drug" that would save the lives of soldiers — so that they could kill other soldiers.

Weeks later I'd read, in a small news story, that a little girl had died because her doctor had been denied use of the pill, which was only available for soldiers. I felt — and I feel — guilty for taking the medicine that might have saved her life.

Awakened my first night in the pneumonia ward, I saw, and heard, another teenage soldier die, under a hastily rigged oxygen tent at the foot of my bed, and I remembered that my brother Bob's father had fallen ill and died — at Jefferson Barracks, I thought, but I'd learn years later that he'd died in Texas, just after leaving Jefferson Barracks.

The ward in which I faithfully swallowed sulfa pills and recovered was about forty feet long. Black troops were segregated by a space between rows of beds at one end of the ward, and there was no conversation between sick white troops and sick black troops.

"They's good niggers and they's bad niggers," had been my Southern-born, mixed-race father's pronouncement. With no black people in my rural Iowa life I'd not thought much about race, my own or anyone else's, but the segregated army assumed that all black people were bad.

# 21

One gunner from a bomber crew bunking near my own, a power-
fully built Jew, threatened one night to fight every one of the thirty
or so men in our barracks. I'd always gotten along with him. I felt
insulted by his challenge to the group of which I was a part, and
I was too innocent to guess the years of mistreatment that had
caused his bellicosity.

Two of my close friends were Jewish, and I went once a week
with one of them to the Jewish USO for dancing and for winning
whatever affection could be won from young women intent on marriage and only minimally interested in men who would certainly
be gone within weeks to another air base and maybe to death.

Once, when I was hitchhiking with a friend to the Jewish USO,
he said something that let the woman who'd picked us up know
that he was Jewish.

"Oh, you're a Jew?" she asked. Then she said to me, glancing
at my Indian nose and black hair, "I didn't know that your friend
was Jewish, but I knew right away that you were."

In the American army I became friendly with Jews on the basis
of tennis competition, intellectual conversation, and some vaguely
sensed community of pariah-hood. One of my Jewish friends had
missed, by one week, becoming what I had dreamed of being, a
pilot, one whose excellent record would have made him not just
a flight officer but a lieutenant. A week from graduation, uniform
and gold bars already bought, he'd ground-looped an advanced
training plane while practicing landings, and he'd been sent to be

retrained as a machine-gunner. Our friendship ended when the military intervened.

My armaments class was watching the firing of a P-47 Thunderbolt plane's eight machine guns. Like an elephant-size panther readying to spring, the big plane rocked back from the guns' recoil, and the plank target was riddled by armor-piercing bullets. When one machine gun jammed, my Jewish friend was ordered to clear its firing chamber, something none of us had ever done, and we knew that one of us had suffered shrapnel wounds when a cartridge misfired and exploded in an open firing chamber. My friend refused to undertake a dangerous job for which he'd not been trained.

He was ordered to put on his dress uniform and report to headquarters. I next saw him in the custody of two sergeants, sweat soaking his uniform as he was marched from training site to training site, taking again the performance tests he, and the rest of us, had already passed. Just weeks ago he had been on the verge of commissioning as a proud air force officer. Now he looked exhausted, tense, humiliated, and worried. My friend was the only one in our class of several hundred who was washed out of armorer-gunner training. When he was sent to fight, half trained, as an infantryman, I felt the humiliation and the guilt any decent human should feel at seeing another human victimized.

Before America's entry into World War II a boatload of Jews who had escaped from Hitler's death camps were denied entry into the United States. Today reading that my country tortures prisoners makes me ashamed.

I feel shame, remembering having shot at an innocent vulture to please a training sergeant and doubtless to gratify some vicious part of my young self. I missed the vulture and disappointed the sergeant. Weeks back he had killed a mother bobcat and adopted her kittens, which were as big as full-grown house cats. Startled by my group's machine-gun clatter, they leaped, dug in their claws, and climbed the highest thing other than cactus, the sergeant.

Having had to feed cattle in winter, I feel guilty for having been on a plane that dived and stampeded a herd into an icy lake, while two ranch hands were unloading hay bales onto a snow-covered pasture. I'd volunteered for the flight, to test a recently repaired bomber. Before amusing himself at the cattle's expense, the test pilot had flown inside an old volcano, now Crater Lake. Glowing snow on the rim above us, our plane's reflection the ghost of my pet possum swimming in a rain barrel, we flew around and around over blue water. The beauty of the snow and water remains in my mind, as does the shame of being an unwilling accomplice to the pilot's cruelty toward two cowboys and their herd of cows.

During combat training I saw machine-gunners on low-level gunnery missions shoot cattle, evidently just for the pleasure of killing a live target, and I heard about, but did not see, a bombardier drop a bomb on a Navajo home, killing some sheep and blinding an elderly man.

Our crew's bombardier told me that he'd been accused of the bombing. Of course I knew he hadn't done it because we were in the same bomber. Also I knew him, and I knew he wouldn't do it. All of the officers on our bombing crew were relaxed and didn't require us to salute them, but the bombardier and I were maybe particularly good friends because we were fellow pariahs, myself an Indian and he a Jew. He told me all I was to know of the story, that the men in command had determined that he was not the bombardier who had done the bombing.

Eight million Native Americans wiped out. White troops ravaging the families of Cherokees who had just helped them win a battle against the Creek tribe. Bounty money paid for each red savage's scalp presented at the courthouse. American tourists, bored with beautiful scenery, leaning out the windows of trains and shooting Indians they chanced to pass. The Reverend Colonel Chivington and his Colorado troops riding back to Denver in triumph, flourishing the severed sexual organs of "bucks" and "squaws" in token of white civilization's triumph at the Sand Creek Massacre. California vigilantes, intent on "ethnic cleansing," intent on genocide, bludgeoning to death Indian women who'd been servants of white families for years. Ishi — "the last wild Indian" — hunted with dogs and guns. Was the gamesome bombardier from my squadron imprisoned for killing sheep and blinding an old man? Or was he forgiven and allowed to use the skill his target practice had given him? Incendiary bombs fell. Two atomic bombs fell. Densely populated Japanese cities burned, as humble American Indian villages had burned.

Although I was called a "Jew lover" or a "spic lover" because of my friends, I experienced little personal discrimination. However, I was black haired, and as my skin tone deepened in summer sun, one fellow soldier in the army of democracy said, nastily, to me, "You damned dago or whatever you are."

For two blessed months I had two girlfriends, both Chicanas, and the fact that I could date either of them without angering the other suggests that none of us was in love. A Chicano bus driver said to one of my girlfriends, "So, you go with a soldier," and she, probably thinking of her reputation, seemed upset.

"You must really love me," one of my Hispanic girlfriends murmured, while I was trying to kiss and fondle her in a movie house's darkness. I didn't love her. Driven by hormones, loneliness, and fear of dying without emotional and biological fulfillment, I had only movie-inspired illusions of love and marriage.

My next girlfriend suffered a pariah-hood not based on race. A beautiful blond young woman, she walked — and would always walk — with a limp, and she danced, not well but as well as I did, despite her damaged leg.

"Yours was the most beautiful girl at the dance," a married buddy told me, wistfully, his wife thousands of miles away.

"The most beautiful girl —" A movie-inspired dream of my time.

I might have thought that I was suffering racial discrimination when a training officer asked me if I was trying to fail in my aerial-gunnery classes in order to escape combat. I'd scored the highest score on the gunnery range for one day's shooting. Now I was being accused of cowardice. I mumbled a denial, and it turned out that the training officer had lied as a test of my military fervor. My ratings were extremely good, and a few days after the confrontation with the training officer I was offered a chance to remain in gunnery school as an instructor and escape combat altogether. Fanatically bent on heroics and appalled by the thought of being that despised butt of male jokes, a teacher, I refused. I wanted to prove myself in combat, as my brother Bob and millions of others had proven themselves.

Bob had survived for nine months as an escaped prisoner of war. He had survived Fascist and Nazi efforts to recapture him or kill him. He had survived the affliction that had killed our brother Leland in infancy, malnutrition. He weighed only ninety pounds when he was brought back to the United States. He had survived yellow jaundice. On recuperation leave he came to see me, accompanied by our brother Ray, and for two days we three brothers saw something of Laredo, Texas. I was allowed a third day because of my brother Bob's combat record, but my pass was withdrawn. A general was inspecting the base, and my services were required for raking sand around a gun pit and making it as neat as a parade ground. Angry, I went absent without leave. I couldn't go to see my brothers in town because I had no pass, but I slipped into the concealment afforded by mesquite and cactus, sat on a log, and started reading the novel I carried in one of my pockets. Absorbed in someone else's story, someone else's life, I forgot that I'd been done an injustice and was angry, forgot that I had disobeyed an order and might be punished.

I came back into my own life when a slight sound near my legs proved to be a four-foot-long rattlesnake, writhing past me and into a nearby pile of brush.

"A rattlesnake it come a twisting and squirming out of the first bundle I pitched into that threshing machine, and them big blades jist cut it into bits about the size of them wieners we had for dinner, only the pieces was still squirming and the ketchup was blood."

"Reminds me, this cousin of mine over in the Sand Hill country, he found him a rattlesnake in the one bundle, and another feller, a snake it found him and it got him right in the hand what was lifting the pitchfork and another feller was nailed when his ankle slipped down between the bundles of the load he was standing on. Then there was this dog, a gritty little thing, went after a rattler and got bit whils't shaking that snake and trying to get a better grip. That little fice, its head swolled up big as a St. Bernard's head, and they dug it a keyhole-shape grave."

Others' stories had been my experience of rattlesnakes, but the snake that had startled me out of a truly gripping novel was the first rattlesnake I'd ever seen, and knowing that a chance move might have gotten me bitten while I'd been absorbed in reading, I pocketed the book, picked up my rake, and resumed grooming the designated bit of desert for the general.

I was eighteen, Bob twenty-six, and Ray twenty. I never learned Ray's thoughts about being in civilian clothes while millions of men as young as seventeen and as old as forty-five were in uniform.

It was not legal for Indians like myself to drink alcohol in Iowa, but during the war a uniform was the only legal document required for drinking.

Alcohol. And women.

A potent pairing in Viking mead halls — from which the first European invaders of North America came. In my midteens, I'd drink a few pints of self-confidence, then dance and pick up girls.

Ahead of me in every way, Ray "cut a wide swath" with women who frequented the Oelwein Colosseum dance hall. "She'd go so far, and then she'd decide that she wanted to be just a prick teaser again," was Ray's version of a woman he'd dated for some time and finally forced to have sex with him, an experience he reported to me without comment, neither guilt nor total satisfaction.

My baby body grown to five-foot-seven, 140 pounds, my brain enlightened by hundreds of hours of schooling in the mechanics of pistols, rifles, machine guns, and cannon and the physics of bombers and bombs, I stepped from the nearly total darkness of a military base preparing for war, and as I entered the blinding lights of a barracks I'd learned to feel was home, I instinctively turned my head to let a sharp-edged sheet of metal the size of this page speed past, leaving me with my tight-fitting army Go to Hell cap turned sideways, my right ear tingling from a glancing contact with metal.

"What the fuck?" I naturally yelled, prepared to take revenge on whoever had damned near killed me, but no, it was all a mistake: a bigoted Southerner and a Northerner had ventured into words that had moved one of them to hurl a heavy piece of flat steel, ordinarily used as makeshift dustpan for collecting ashes spilled in front of the little coal stove.

It was all perfectly okay. Everyone was laughing to see me with "that look" on my face, with my hat turned cockeyed, as if I thought I was Napoleon or somebody, all of us relieved that no one had killed anyone and all of us soon to join half of the world in sleep and then rise and train to kill strangers.

I grew to manhood in a community like most, where men have to fight to get respect.

Ray was a fighter, like our dad. In a neighborhood disagreement a man probably then in his thirties called my father, then in his midfifties, "a liar." My father hit him. A friend of the first man attacked from behind. My brother Ray, then in his early twenties, hit the second man in the mouth and put him out of the fight—and suffered infected knuckles from the defeated's snuff-stained teeth. A third man attacked my dad from behind, but a friendly neighbor grabbed the third attacker, dragged him across a table, and told him, "You stay out of that," words that survive him, warrior words that he had, as idiom put it, "made good." My father and brother then beat their opponents into surrender and into a family story.

As Dad's eldest living son, Ray had to be heroic, starting with early boyhood, his small heroisms the routine ones of bearing bigger loads than his younger siblings could bear. "Your brother lived a hard life. There wasn't an ounce of fat on his whole body," the undertaker's helper told our sister after Ray died of a heart attack at age fifty.

Ray drove our huge horses steadily and capably, while his younger brother Ralph tried what would be his main strength in the struggle for world survival, his voice, whining eloquently, "I want the gines," meaning the lines, with which Ray was keeping the big black team in the road and not in the ditch.

Ray mastered four rebellious horses and kept them from trampling me under their muddy hoofs and under the big disk blades, which would have cut my flesh into bacon strips. At sixteen Ray, possibly nursing a hangover, tried again and again to back our tractor into line so its pulley drive wheel would power our threshing machine's blades and cannon-blasting straw blower. Again and again Ray got it wrong but persisted, though every grown man in the threshing ring angrily yelled for him to "Let somebody else do it," and Ray finally got it right.

Again and again I watched, awed, as he met the challenges of the farm work that awaited me.

"You just don't have self-confidence," Dad told me again and again, weakening whatever confidence I had. Ray had confidence. Horses knew it, neighbors knew it, and Dad knew it. Dad "never swung on a man without seeing the bottoms of his feet." The bigger they were, the harder they fell. But Ray was nearly choked to death in a tavern fight while I was only half a block away, dancing and drinking beer and having a good time.

"He got me by the throat and choked me till I passed out and would have died if somebody hadn't pulled him off me." That honest confession and lesson stay in my mind as a moment when I knew that my big—and long-envied—brother loved me and valued me and cared about what happened to me and was just as vulnerable and human as I was myself.

Drunken fights were common where I grew up. At a dance I followed my drunken friends past a fellow and a girl. He accused them of jostling him and pushed someone. All three of my friends started toward him, and drunkenly mouthing, "Not everyone on one," I stepped in front of my group. The guy I'd presumably saved from a group assault drunkenly misunderstood my intention and pushed me so hard I staggered backward, came up against a pillar, and, filled with rage at the injustice, charged. A huge hand grabbed my shoulder, and I was propelled backward to bump against the same pillar, rage fading as I saw an enormous policeman moving in to reestablish law and order.

World War II aerial-combat losses were devastating, and older men joined with us teenagers and twenty-some-year-olds in bomber-crew training. Men from farms in North Carolina would sit on barracks steps at night and sing the mournful love ballads I'd grown up hearing my father sing. The older soldiers were missing their wives and children. One of the older soldiers was so terrified by his first flight in a bomber he wrapped his arms around a vertical gunnery-turret axle and had to be pried loose after he was back on the ground.

The bomber that had taken off ahead of ours crashed. Black smoke rose from rocks and snow only two hundred feet below our bomber.

I saw one man running to get away from flames before high-test gasoline could explode. A half-track vehicle was speeding over the rough terrain to attempt rescue.

"Take crash positions!" crackling into my headphones, I felt no fear. The situation was, I suppose, not real to me.

Two of my crewmates were fighting to wedge up against the bomb-bay bulkhead, which was actually the assigned position of only one of them. One was Lutheran, one was Catholic. The pilot had asked my advice on how he should deal with their enmity. I remembered a rough game and some fights when my high school had played a Catholic high school's basketball team, and I remembered that Catholic kids and Protestant kids had fought with fists, clubs, and knives just twelve miles from my home. I'd had no advice for my pilot, but seeing my two crewmates making a bad situation worse, I dropped the parachute I'd been holding to pillow my head against my side of the bomb-bay bulkhead. Spreading my thick-soled, fleece-lined flight boots wide to keep myself balanced upright on the steeply angled floor, I edged toward the two, who were wrestling, their bodies awkward in flight suits thickly padded for 30-below-zero high-altitude flying. They were lurching over the airplane's corrugated aluminum floor, in danger of plunging out the waist window and hurtling hundreds of feet to splatter against the lava ridges, of their God's Creation, blurring below.

I slammed one guy down beside the rear bomb-bay hatchway, my own designated crash position, from which I had just leapt up. I slammed the other into the crash position they'd been fighting to take, to the other side of the hatchway. Then I simply sat down and waited. I had, I felt, been heroic, had done what movies, recruitment propaganda, and presidential speeches had told me I should do, in order to eventually win a medal, win kisses, and win some winsome looks from pale women.

I was posturing to convince myself. My posturing was spared the ultimate test that time, but there would be others. That time our pilot, who'd survived being badly injured in one crash, skill-fully flew our crazily jolting bomber, carefully using the rudder controls to compensate for our ailerons' being frozen. Mushing slowly in a wide turn over the rocky mesa, he guided our plane back into line with the runway, and we landed safely.

Only one man had escaped the bomber we'd seen burning. The base safety officer had climbed onto the wreckage to try to save others, but explosion had propelled a sheet of metal and nearly scalped him. He was a true hero. Eight men had burned, and I'd narrowly escaped the same death, but it felt somewhat unreal, like the earth itself when seen from altitude. You know what you are seeing hundreds of feet below, but only the few inches of cor-rugated aluminum floor beneath your flight boots seems real.

I'd heard stories of World War I soldiers sitting on dead German soldiers while eating rations. I was eating a peanut butter and jelly sandwich when I saw a bomber go down in flames, burning the men inside. At some point I'd decided to eat the sandwich while still on the ground because sandwiches froze in the subzero temperature of altitude and one had to slip them into one's fleece-lined flight jacket and under an armpit to thaw them. I only became aware that I was simultaneously eating and witnessing suffering when I saw that the copilot was shocked by my callousness.

In pre-dawn dark I crawled up through our bomb-bay, and,climbing into our airplane's aft section, I stumbled over a sleeping ground-crewman who was supposed to be chipping ice from the plane's controls and getting it ready to fly. I gave him hell, but he only answered, "I just want to get back to my wife and kids, and I don't give a damn about anything else."

After that my crew did double duty. I not only checked out the bombs and machine guns, but I also helped the flight engineer to pre-flight the engines and the controls, work that the ground crew should have done.

Sometimes our best efforts were not enough. Snake River fog closed in while my crew was headed back to base. To get under the fog, our pilot went low and followed the road leading to our base. A bus driver looked up, and thinking that we were going to land on top of him, he drove into the sagebrush. We found our way back to base, and just after we'd landed and gotten out of our airplane, another low-flying bomber roared over us and missed the runway. Trying to get back into the air and turn at the same time, the huge ship stalled for lack of power, slipped sideways, crashed, and burst into flames just a few hundred feet from where we stood, safe and horrified.

Gasoline exploding, nine people burning to death were hidden by flames, smoke, and melting aluminum airplane skin. I remembered a high school friend's story of an elderly neighbor's body after his cookstove exploded, his own flesh the last thing it would cook, his thighs like split frankfurters. My brother Bob once told me of riding on a German tank, after his company had been captured. Now in retreat the German panzer unit had transported their prisoners through a twenty-square-mile battlefield, strewn with the burned-out hulks of German and American tanks.

Our pilot was an eighty-miles-per-hour automobile driver, who gave us rides into fun-time Boise, where his wife worked as an actress or entertainer. He'd been a professional basketball player, and solely because of him our crew won all of its games.

His flying skill saved our lives more than once, but unexplainably, one night he endangered our lives by landing in the wrong direction. I was standing, talking with the navigator beside one waist-section window, when he grabbed my shoulder and slammed me down onto my thick flight-suit-padded knees, a position he too assumed, for fear that a rough landing would throw us out the window. As our plane hit the ground and rolled at terrific speed, I saw the lighted wind T pointed in the direction from which we'd come and realized, as the navigator had, that we might crash head-on into a plane landing in the correct direction. Our landing speed increased by the tailwind, we hurtled from one end of the runway to the other before our brakes stopped us, but no plane crashed into us head-on, and instead of losing our lives, we lost some sleep, while command officers held a lengthy talk with our pilot. Another time our pilot suffered blurred vision, possibly a consequence of the crash he'd been in, and had to let the copilot land the plane.

More than two hundred were killed while I was in training, two of them my friends. Their deaths became real when I saw one wreck afterward, its huge wings and body a twisted silver cross.

My best friend from my first crew died while flying with another crew. Their bomber went into a spin so violent no one could parachute, and the plane crashed and burned. My friend's body, for five decades and the spans of several more wars, has been, with possum and cabbage trimmings, a part of the earth, but some of his cheerful generous nature perhaps still lives in the minds of those of us who knew him.

I was eighteen. I was the armorer, the specialist gunner, and a corporal. The navigator was an officer, a second lieutenant, and knew maps, sextant, and compass, but he knew little about the machine gun he had to man when not navigating. The first time he fired a .50 caliber machine gun he failed to notice that a ground crewman had forgotten to insert the pin securing the gun to its swivel mount in the side window. When he pressed the trigger, recoil drove the gun back against his flight-suit-padded chest. Luckily he was not hurt, and I resumed teaching him, in the space of a few minutes, all that thirteen weeks of training had taught me about killing other human beings.

I was not destined to kill. In fact, I twice maybe saved some human lives.

Its sear pin worn out, a .50 caliber machine gun fired thousands of armor-piercing bullets from my plane's tail turret back through a flight of ten or so bombers, each bomber crewed by nine men. The tail gunner scotched his out-of-control gun by shoving the wooden lid of an ammunition box in front of the bolt lever. So long as he held the box lid, everyone was safe, but if the box lid slipped, many might be killed.

I'd helped Dad in giving first aid to rusty farm machines. Now I was an armorer, a doctor for gunnery maladies. With who knew how many minutes or seconds left before the tail gunner's cold fingers would slip, letting bullets bigger than bear's teeth bite into human flesh, I considered twisting the steel-linked bullet belt, but that wouldn't stop the cartridge already held in the bolt from slipping forward and firing at least one more, maybe fatal round, and anyway, twisting the belt might not work, the power of the gun twisting its belt straight and out of my thick-gloved hands, which were already numb from intervals of going gloveless to work.

I made the tail gunner's temporary cure permanent by grabbing another ammunition-carton lid and, with it, battering the butt plate off the machine gun, after first warning the waist-section gunners to stand to one side so they wouldn't be pierced when the recoil spring shot its guide rod straight as a steel arrow back through our bomber, to bounce harmlessly off of an aluminum bulkhead.

At age eighteen, a trained armorer gunner, and supposedly expert at everything to do with the B-24 bomber's equipment for killing, I was ordered into the polar cold of an open bomb bay to refasten a bomb to its rack or to pry it loose and let it fall before our fuel ran low, forcing us to leave the bomb range. Awkward in a thick leather fleece-lined flight suit and hampered by the bulk of the parachute buckled to my chest, I tested, with one thick-booted foot, the slipperiness of the icy catwalk between the bomb stanchions.

Then, thick-mittened hands gripping slippery, frost-covered bracing, I inched toward the bomb, which was dangling from one end of a jammed bomb shackle and swinging in wind blasting up between the open bomb-bay doors. The bomb had only a small black-powder explosive charge, but that might make hundreds of gallons of high-test gasoline explode.

I sat on the catwalk, legs awkwardly clamped around a vertical brace, and using something, I think an empty machine-gun cartridge, I tried to pry the bomb-shackle lever and release the bomb to fall harmlessly. Again and again I tried, while again and again dodging the bomb's ninety pounds of steel shell, which was swinging like a giant home-run hitter's gigantic bat. Finally, I tried to grab the bomb and lift it back into the second of its two bomb-shackle clamps. The steel was frosty and slippery. My mittens were thick and frosty and slippery, and it was too cold to take the mittens off and work barehanded for more than a few seconds at a time. More and more exhausted, I was in more and more danger of slipping off the catwalk and plunging thousands of feet toward the snow-covered bombing range. I was afraid that my fingers might be too numb to pull the parachute ripcord, afraid that even if the parachute opened, I'd sink into smothering snow in gullies of the mountains below, the parachute slowly settling after me, a big white blossom, the only one to grace my lonely white grave.

I saw my best friend inching along the narrow catwalk as I had done. He had been ordered to help me secure the bomb. Eyes blurred by tears in cold wind, I watched my friend's leather-suited body move toward me. His eyes, pale blue and blurry with tears, met my terrified stare. Then he looked away, and, mittened fingers gripping metal bomb stanchions to keep wind from blowing him out of the airplane, he stepped over my struggling body and slowly, cautiously made his way into the aft section of the plane, where our pilot wouldn't see that he had disobeyed orders and where, I guess, he waited, hoping I wouldn't fail to prevent explosion.

Finally, my hands caught the bomb at the apex of one of its swings, shoved it a few inches higher, and gripping tight with my tired thighs and letting go of my only handhold, I managed to get the bomb back into the mechanical clutch of that magical silvery facsimile of a human hand, the bomb shackle. My fingers numb inside thin rayon gloves that kept cold from freezing skin to metal, I threaded the gleaming copper safety wire back into its hole in the fuse of the bomb — managed to embrace the bomb stanchion braces, get my thick-booted feet under me, get upright, and stumble cautiously back seven or eight feet into the rear section of the airplane.

In trying to think well of the eighteen-year-old I was, have I exaggerated? Was the bomb striking sparks in the fuel-vapor-laden air, or were the sparks only what I and all of my crewmates feared — or only flashes off the copper wire arcing free and not in its hole to secure the fuse from exploding? None of what I did, while terrified, amounts to heroism worthy of note, and certainly I made no mention to my crewmates that I'd possibly saved their young lives and my own. Neither did I blame my friend. In his place I might have done the same. I did not report him to the pilot, who might have reported him to the squadron discipline officer, who might have taken him off flight status and shipped him off, as my Jewish friend had been shipped, to become cannon fodder in the fields of Europe. His early childhood had been damaged by his parents' divorce, mine by my parents' undeclared war and my father's drunken violence.

A famous humorist, Max Eastman, once said that all humor is based on the play of young animals, who imitate fights to feel released from fear of actual peril. When an officer from another crew accidentally popped his life-saving parachute while on the ground and had to carry it still strapped to his chest and bundled like laundry in his arms, all of us, our fear of having to parachute from burning planes relieved, joined in a laugh.

All of my crew wore parachutes strapped to our chests. Old combat-crew wisdom said that if the rip-cord release failed, we could rip pins loose and deploy chest-fastened chutes before we hit the ground. Parachutes worn in back were impossible to reach if their ripcords failed. Valuing comfort more than safety, we gunners in the aft section of the bomber, and out of our officers' scrutiny, could take our chutes off and forget about them until we'd landed and had to take them back to the parachute riggers. Often we'd use our chutes as pillows. After a fun time the night before I could sleep anywhere, even in 20- or 30-below-zero temperatures. With the parachute as pillow and my thick flight suit as blanket and mattress, I'd curl around oxygen bottles atop the ridged metal roof of the bomb bay and catch a few minutes of sleep before I was needed again.

The pilot of the plane that imploded an A-bomb over Hiroshima has been quoted as saying he slept on the return flight to be rested enough to make a safe landing.

Due to oxygen deprivation and exhaustion from a night in town, one of my crew members fell asleep while standing with me and another crew member near the edge of a camera hatch that I'd opened, preparing to photograph bomb hits. As our buddy swayed, asleep, standing, teetering toward a fall of thousands of feet without his parachute, the other crew member and I laughed, but we were both tensed, ready to grab him if he actually started to fall.

"Dear-Johned," or as rejected lovers say these days, "dumped" by my girlfriend, I stood in front of the open camera hatch, not contemplating suicide but considering faking a fall and parachuting, a ploy that had, a rumor said, gotten another man a furlough home. Fear, devotion to duty, whatever—I closed the camera hatch.

Despite their lofty status officers of both of the crews with which I flew encouraged informality—no saluting—first names—or nicknames, Hap for my first pilot, Pappy for the second, Solly or Sergeant Red Nose for me. The latter warrior name was bestowed by the tail gunner, who was nearly twice my age and resented my wearing one more stripe than he'd won. Solly was the name one of my Jewish buddies coined because he'd misheard my last name as Salzburg and because my sundial-blade nose made him think that I was Jewish.

"You bastard," people said to their best buddies, without meaning anything except friendship. "My good old asshole buddy," men said, not meaning the anal intercourse implied. "You cocksucker," men laughed, not meaning anything derogatory, though they called some civilian men hanging around military bars "queers" and meant it as a supreme insult. "You sonofabitch," men said, not meaning anybody's mother. "You motherfucker," men said, not meaning anybody's mother.

Under orders to rush us into combat against Germany our instructors faked the final few training quotas by ordering us to aim guncameras at sunlit clouds so that it would seem the film had been fogged. One week from finishing training and going to Europe, I spent much of my meager flight-corporal pay to have a portrait made. The portrait camera aimed at me should have shown my girlfriend, my family, and the world a fearlessly smiling, slender eighteen-year-old wearing the uniform of his warring nation. I had my self-conceived and no doubt conceited military-movie grin's parade row of perfect front teeth on full display. My necktie was straight enough to have satisfied the most meticulous of inspecting officers, but the photographer had perched a studio-prop parade cap on my black Indian hair and failed to notice that its badge had accidentally swiveled in the box, the American eagle not proudly upright with arrows clutched in its claws but drunkenly askew, about to fall on its butt. It was the photographer's mistake, but, a poised middle-aged man of commerce, he faced down a sullen teenage farm boy and exacted an additional fraction of flight corporal's pay for a second set of portraits.

A common cold keeping me on the ground during our squadron's graduation-parade flight, I felt what millions of Europeans were feeling, the awesome teeth-jolting vibrations of hundreds of engines, their roaring foreshadowing that of exploding bombs.

I was under orders to board a troop ship and cross the Atlantic to combat, but the ocean I actually saw was the Pacific, off California, the awe-inspiring beauty of hundreds of miles of sunlit sand and emerald water a contrast to the temporarily halted, quarter-mile-long train, grimy under its own smoke. Hundreds of soldiers armed with .45 caliber automatic pistols had anticipated killing reportedly civilized Germans, but veering from Idaho down to California seemed to mean that we'd be bombing reportedly savage Japanese. My escape kit's fake-passport photo showed a deeply tanned black-haired kid, who'd often been mistaken for a dark Italian. A plea was printed in French on silk, intended to persuade resistance fighters to risk their own lives to save mine.

In Salinas I was ritually kissed on the cheek by the American equivalent of a Greek goddess, one of several dancers who'd descended from stage and raced through the audience bestowing lipstick on some of us blessed by having been seated on the aisles. Envied by less fortunate buddies, I kept the symbol of my ten-second love life until forced to shave for inspection before again boarding a train.

I saw Los Angeles as a city dimmed to near darkness in fear of Japanese submarines. I saw Albuquerque as a snow-covered railroad station, beside which other Indians huddled in thin store-bought blankets, hoping to sell jewelry.

In Denver, where a few months before I'd learned to disassemble, repair, and adjust machine guns and cannon, only one person was visible on the long train platform. Beautiful, she seemed more so as she moved, vividly dressed, over snow and handed steaming coffee up to windows jammed with eager young men.

A military secret, that our shipment had been canceled, was revealed when a train crewman said that no food had been taken on for travel beyond the evening meal.

In an air base near Kearney, Nebraska, I legally saw the bomber I could have been imprisoned for photographing—saw in fact a row of "Super Fortress" B-29s, a B-24, the plane in which I'd had been flying, parked under one wing of one of them.

My life, though I didn't know it, was taking a turning point—was possibly being saved.

Another life, one that millions of Nazis, Fascists, and Japanese would have sacrificed their lives to end, ended naturally while I was drinking beer in Kearney, the little town named for a fort established to control occupied Indian lands. Unable to find dates at a local dance, the young women understandably reluctant to become emotionally involved with migrant killers who'd soon be across the Atlantic Ocean, four or five of us were lingering in a tavern—preferable to lonely bunks in a barracks—when a sleepy ten-year-old boy entered to sell a one-page "extra" edition of the Kearney newspaper, its headline "PRESIDENT ROOSEVELT DEAD."

Drunkenly stunned, we spent the rest of our money on more beer. Then, to rebel against a great man's mortality and our own, we stole a military policeman's jeep from where it was temptingly parked in the lightless, wartime-blackout street and drove morosely back to base to try to sleep.

I was under orders to join in "blockbuster bombing" German factory workers' homes and factories and other targets—all of which I was, with the ruthless innocence of youth, enthusiastically and idealistically eager to do—and to suffer an unrealistically romantic and painless movie hero's death. Faced with imminent danger, love-sick, and closer to home than I might ever be again, I risked punishment by stretching a weekend pass and hitchhiking to try to win back my girl, who was, I correctly feared, interested in someone some thousands of miles closer to her home than where I was soon supposed to be.

Love situation not improved by on-site eloquence, I hitchhiked, already late, my pass expired, and in the middle of the night I caught a ride with an elderly couple.

Asleep on the dark back seat, exhausted from trying to fulfill my eighteen-year-old's beautiful confusion of lust and love, I was grabbed by a huge cop, dragged out of the car, frisked for weapons, and ordered to produce identification.

My weekend pass clearly stated that I was still maybe eighty-some miles further from base than I was authorized to be and hours past my document's expiration time. Afraid that the cop would slam me into jail, arms up to the glittering stars, not to pray but to obey the man in command, the man with the gun in his hand, I heard him telling the frightened old couple that he was waiting to get a name from the radio to match it with the name on my weekend pass. Then I heard that a soldier about my size and build had murdered his girlfriend.

My bomber lost in fog, Marconi's miracle invention, the radio, had already saved my life, and it saved me again. The police-car radio informed the big cop that I was not the murderer, and no longer suspected of murder, I was free to fly to kill thousands of strangers.

In Omaha I lived through my second scare of a long—and love-less—night. A military policeman grabbed my arm, but he turned out to be a good Samaritan, concerned that a more officious MP would get me for not wearing my cap when out of doors, the railroad station under a roof but not regarded as inside.

Cleared of murder, the charge that had sent my father to prison, and forgiven having been bare headed, I was lucky my childhood bedtime stories' magic third time. A tired gate guard not noticing or not caring that I was arriving several hours later than the time printed on my pass, I made it back to a hot shower, my bunk, and then black coffee, eighteen and ready for whatever came next.

What was due to come next was to board a big ship and sail past German submarines and live the thrillingly and chillingly predicted five minutes—of firing half-inch, armor-piercing .50 caliber machine gun bullets at German fighter pilots, who'd be firing machine guns and cannon back at me, trying to prevent the blockbuster bombing of thousands of blocks of German homes. Five minutes of combat, and then I'd return, in a flag-wrapped hero's casket, to the sound of a bugle's beautifully mourning my patriotic—and dreamily painless—passing, while my faithless girlfriend would realize, too late, that she'd loved me.

What really came next was someone in Washington DC's dispatching orders that the bombardier and myself should retrain for a month and then fly in a B-29 Superfortress bomber.

I left my B-24 Liberator bomber crew. Of our number only the ball-turret gunner, my best friend, would die, and only the nose-turret gunner would engage in combat—not with Imperial Japanese troops but with Filipino freedom fighters, who didn't like American reoccupation any better than they had liked Japanese occupation.

# 22

While training to command the lethal electronic gunnery of a
B-29, I and all of the other trainees had to survive what was still
a military secret, the unreliability of the huge 2,000-horsepower
engines required to keep an enormous plane and an enormous
bomb load airborne. If two engines went out on the same side, the
airplane would be wrenched around, and when this happened near
the ground, the plane would crash. That is how one of my friends
died, and that is how I came close to being killed.

One engine caught fire and had to be shut down. Then a second
engine exploded and had to be shut down. That left us with two
engines, but since we had an engine on each side of the airplane,
we were in balance and could still fly. However, the explosion had
ruptured a hydraulics line. With no hydraulics the plane had to land
without flaps to slow its descent and no brakes to slow wheels on
the ground. Just before we sped off the end of the runway, a third
engine exploded. If this had happened seconds earlier, the plane
would have crashed while landing. The exploding engine was like
an anti-personnel bomb—like the one that crossed the Pacific on
a Japanese balloon and killed a Sunday-school class in Oregon.
We were lucky; piston fragments pierced the B-29's midsection's
thin aluminum skin but hit none of us.

America developed a new respect for firefighters and ambulance
crews after the destruction of the World Trade Towers. I remember
vividly, and with deep gratitude, fire trucks, with their chemical
flame retardants and tanks of water, and ambulances, with their
red lights flashing, slogging through sand, while the rest of my

crew and I jumped into the sagebrush and ran, afraid high-octane gasoline would turn the bomber into a colossal bomb, as fatal to us as the magnesium-fueled fire-bombs we were training to drop on highly combustible Japanese homes.

We air soldiers were training to kill thousands of our fellow humans, but "the enemies" were thousands of miles away. Young, sleep deprived, sex deprived, and drunk, men fought one another over trifles. Sober but in need of the three or four hours of sleep I'd hoped to get before flight time, I was rolled out of bed and onto the barracks floor. The drunken prankster, who was busily rolling other airmen out of sleep, was a friend of mine, but furious, I tore into him with my fists. He outweighed me by twenty-some pounds, and when he hit me hard enough to hurt, I instinctively applied my newly acquired army judo training and threw him down a stair's steep steps. Luckily, he was not killed, only — drunkard's luck or whatever — jolted into some degree of sobriety.

I slept and awoke when the morning whistles blew. I put in my ten- to fifteen-hour day at training to kill those I was supposed to kill. The soldier I'd thrown down steep stairs and I went back to being friends, as, many years and many deaths later, the United States and its surviving enemies would do.

B-29 training flights often lasted ten hours. Our morning flight would noisily get up at maybe four o'clock, while the afternoon flight was trying to sleep. Then, while we were trying to begin sleep early, the afternoon flight crews would be noisily enjoying life. Once buddies and I decided to skip sleep altogether and continue our evening of drinking and feminine companionship in Albuquerque. Then we had to keep elbowing one another in the ribs so the pre-flight officer wouldn't see us falling asleep.

The pilot taught each crew member to fly, so that if he and the copilot were killed, someone could bring the airplane back to base and land. I got to fly the B-29 just once. It was difficult because the pilots' seats were far forward, and one couldn't see the wings and keep them level with the horizon. I did pretty well, and I felt proud, I felt as I'd felt as a small child when first given "the gines" to drive horses. We plunged toward the runway, only plexiglass between us and the concrete toward which we were hurtling. I felt panic, but I kept the plane level and stable until the pilot took back control. When told to, I stomped down hard on my set of brake pedals, and that was the extent of the life I'd dreamed, the life of an air force pilot.

Looking back on my two and a half years of military service, I bless my college-trained buddies, who accepted me as a younger brother and potential equal and either loaned me books or directed me to books available in air base libraries.

Among other things I learned that poetry was not just for sissies; it was a part of the reading of a buddy who'd been an East Coast boxing champion. In matches held for entertainment, after a day of learning to fight with machine guns, he had won against opponents forty or fifty pounds heavier than himself. A gang bar fight, centered on my poetry-reading fight-winning friend, was avoided by some talk and some drinks, just a few months before World War II ended. I was relieved that the bar fight didn't take place because it would have been against Hispanics. A black-haired, deeply tanned, mixed-blood Indian, I was often taken to be Hispanic, and my girlfriend at that time was of mixed blood, Indian and Hispanic.

A few nights after the averted gang fight a buddy and I came out of a different bar and saw our East Coast boxing-champion friend spin and fall to the sidewalk across the street. Shot, I thought, having seen a few movies, but it turned out that one of the best fighters in the United States had, by the simple lifting of fingers clutching whiskey, knocked himself out.

After his 160 pounds of bone, muscles, and comatose brain were dragged onto a bus, into a barracks, and into a cold shower, we, his saviors, had to dodge or roll with the punches of our furious friend. That is my best sense of what a string of stunned boxers had experienced.

A thief got a better sense when, after stealing the wallets of a row of sleeping men, he slipped his hand under the pillow of a knockout champion who was also a light sleeper.

Another of my buddies had played baseball at Colgate University and had had a successful tryout with the then–New York Giants. The war ended his baseball career, not because he suffered combat wounds but because he slipped off the edge of the bunk above mine and his foot crashed through a window, severing his Achilles tendon.

After my Colgate friend and I were ordered to different air bases, I lost track of him for two years. When we renewed acquaintance, near the end of the war, he rebuked me for having become a hard drinker with a shallow attitude toward women and toward life. The rebuke from someone I'd respected stayed with me, even though I continued playing the role of a tough guy.

World War II put millions of American men and women between ages seventeen and forty-five into uniform, and two married men in their mid- or late twenties sought me out as a friend. One of them invited me and another buddy to share a meal with himself and his wife. Feeding us during food rationing was extremely generous, a fact I've only remembered and appreciated these many years too late for appropriate thanks. The apartment was a one-car garage, the only place available to rent in a city jammed with the families of soldiers, some permanently stationed at the air base and some, like my friend, wanting to be with their wives for what might be the last few weeks before death in combat. All of us traveling home for a few days' leave before flying to war, I saw my friend and his wife asleep sitting up on a train, and I remember the indescribable beauty of the faces of two people who were deeply in love. From this and other experiences I learned more than I've ever learned from books.

One morning the two captains who conducted briefings informed us that atom bombs had been dropped on two Japanese cities, and the war was essentially over. Walking back to our barracks, one of my crewmates asked another what he thought about the briefing. We all agreed that the officer had probably told us a wildly improbable story to test our willingness to fight.

We only believed the story when we read it, with the rest of the United States, in the next day's news. We'd been ready to fly to the Pacific island of Tinian and, from there, to fly over hundreds of blocks of flimsy, highly combustible Japanese homes and set them aflame. That sort of bombing had already created one "fire storm," which had incinerated Dresden, a massacre greater than the ones perpetrated in Hiroshima and Nagasaki.

The war ended, and I had a better chance of living longer than the rumored "five minutes" over factories, railroad stations, and houses. Millions of us who had been soldiers could now count on the approximate four minutes between last breath and brain-cell expiration.

"When Worlds Collide" had been the name of a newspaper supplement story about an asteroid's crashing into Earth and destroying the human race. Age ten, I'd read the story and been sleepless and desolate for most of one dark night. I would live to know that within myself two worlds had collided, the Indian world of hunting and planting and harvesting, in harmony with nature, and the white world of greedily ravaging nature and pirating weaker countries' goods by means of scientific war.

During my twenty-nine months of combat training I had hitchhiked thousands of miles in the cars of American patriots. The war over, a buddy and I waited, still in uniform, for twelve hours beside the road between Albuquerque and the Carlsbad Caverns. A ride finally offered, we canceled our order for breakfast, and for the first of several times I heard the phrase, "Damned soldiers."

Two atom bombs had been dropped, incinerating thousands, and I'd only killed once, while talking with a friend, who was guarding the main gate of an airbase near McCook, Nebraska.

"Hey, look, a little black and white kitty," my big-city friend said and was moving to meet and pet the animal, until I dragged him back into the guard shack and explained about skunks. Then, since the skunk was staggering and might have rabies, I phoned the officer of the day and got permission to fire my .45, Wild West–style revolver.

With one carefully aimed shot I did the only killing I'd do in twenty-nine months of military service.

Assigned to a night of guard duty early in my military training, I'd slung my rifle on one shoulder, leaned against a light post, and read a pocket-sized novel, *The Red Badge of Courage*. Like the young main character I desired a war wound, my "Red Badge" to prove myself worthy beyond anyone's questioning, but the war had ended, and I was, for better or worse, just myself.

Let's pretend. When I enlisted at age seventeen, I was posturing, but I intended to become the man I was pretending to be.

My brother Bob a prisoner of war, I had wanted to kill his captors, the Germans, who'd been so evil in the official history books of twelve years of state schools. The fact that Bob's father had been a German American who'd died in the U.S. Army in World War I didn't mean much compared to all the newsreel film propaganda, accompanied by stirring background music, which made me feel I was part of something Big, even though I was only five-foot-seven, and made me feel I was an important part of something Important. In school after school I learned more and more complicated ways of killing fellow human beings and ended the war in New Mexico, still training to electronically machine gun and cannon any kamikaze pilots who might try to prevent my Harvard-educated bombardier from electronically bombing Tokyo's men, women, and children.

Survivors feel the guilt of having survived, I've heard or read, and like most murderers whose death sentences have been, at the last moment, commuted to imprisonment for life, I gratefully plead guilty of having outlived, by many years, some friends, some enemies, and some millions I never knew.

"The war is over," a pilot is said to have said, two years before combatant governments would say the same, "The war is over for me," rudder pedals having, minutes before, sheared off his feet and left them bloody in the soggy fleece-lined flight boots meant to protect from cold — feet amputated like those of a pheasant caught by the hay-mower sickle's sharp saw-tooth blades — the pheasant having instinctively crouched and stayed motionless so as not to be seen by the thunderous, earth-shaking monster the tractor-drawn mower must have seemed, the amputee pilot having mistaken altitude or his navigator having mistaken a map's identification of hilly terrain.

"Died for God and Country, Gave His Life That Others May Live, A Hero's Death, Collateral Casualties, Killed by Friendly Fire, Acceptable Losses . . ." and now one hears that twenty-some thousand unnecessarily die each year due to medical errors in hospitals.

"Sign up for reserves, no meetings to attend, nothing, and when the war with Russia starts, you won't have to start over as a private. You'll keep your rank and go back to flying in B-29s."

Although I had, as all Americans had, read daily newspapers' veneration of our comrade, good old Uncle Joe Stalin, I signed to fight communism, no wiser than I'd been at seventeen, when I'd signed to fight Nazism, even though I'd learned through experience that much of what I was being taught to hate was also prevalent in the dictatorship that had maintained life-or-death control over me, the American military.

An Italian scholar, Fedora Giordano, has written that much of my fiction and poetry grows out of having lost a chance to live the traditional Native American role of warrior, and she may well be right. "Teenagers are crazy, and you can turn them into good soldiers," an officer has written of his combat in Vietnam. I'd repeatedly volunteered for war and—law of chance—had not gone into combat. I'd had my courage tested a few times and had passed the tests. I'd witnessed some of the two hundred deaths my training squadrons suffered, and for years after the war I'd hear airplanes explode inside my head.

I was deranged from missing the war that was to have redeemed my being a failed baseball player and a twice-disappointed lover. Twenty years old and back on the farm, which had nourished my body while war propaganda nourished my teenage dreams, I took revenge on the model airplanes that had twirled, leashed like vicious little dogs, on their threads in the breeze above my dreaming head. Hours of my young life had been devoted to con-structing the fragile, tissue-paper-skinned warplanes—the Defiant, the Warhawk, and the Spitfire—but on the blessed black glaciated earth of Dad's fall-plowed field, I burned my idealistic dreams of military glory and sacrifice.

Then, like a marauder from the mobs that had plundered my Cherokee people—like any invader—I "cleaned out" the pantry, where rusting tin containers had kept mice turds from peppering the flour, which had kept me alive. I hauled to the trash heap all the clutter, unable to imagine that I was destroying treasures, now worth hundreds, maybe thousands, as antiques, their sentimental value to my mother and aunt inconceivable to the deranged young Spartan soldier I'd become.

Five years later, the United States losing the Korean War, I was ordered to put my affairs in order within two weeks and return to active duty as a B-29 machine gunner. I'd gotten the top grade in a "European Backgrounds to American Civilization" exam; I'd studied with Robert Lowell, who had first volunteered during World War II and then gone to prison rather than serve, after he'd learned about the blockbuster bombing of civilians. I decided that I would go back into the air force, rather than go to prison, but I would only go if I were allowed to retrain as a medic.

World War II had ended before I could test my resolve to be a combat hero or die, and my resolve as a moral objector to the Korean War was not tested. Computers had proliferated in the few years since one had directed the guns of my B-29 bomber, but computers were not perfect. One at my command base in Nebraska extended my enlistment indefinitely, but another, in Washington DC, sent my honorable discharge on the date it was recorded, May 8, 1951.

My baby brother, Rex, was destined to graduate magna cum laude in mathematics and science and to become a medal-winning air force command pilot. Even after I'd achieved some success as a fiction writer, poet, and professor, the mother of one of my high school friends asked me, "What went wrong for you, Ralph? I've always thought it was your starting first grade so young and starting high school when you were only twelve. What do you think?"

"I think," I think I replied, responding to the sympathy, "that you may be right."

"A quiet fellow but one worth knowing," one of my peers summed me up for the yearbook that was printed the year I graduated from high school at age sixteen.

A few years back Rex had moved through darkness to capture or shoot whoever had invaded our farm, to steal war-rationed gasoline or war-rationed meat for the rich to buy on the black market in Chicago. Knowing, from his days of hunting, to place feet between twigs blown down by summer winds, Rex had closed in on a huge shadow. The shadow whistled, and then Rex heard the no-longer-quiet footfalls of whoever was stalking him from behind turn and head for the concealment of our cornfield.

While I was deciding to risk prison or the life of a combat-unit medic rather than to take part in the burning of civilians in North Korean industrial cities, Rex lost his high school sweetheart and, in burning her love letters, set our house's shingle roof afire and had to climb a ladder and save our home with buckets of water.

Graduated from college and faced with being drafted into the infantry to fight in Korea, Rex enlisted in the air force. Finishing near the top of his aviation cadet class, he was granted a regular rather than a reserve commission and went on to serve his country as an interceptor pilot, as a nuclear bomber pilot, as a battle-decorated supply and hospital plane pilot, and as an engineer overseeing the quality of planes sold to the air force. During his training for becoming a combat pilot and an officer and gentleman, he was taught table manners even more exacting than the ones our mother had encouraged. These manners were of use when he served two years in the American Embassy, in Rabat, Morocco.

My brother Rex is a veteran of America's War against Vietnam. I was among the Americans protesting that war. In the peace movement honorably discharged soldiers, who had fought heroically, spoke eloquently to end the war, thus saving the lives of those still engaged in America's failing attempt to conquer and rule.

A popular journalist's book calls my World War II generation "the Greatest," but America's resistance to the War in Vietnam was, I feel, a triumph of America's best values over values shared with tyrannical regimes of the past. Memoirs written by a number of Vietnam veterans constitute a great body of literature, one that should be of value to ongoing generations.

# 23

I've survived birth and some other potentially lethal occurrences for many decades. So who has survived?

"What's in a name?" wrote Shakespeare, whose own name is spelled different ways.

"An old professor said I should spell our name 'Salisberry' because 'bury' is to put someone in the ground." Dad's "old professor" would have been, almost certainly, no linguist, but "Salisberry" became the spelling Dad decided was his, though all or most of his family ended the family name with "bury."

"Salisbury" was the spelling of teachers, of air force officers, of anyone who was not told otherwise, and after the war I legally changed my spelling to Lord Salisbury's spelling, the Bishop of Salisbury's spelling, Shakespeare's spelling of King Henry the Fifth's immortal words, "Go forth to battle those Frenchmen, good Salisbury, and give 'em hell."

"'Salisbury,' just like the steak," my fellow Americans say, pleased at having found an association for mastering or mistressing a slightly out-of-the-ordinary name. Some are sometimes somewhat embarrassed to have written Salisburg, mistaking my supposedly Indian nose for what they were accustomed to disparaging as Jewish.

Who has survived? And what has he survived?

"Ralph James Salisberry" cleared me of the crime of murder when I was an idealistic eighteen-year-old volunteer soldier, menaced by a policeman's gun near Omaha, Nebraska.

When I was a presumably respectable citizen at age fifty, "Ralph James Salisbury" cleared me of the crime of child molestation.

I saw hatred in the eyes of a young woman who'd enlisted the aid of another young woman before confronting me and telling me that they had called a policeman and that I had better not try to escape. Why would I try to escape? I demanded.

Then I reassured my three-year-old child that the two young women were okay, though the eyes of my accuser seemed ferocious. The second young woman seemed merely worried and distressed, perhaps from uncertainty about her determined companion, perhaps from uneasiness that she'd been persuaded to leave her employer's cash register unguarded in the caramel popcorn store a dozen yards from where she was standing.

The blond policeman was maybe the age I'd been as an inexperienced college instructor, and being young, the young man was very attentive to an attractive, intense young woman. When my turn came, my story was simple. I'd just put my wife on a bus that would take her to her temporary work in the schools of a nearby city. Our daughter had asked me to stop and let her have fun on the swings, slide, and jungle gym outside the popcorn store. I volunteered my driver's license and my photo identification card from the university, but still mesmerized by the intensity of my accuser, the policeman insisted on detaining me even after his radio said that I was not in the database for any crime. I suggested that the policeman accompany me to my child's pediatrician's office only half a block away.

After the still rather dubious and maybe disappointed young policeman was convinced that he had an innocent father in custody, I said that the young woman who'd called him had perhaps been put into a state of fear because a rather strung-out and violently muttering huge man had passed moments before the young woman had battened onto me. My accuser had been "very certain" of her identification of me, the young policeman said, and I think now of news about innocent Americans being sentenced to years in prison or to execution because they were falsely identified.

As we retraced our steps to the playground, I suggested to the young officer of the law that he continue talking to me in a friendly manner because I was worried that my child would no longer trust policemen. That sinking in, the young man, probably not a father, rather awkwardly and unconvincingly did his best. Perhaps he should contact the young woman and tell her of her mistake and make another false accusation less likely, I said, but I am not confident that he did.

The caramel corn I purchased from the milder of the two young women was my final effort to rescue my daughter from an unsettling experience, to rescue her from what were possibly the good intentions of a young woman — intentions as laudable as those that had moved me to enlist for one of America's misguided imperialistic wars.

Four or five years later my daughter, perhaps nine, and her friend the same age were accosted by a middle-aged man who tried to lure them into his car. The daughter of a streetwise mother, our daughter's friend took my daughter's hand and ran with her, not in the direction they'd been going but in the opposite direction, so the driver would have to turn his car in the middle of the street in order to pursue.

The child molester apprehended, through the children's memory of his car license number, my wife and I and the other parents refused to let our daughters testify in court. The abuse they would suffer from a well-paid defense lawyer was something we could avoid, where so much that is wrong with our society, our species, our world, cannot be avoided, still less improved.

One of the shortest biographies ever written, Ralph James Salisbury, born January 24th, 1926, has gotten me paid, gotten me married twice and divorced once, and gotten me past passport authorities in Canada, Mexico, Germany, France, Finland, Norway, Sweden, Italy, Greece, India, the former Yugoslavia, the former Soviet Union, and the former East Germany, where the absence of "Ralph James Salisbury" could have sent me to prison when an East German border guard noticed that I'd neglected to sign my passport.

Jet-lagged and exhausted after weeks of little sleep while I'd worked to read the final projects of the young poets and fiction writers who were my students, I stupidly reached into my coat for a pen and simultaneously reached to take the passport back from the East German border guard. Later, too late, I'd remember a drunken U.S. sailor's reaching into his peacoat for his identification document, doubtless thinking that was what had been demanded of him. The habitual obedience response triggered the self-defense response of a jittery Dictator Franco–era coast guardsman, who shot the young American sailor dead.

At the tense East German border, where many had been killed while trying to escape to the West, I escaped trouble because a kindly young soldier — as young as the young soldier I'd once been — took a worried look at his officer, then far down the line of Americans being detained, and told me to wait and sign the passport after I was safely back on the bus. I never studied German and can only converse haltingly and ungrammatically, but I understood the young guard as well as I've understood any poem I've memorized. The German word for "thanks" I knew but could not say, for fear of getting the guard and myself in trouble. How much I have to be grateful for from so many — from my family, from my teachers of eighteen years, from my students of fifty-some years, from my editors, from my readers, from a multitude of life-loving, human-loving strangers, and how meaningless my necessarily belated and necessarily anonymous thank you must be, as I stroke the head of my cat in passing and as I lovingly, reverently shape into morning prayers the lilac-fragrant air I would share with all of the living and share the odor of decay, which bonds root with blossom in my nostrils, my brain, and my mouth — and bonds all I have been to what I will be.

How would you like to visit Robert Frost in his home and have a conversation with him? How would you like to not meet Flannery O Connor?

Last night, near dawn, Ingrid and I conversed with Robert Frost. You mean you dreamed of meeting the great poet, you may say, and perhaps that is what I mean, but dream or reality, Frost was delightful, warm and engaging, and making small jokes the whole while, and I enjoyed my visit or dream, and I am now enjoying remembering and sharing, first with Ingrid and now with this page.

In what most of us call real life I was part of a large audience, five hundred or more, who listened to Frost as he read from his poetry and delivered some ideas about poetry. "You can't just come straight out with stuff, you've got to get yourself a little rigmarole," he said. The Man and the Mask, Yeats wrote. The Man and the Mask. The mask and the man. A little rigmarole.

"The function of irony in writing is to let you get as close as possible to the unbearable," W. S. Merwin said years ago, while chain-smoking cigarettes he had rolled with a small hand-powered machine, and when I quoted him, years later, he did not remember having said an important thing really well.

"You've got to get yourself a little rigmarole," Frost advised young writers at the University of Iowa, where I had just registered as a

twenty-year-old junior. And where I would not meet Flannery O
Connor.

My small part in World War II nearly ended, I had begun keeping journal notes. Before I reached twenty-one, a college literary
magazine's publishing one of my stories and five of my poems
encouraged me to believe that I might be worth something. At
twenty-two, two years into a university education, I entered the
nationwide short story contest of *Tomorrow Magazine*, a competitor
of the *New Yorker*, the *Atlantic Monthly*, and *Harper's*. The publishers
of *Tomorrow* would not win their economic competition, and my
story, "A Pair of Boots," did not win their contest, but it was printed.
The money — $150, roughly the equivalent of $3,000 today — was
enough to pay for a university semester's worth of rent and food
for myself and my then-wife, Joyce Hurlbert, the mother of our
two sons. Publication by an internationally circulated magazine
and the approval of instructors and fellow students gave me an
ego boost, which I needed after having failed at becoming a Big
League baseball hero or a war hero.

Flannery O Connor, two or three years ahead of me in the University of Iowa Creative Writing Program, failed to win the *Tomorrow*
contest, but her intensely moving story "The Woman on the Stair"
was printed. She was a graduate student. I was a junior. I never
met her. In her short life she grew to be one of the finest writers
of my or any other time, and she set an example that all human
individuals need to follow. She did not live long, but she did not
waste her life.

Karl Mattern, a migrated German artist I knew in my midtwenties,
once told me he used pointed twigs instead of steel-tipped pens
for ink drawings because intervals of sharpening wooden points
kept him from becoming too glib. In an interview published by
*Western Review*, a magazine for which I once worked, William

Faulkner said that he wrote with one finger, "hunt and peck," on a typewriter because the effort slowed him, gave him time to think before he wrote.

On an electronic computer's memory chip I am writing about myself as a writer — a dog chasing its own tail — and I write that, with a stub pencil approximately the length of an army rifle cartridge, I drew cowboys and Indians, hunters and hunted, soldiers and warplanes, all crowded together in whatever space was left on the only drawing paper my family could afford, the blank backs of outdated mail-out grocery store ads. Most of my poetry and much of my fiction have been composed with a stub pencil. The pencil a one-legged skater, trying not to stumble, I scribbled nearly undecipherable words in my effort to keep up with the impulses of creating. However, a high school typing class had taught me touch recognition of letters, and I eventually found myself able to compose fiction and to revise both poetry and fiction on a typewriter. Now I finger the keyboard of a computer, whose speed more than equals the speed of my mind.

# 24

Late one night, just arrived from formerly Nazi now democratic Germany, fifty-nine, I stood on the Paris Metro and faced a huge young opponent, who'd just tried to steal my wife's camera. I knew I'd let out a war cry to get my body and mind together, to turn fear into fury and fight like hell to defend my wife and eleven-year-old daughter, but I also knew I'd suffer a beating and maybe get killed. My opponent said something. I remained silent, ready. One of the big man's two big accomplices signaled from the subway car door he was blocking. We were coming into a station, and the Paris Metro police carried pistols. When the car doors opened, the two blocking the doors fled, and the one facing me fled with them.

Thunderbolt, bullets, the crash of metal against metal, against earth, rejection in love, failure to succeed, failure to win approval when one does succeed. We struggle against or flee whatever threatens our bodies or threatens our essential sense of ourselves. If we survive, we should learn what we can and try to be worthy of what is our best. These are not thoughts that led me to teaching. They are thoughts that come after years of trying to teach.

Four years and one month old I was given my first glimpse of my first in a lifetime of students, Rex, my newborn brother. I still feel the iron rung at the foot of my parents' bed gouging my feet through the soles of my shoes as I strained up to see over the gleaming brass bed railing. I think I remember that the room was cold, I think I feel the cold, in flesh many years from the lived moment, but perhaps I only know the room was always cold in February, the month of my brother's birth. I was witnessing the moment I had lived four years and one month before, and I think I have kept an impression of the event.

My mother's loving face was still haggard from a hard birth. Her image is strikingly young in my mind as I write. She was then in her midforties, her auburn hair, a lock of which survives, dark against a white pillow. Her body, exhausted and wounded by birth, was resting and warming her baby beneath heavy quilts and beneath a thick sled robe, into which horses, a bay and a gray, were woven.

My first student. Rex. My baby brother. I taught him to walk. I put all of the dining room chairs on their sides, as we children often did in playing house or in making fences for the little calves we sometimes pretended we were—although not to the point where, bellowing pitifully, they disappeared into a truck to become veal. I started my toddler brother around the ring of chairs, teaching him to hold on to the chairs and to make his little legs move in the motions of walking. That was, excluding shoving little bewhiskered kittens' distressed faces into saucers of milk, my first effort in an endeavor to encourage survival, teaching.

Long before there were any equal opportunity programs for impoverished young Native Americans, I was educated, through six university years, because of my twenty-nine months of military service. Faced with the necessity of supporting a wife and baby, I was working as a janitor, and applying for work in a vacuum-cleaner factory, when another member of Robert Lowell's poetry workshop kindly offered to have his wife put my name at the top of an employment-office list for college teaching.

A few weeks later I got a job offer from an old Rhodes scholar, Thomas F. Mayo, who was a first cousin of William Faulkner, had taught "Willie" in grade school and believed in the worth of writers.

My eighteen years as a student were at their end, and my fifty-five years — and who knows how many more — as a professor were about to begin. Diapers, bedding, books — '39 Studebaker Commander's springs sagging from all that was packed inside, I was following miles of the Cherokee Trail of Tears, following my brother Bob's father's trail to death in Texas.

In my family males had squatted over the animals' manure trough while females utilized the smelly privy, which we called "the back-house." In country school there was a girls' toilet and a boys' toilet. In high school running water had made going to the bathroom more seemly, but segregation by sexes had been the rule. While driving through Arkansas at night, I encountered for the first time racially segregated waste elimination, "Men" and "Ladies" on two doors, "Colored Only" on a third door.

I would soon risk my life by defending the rights of black people, but I only realized that I was legally "colored" when, months later, I read that a Cherokee killed in the Korean War had been denied burial in his white wife's family's burial plot. Another news story was about an eighth-blood African American who'd been imprisoned for being married to a white woman. Then I realized that I was a quarter-blood Indian married to a white woman and subject to imprisonment for miscegenation.

Affordable housing almost nonexistent in Bryan, Texas — last headquarters and last home of General Hood, the Lion of the South — I first rented rooms over a garage. The heat in that unin-sulated space was intense, and when the landlord failed to replace the hot water heater, leaving my wife and me to launder a small baby's diapers in cold water, I used what time I could spare from my teaching and found another rental, the upstairs of a house owned by a cheerful middle-aged salesman and his friendly, helpful wife, who would sometimes babysit our child, perhaps thinking to one day have a child of her own.

She was from what was called "a good family," and she bossed gently the black woman who "did" for her. The "colored maid" washed dishes and floors, did laundry, and cleaned the bathroom. She got permission to take time off from work and walked to the gasoline service station, a quarter of a mile away, to use the "colored" rest room. The idea of a black woman's sitting on her toilet was more than our kindly landlady could bear, although, she confessed, she'd been nursed at the breast of a black woman and still loved that woman "dearly."

My landlord was, as I'd been for all of my adult life, a hunter, and on his living room wall was the head of a javelina, a wild boar he had killed. I remember the huge head, splayed tusks flared menacingly in the shadows above my own head. I remember that image of a wild life I had lived, a life still thriving for others only a few miles from where I spent all of my time in correcting writing and expounding grammatical principals, which meant nothing in the abstract but made such natural sense when emerging without thought in one's own writing.

The state college president's opening address to his state-employed professors commanded that we be obedient to the state's constitution and laws and "respecting of community values," avoiding social and political strife and upholding Christian morality at every turn.

I had to teach grammar, something I hadn't studied myself since, probably, eighth grade, my natural writing ability from then on exempting me from basic English study. My hero Ernest Hemingway felt gratitude for having worked as a journalist under the tutelage of a good style editor. Resolved that teaching would teach me practices of use to a writer, I read the textbook and tried to keep ahead of the department's schedule of student assignments. Teaching an overwhelmingly large class was hard. But whatever was the case with my students, I learned a lot, painfully.

Luckily, the English Department had made learning-by-doing the premise on which writing classes were based. Unluckily, it was impossible to red-ink writing flaws and to write insightful comments on all student compositions. Luckily, an older instructor told me that not even the department head himself read all of the papers his system assigned. As many as possible were read. The remaining quantity was on record as "requirements," to impress the dean at budget time.

Unluckily—or, as I've lived to believe, blessedly—the book of essays picked as a reader held several weeks' worth of emphasis on race relations, and—my teenage Kentucky accent gone—my "damyankee" accent strongly hinted at my personal egalitarian view even before I spoke up for the logic of racial equality, as the course required me to do. The English Department was a bastion of democracy in a state whose residents had lynched, with impunity, African Americans.

Texas A&M's proud legend was sending more second lieutenants into the army than did West Point. My only previous knowledge of the school had come at the end of World War II.

A buddy, with whom I was sharing the duty of guarding the main gate, said, "I'll call the base commander, and as soon as the colonel hears that I was a sophomore at his old school, Texas A&M, we'll get our flight pay back."

I didn't quite believe him, until he picked up the guard-shack telephone and asked for our commander. While I listened, awed that just going to the same college could give him such status, he articulated into the army green mouthpiece, "Sir, this is Pisshead Peterson." A very long pause. "Yes, Sir. Sorry, Sir."

Teaching where Pisshead Peterson had studied for two years, I learned from students that for each of the traditional names for class levels, freshman to senior, there was an obscene, in-group nickname, Peterson's that of a sophomore.

Students' nickname for me and most of my intelligent, egalitarian, law-abiding, constitution-honoring English Department colleagues was "nigger-lover." However, at least one history professor was "a good old boy" and "thought right" about the "race question." His classroom just down the hall from the office where I'd be grading literature or beginning logic class papers, the popular purveyor of American history's voice would make my closed door shake, "Damned niggers!" about as scholarly as the lecture got. One day I heard racist epithets and verbal abuse and encountered a neck-tied and white-shirted white man, as huge as the drunks and the tavern bouncer my cousin and I had seen in action thirteen years back. My wife and child's livelihood depending on my not being thrown into jail or lynched, I had to keep silent and witness the humiliation of a big athletic-looking black janitor, who could only murmur, "Yes, Sir," eyes down on his broom, as he heard himself, and all others of his race, being called filthy names. I, and millions of other Americans, shared the humiliation of submitting to insane, lynch-mob-backed brute force.

"Could I buy you a coke?" a black janitor asked, and aware of his low pay, I didn't know whether to offer to buy him a coke instead and risk insulting him. "Yes, thank you," I decided.

Falkner's scholarly, humane old cousin was known to help black janitors and cleaning women, giving them advice or at least an open ear and even loaning them money in hard times. He was in the tradition of white gentry who had done what they could for slaves. I was a well-intentioned damyankee, and my salary was so low I couldn't have loaned anyone money, but what the black janitor wanted was advice. In the army he'd been trained as an auto mechanic, and he had his own tools, but the only job he could get was that of a janitor. Two choices were open to him, moving his wife and family to Denver or to Kansas City. All I knew about Denver was from my experience as an eighteen-year-old in uniform during a time of intense patriotism, but from my brief time of living in Kansas City, I knew that discrimination against black people was prevalent.

In a few weeks I got a letter from Denver saying that life was better there.

Camouflaged by pale skin and gray eyes, I did not proclaim myself to be an Indian. Like my father, who had wanted to live the celebrity life of a handsome traveling musician and not suffer discrimination as a Native American, I maintained the stature six years of university education had conferred.

My relative youth, twenty-six, was an advantage in teaching. Students could relate to a big-brother-aged professor, whose enthusiasm somewhat enlivened the subject of English composition. However, I stumbled embarrassingly sometimes, and only a willingness to spend hours of individual instruction in writing prevented my utterly failing as a teacher.

The students were uniformed and regimented young men who'd graduate as second lieutenants and be sent to fight in Korea. My World War II veteran's status and sergeant's manner were definite advantages. Like the Southern society it served, Texas A&M was institutionalized madness. Verbal abuse from racist history professors was not the only mistreatment black workers suffered. Students whom I came to know as friends confided their distress, as Christians, when attractive black women were interrupted in their sweeping of hallways and sexually assaulted in the student dormitories.

A student who published a letter calling into question some army cadre violations of law was beaten and dumped, with all of his belongings, beside the highway. The college president at first issued a statement that the kidnappers would be punished, but several army command aircraft flew into the small airbase adjacent to the home of a friend of mine, and the president changed his position, saying that the young men involved in the incident were being punished sufficiently by their own consciences and adding that their student victim could come back to school if he wanted to—if he were willing to submit to further abuse. He chose to forfeit the money he'd paid for a semester's tuition.

There have certainly been some high points in my years of teaching, from 1951 to now, and I've often humiliatingly failed.

One of my friends threw a martini party to loosen all of us freshmen professors up before the official reception welcoming us to the department. Unused to hard drinks, I became, it seems, unusually libidinous. The attractive wife of a colleague told her husband that I was a writer who really had something going for him. The husband told me that he had asked her what it was she thought I had. I was embarrassed, and I was too unsophisticated to try to make amends.

My wife and I became friends with one of my older students and his wife. My student was the son of two artists and not respectful of meaningless customs. When I complained about having to wear a necktie and jacket to attend a party honoring my department head, my student asked me why I didn't go in shirt sleeves. Not wanting to appear hypocritical, I did as my student suggested. No one reproved me, but my colleagues' manner was as icy as it could be on a sweltering day.

Swimming with my student in an old quarry, I jokingly suggested that we swim the considerable distance to the shore where our wives were preparing a picnic. "Okay," my student said and began to swim. I'd been kidding, but he, it turned out, was a member of the college's distance swimming team. Sheer walls lined the quarry for the entire distance. I either had to back down and walk the shore or risk drowning. Like a prideful damned fool I risked drowning, and after some minutes of floating and treading water—not quite as shameful as not trying—I arrived, exhausted and grateful to be alive to do still other foolish things.

Diving into the quarry was the next foolish thing I did. I dived deep and got tangled in some old mining cable but managed to grope my way free before I ran out of breath.

The quarry's banks were a mineral called bentonite, a chalky white substance, and, the water reflecting blue sky, the beautiful place reminded me of flying over Crater Lake in winter.

One of my friends, a recently divorced Texan, was arrested for being a white man waiting for a bus near a whorehouse in the black section of town. Fired from his job, he disappeared, and the old gentleman brought back from retirement to fill the vacancy found neat stacks of student compositions. My friend had dutifully assigned every paper the department syllabus required, but he had not graded even one.

Teaching essays on "the racial equality question," I unwisely but unavoidably had to declare my position, the position of an American citizen who had believed in the American constitution and had volunteered to fight and risk death for it—the position of a "damyankee nigger lover," but I tried to make it clear that I was teaching skills, not attitude.

Teaching a beginning logic text's essay on the logical bases involved in race prejudice, I faced the hostility of twenty-some students, who felt threatened and enraged that anyone should question the rightness of their and their parents' and their region's accepted views. With a patience dictated by respect for overwhelming opposition, I slowly, Socratically tried to put into logical perspective the proposition that black people were inferior to white people.

"A white man is better than any nigger!" one of my students declared, his declaration probably what nearly all of my students had been taught from earliest childhood.

I adduced a doctoral student of nuclear physics who'd lived near me in university housing at the University of Iowa. Did all agree that my neighbor was better than a literature student like myself in knowledge of nuclear physics? All warily agreed with the obvious.

Did the fact that the nuclear physics scholar was black make him inferior to me in the knowledge of nuclear physics?

Reluctantly, all agreed that it did not.

Did the fact that the nuclear physics scholar was married to a beautiful blond woman change what all had agreed to? I suppressed my writer's urge to tell the truth, the whole truth, and nothing but the truth. I did not mention the potential creator of nuclear weapons' marital status, but a student asked the blockbuster question that might have ended all discussion in dormitories, "Would you want your sister to marry one?"

Sidestepping the irrelevant question, I said that my sister was already married and hadn't asked me who I might or might not want her to marry. Is there anyone here whose sister asked him whom she should marry? Silence.

"Back to the proposition, a white man is better than any black man. Is it based on logic? Is a black man near to winning the highest degree a university can award in nuclear physics a better nuclear physicist than I am?"

All agreed that he was, and at this point a handsome young future officer and gentleman, who had spent the hour in staring disdainfully out a window, felt threatened by the unanimous agreement of his peers.

"You mean you think a nigger is as good as you are?" he demanded.

This was definitely not a time for proclaiming Indian blood. "All of us have come to the logical conclusion that a black nuclear physicist is not only as good as but better than any of us in nuclear physics," I responded, and after reviewing the logic with which the rest of the class had been engaged for an hour, I asked the red-faced and deeply troubled young man, who had more than once proved his intelligence, "Don't you agree that the black man I spoke of is better than you are in nuclear physics?"

Silence. Then the young Southern gentleman said, "I cain't say it. I just cain't say it."

Whether he ever said it or not, he'd soon have a chance to feel it in the newly integrated army, then discovering that the colored populations of North Korea and China had soldiers who were sometimes better than Caucasian American or African American soldiers.

"You're the only man I've met in this goddamned place," one student told me in front of a class of thirty students and shook my hand. The young man was a mixed-blood Apache. He had endured a year of harassment and earned good grades in the classes his tuition money had paid for. Leaving school and returning to his parents' ranch, he had hurled his final defiance, his warrior insult, into his enemies' faces and in doing so gave me a tribute I can only try to deserve.

"Careful with that nigger-lover talk, or you'll end up getting lynched," a neighbor with whom I'd been friendly warned, and some months after the student letter-to-the-editor writer was beaten and dumped by the road, I got a threat that I'd be lynched. How many generations of freedom-seeking individuals had received such threats and then, some night, had been castrated, shot, hanged, tortured with blowtorches, doused with gasoline, and set on fire, tied by the legs between two horses and split, dragged over a rocky road behind a speeding car?

I remembered Dad's story of arriving in a West Virginia town, intending to sing and play the banjo for an audience there. Instead he found himself holed up in the town's only hotel, his pistol in his hand, guarding one door, while the hotel owner and the town constable guarded the other two doors, all of them, including the marshal, in danger of being lynched by a mob of miners whose previous coal-mine strikes had been put down by an army of hoodlums, which the company had hired and called detectives.

Taking my own lynch threat seriously, I thought I'd better get a gun. Unfortunately, my pay was so low, I couldn't buy one. A friend told me that he had discovered a .32 caliber revolver in a space behind the drawer of the desk in the office to which he'd been assigned. He already had a gun and felt that he didn't need another. I traded him an electric motor for his revolver.

When a gasoline bomb bounced off my front door and fizzled and did not explode, I went out into the night, as my father had often had to go, gun drawn, ready to defend my family. The thugs slammed their car doors and got the hell out of there when they saw that I had a gun.

# 25

I slept with the pistol beneath my pillow, as ready as was possible to repel any intruders, and I applied for a job north of the Mason and Dixon Line, at Drake University.

Walking down a hall to my job interview, I saw a bulletin board displaying a headline, SENATE CENSURES JOE MCCARTHY. It was good to see the downfall of a man who'd been traitorous to all our republic professes. I saw black students walking to class beside white students, and when the job was offered to me, I took it.

The farm where I'd grown to manhood only one hundred miles away, I visited and tried for the first time the revolver with which I'd driven off a carload of attackers. The firing pin was worn down, and the revolver was as useless as the rusty Wild West six-shooter washed up by rain during my childhood.

Ironically, the electric motor I'd traded for the defective pistol also proved to be defective, and the friend to whom I'd traded the worthless electric motor became the director of rural electrification during the term of President Carter.

"Never throw down on a man unless you mean to kill him," had been a part of my father-son education, and learning that my only protection weapon could not shoot, Dad gave me the automatic pistol, with which he had protected our family and had, when drunk, shot a circle of splinters around my four-year-old feet.

In accepting the job at Drake University, I turned down a promising interview at Cornell College, an hour's drive from the farm where I was born. If I'd taught at Cornell, one of my students might have been a young Phi Beta Kappa winner and poet, Ingrid

Wendt, and at the ages we were then, we might not have fallen in love, might not have married, have had a daughter and by now a granddaughter and a grandson.

I chose Drake University over Cornell College because Drake was located in Iowa's capital city, Des Moines, and I wanted to learn something about the society in whose army I'd served, the society in which I'd just fled threats of lynching. Fortuitously, my next-door neighbor was Frank Miller, the political cartoonist for Iowa's largest newspaper, the *Des Moines Register*, and just two doors away was Jack Magarell, who'd been number-two anchorman for Iowa's largest TV station and was, at the time I knew him, the *Des Moines Register*'s statehouse reporter.

From a news story's reporting a jailing in my hometown, West Des Moines, I learned that Indians like myself did not have the right to drink in 1950s Iowa. I'm not sure if we had the right to vote. I know that during my childhood it was not legal for anyone to vote without having paid, first, a poll tax. Dad paid his poll tax by working, like a prison chain gang prisoner, on a county road, clearing brush from overgrown ditches.

Like the rest of his family—and like most Southeastern Indians, so I've read—Dad was a Republican, in solidly Democratic—or, in journalistic parlance, Dixiecratic—Kentucky, but two things changed him into a fervent Democrat. The first was Herbert Hoover's help-the-rich-to-prosper economics; the second was Dad's experience as a local vote counter. Iowa was overwhelmingly Republican, except for a few pockets of factory workers, but since Dad was a migrant Iowan, the election board persuaded him to serve as a Democratic vote counter. When Dad saw his Republican coworkers deface Democratic ballots to invalidate them, Dad angrily became a Democrat for real.

President Herbert Hoover had been born in West Branch, Iowa, only an hour's drive from where I was born. Hoover was "the man who fed the Belgian babies after World War I" in the minds of most of the neighborhood mothers, even though their own children had little food. Reportedly slim, handsome, and highly successful in illicit love during his younger days, Hoover was fat in the midst of America's starvation. My rebellious renegade Indian father called his president "that damned Hoover," and I got into trouble in school because I thought that "Damned" was Hoover's first name.

Reading Damned Hitler's dying prediction that *Amerika* would fulfill the destiny that Nazism had begun, I wonder if it might not be healthy to rename all of our leaders—that Damned Washington, the slave owner; that Damned Andrew Jackson, whose legacy includes unconstitutionally defying the U.S. Supreme Court and sending troops to break the United States' treaty with the Cherokee nation; that Damned Abe Lincoln, who became the Great Emancipator of African Americans but found nothing wrong with continuing to oppress Native Americans; that Damned Eisenhower, who used his military career to bring the military-industrial collusion into prolonged power and, nearing death, warned against the conspiracy for which he had been the front man; that Damned Truman, who possibly saved my life by using two atom bombs to commit two of history's most colossal massacres and end World War II; that Damned Johnson, who continued, in Asia, a European imperialism that would lead to America's bloody defeat in Vietnam. That Damned George W. Bush, whose greed for more, more, always more oil money, always more tax money for the rich, has provoked Muslims to wage war against imperialism around the world. That Damned—choose your own candidate. Let's make Presidents Day a tell-'em-off, feel-good day, a relief from sedulousness, sanctimoniousness, conformism, and timidity—a relief from voting persuasive liars into power again and again.

A hundred miles from where my father had become a Democrat, I got to know the men who staged a patiently worked-out coup to take over and reform Iowa's Democratic Party. The voted-out party chairman was sent to prison for accepting Republican bribes and embezzling union funds. The newly constituted Democratic Party began winning elections.

Duke University had declared the then–vice president, Richard Nixon, too dishonorable to deserve an honorary degree. Nixon was being groomed to run for the presidency, and receiving an honorary degree from Drake University, with a name similar to Duke's, was supposed to blur voters' memories of Nixon's disgrace.

When many professors objected, the Drake administration agreed to a vote. At the faculty meeting a request for a secret ballot was denied, and a university official's secretary was at the front of the room, taking down the names of those who spoke against Nixon. She later got a different employer and spread the word of what she had been forced to do. Even with all the intimidation, observers determined that a voice vote had refused Nixon the degree. The man in charge of the podium declared the opposite.

Outraged by officials' bullying tactics, I leaked a news story. I asked for anonymity because I did not have job tenure and was financially vulnerable. The newspaper ran the story, quoting anonymous sources, but on campus that day student after student congratulated me.

This was one of those moments when I felt proud of being a teacher and proud of being an American citizen. It was also a moment when I realized what my salary from then on would tell me. Racists' bombs and bullets weren't the only dangers growing out of university teaching. I began to look for another job.

At a political rally for vice-president-to-be Hubert Humphrey news arrived that Fidel Castro had overthrown the U.S.-backed dictatorship that had ruled Cuba. Humphrey, fearful of worldwide communism, declared his apprehensions, but a black friend, a medical student, and I were delighted, not because we had inclinations toward communism but because the rule by military force and torture had been replaced with a government that clearly had the support of the majority of Cubans.

Because of my magazine publications I was invited as one of two guest speakers on a radio talk show, with listener questions being telephoned in.

A writer of juvenile fiction and I were supposed to be talking about our writing and about ourselves as writers. He and I had little in common. His goal was to write books that would sell, but one of his answers to a call-in listener got my attention. Asked about the United States' hiring of the German rocket scientists who'd designed rockets planned to destroy U.S. cities, the forthright writer of popular fiction replied, "We should hang the sons of bitches."

Simple-minded as his moralistic view was, it underscored the hypocrisy of imprisoning or executing some enemies, designated as war criminals, and giving well-paid jobs to rocket scientists and employing former Gestapo officials to continue persecuting Germans and other Europeans thought to be communists. The mention of atom-bomb rocketry reminded me that a part of my training for bombing Europe included a plan for bombing a German "heavy-water" atom bomb facility located in Norway. Years later I'd learn that heroic Norwegian resistance fighters had packed dynamite on their backs, killed German guards, and destroyed the German capability for developing A-bombs.

Naive as talk of executing useful former Nazis might be, equally naive was my hope—and the hope of a botanist who called in to the radio talk show—that humans might farm and live in harmony with nature and not continue centuries of conquering, and destroying, themselves. This was 1954 or '55, and after the radio phone-in show an influential newspaper editorial writer angrily railed against us "nuts," who were "enemies of progress."

A year or two late, Rachel Carson's book *Silent Spring* got the societal prestige of *New Yorker* publication, and all of us nuts, Indians and others, seemed civilized and respectable.

Connecting what came to be called the ecology movement with what had long been Native American tradition happens naturally with those of us who grew up learning to live in harmony with nature.

Under my father's instruction I labored long, hard hours at putting cornstalks and oat and hay stubble and the excrement of animals back into the earth. Most of our neighbors blackened the skies by burning stalks and stubble to make plowing easier. An unimaginably huge glacier had bestowed rich loam, but when that loam was depleted from overuse, an industry-serving government agency recommended artificial chemical replacements, which polluted drinking water and caused health problems. Using chemicals was easier than plowing natural organic matter back into the soil—and it made industrial profits—but the ill effects on farmers' health became immediately apparent. My brother Bob showed me his hands; they were covered with blisters. The effects on organs and genes of future generations are still unknown.

# 26

Oh, help me, Lord, help me, help me, help me, cause I'm a poor sinner, a poor, poor sinner.

Don't go troubling Me about your picky little troubles, if you're a poor sinner, then try something you're good at.

That's a part of my life story as it might have been told by my storytelling dad or by one of the Cherokee heroes of my youth, the celebrated humorist Will Rogers.

Sexual adventures, misconduct, explorations, infidelities, experimentation, or just plain lechery, I say, aware of wife, children, and family and keeping to, I hope, a dimly perceived modicum of tact, and, hey, already irony has taken me a mile at least from myself, my center, my nature and from anyone's possible empathy. My ironic diction's a killdeer dragging a hopefully seemingly broken wing to distract destruction from little morsels innocently chirping for food, unaware of hawk beak, snake's fangs, fox's teeth, or cat's claws.

"The only facts when you get down to brass tacks / are birth, copulation and death," T. S. Eliot's Apeneck Sweeney says, and my next few paragraphs are not going to be focused on birth or death.

"You'll be married by the time you're twenty-one," a kind, big-brotherly, married friend predicted a few weeks after the United States' two Weapons of Mass Destruction had given us hope of living normal life spans.

In the summer of my twentieth year I began dating a twenty-year-old deputy sheriff. No, I have to hastily say, to those inclined to suspect all poets of more than normal feelings about their own gender — no, my date was a receptionist in the sheriff's office, and she'd been deputized so that her signature on paperwork would have legal status. During some weeks of passionate, beautiful dates, I fell in love.

Lovers' lanes are not typically paved, and stuck in loose sand one moonlit night beside a shimmering lake, I proved my manly ingenuity by improvising a shovel from the luggage-compartment tool-kit cover. Winning loving praise strengthened my feeling that I was capable of taking care of a wife.

Now elderly, my youthful first marriage ended in divorce, my second marriage now in its fortieth year, I can still see what I saw at age twenty, the soft glow of a young woman's face raised to my young face, in something like adoration, the slender moon, a solitary swimmer in a lake — a lake where I'd once snickered, with other teenagers, at sight of an aged man walking from dressing room to water's edge, his black, old-fashioned suit complete with jersey top and shoulder straps — complete, except that moths or years of uric acid had eaten out the crotch, a fact of which he was apparently unaware. He must have noticed that the laughter was directed at him, but perhaps he thought it was the laughter of nearly bare young people, who'd have thought his out-of-style suit funny even if its crotch had been intact.

Without pausing, the old gentleman waded into brown water, and when he could wade no longer, he began a flawless backstroke, which moved him, brown water turning silver from his steady, graceful swimming, around and around the lake.

No longer a snickering teenager, twenty, and serious after recent escapes from death, I confided my marital intentions to my father, who'd have to give his consent if I were to marry before I turned twenty-one. Although Dad had never met my intended wife, he strongly advised me to wait a few years.

Another father, who lived in a place called the Vatican, had had something to say, and the father of my beloved would echo the church's decision, I feared, and I made up my mind to become a Catholic to win my love.

This youthful resolution was not put to the test. My girlfriend decided that we should break up because I was going to college, and she was not. "But I still love you," she murmured, and left me desolate for a time.

Of my several youthful affairs following the painful loss of a woman I'd deeply loved, I remember, with some guilt, a woman slightly younger than my young self who urgently wanted to marry me. She was attractive, and she pleaded for me to recognize that she was as intelligent as she felt me to be. The anguish of recent love loss, resistance to being the hunted instead of the hunter — for whatever reason I broke off the brief affair without any consideration or kindness and fled to college — where I fulfilled my married air force buddy's prophecy and married Joyce Hurlbert, whom I'd met in a class.

Of the mother of my two sons I make no criticism, and I have no regrets for the marriage. The word "incompatibility" comes to mind, and doubtless it could be applied to me.

Living that grown-up male version of the utterly selfish "terrible twos," thirty-nine and getting a year's head start on the "life begins" again and again and again "at forty," I went, for the first time in my life, to the city where, nearly two years before, my short story had failed to make *Tomorrow* a winner in the competition for the *Atlantic* and *Harper's* readers, the city in which by now one of my poems had appeared, in a magazine parochially named the *New Yorker*. I rendezvoused with a woman I'd never met, a poet who, it turned out, was then sleeping with a fiction writer. Despite some pleasant dalliance, I stiltedly understate — keeping to the camouflage of nineteenth-century style — despite some pleasant dalliance, I began to realize that my intended conquest, amor, or sex-partner-to-be was not interested in me as a lover. She was interested in me as an editor who had published her poems and might publish more.

At an evening cocktail party I, all whiskey-unwise, denounced the cynical senior editor of a big New York press. Amazingly he did not use his greater size to reject my opinion of him. Instead he began to drunkenly confess that he knew he was a literary pimp, selling sex in fictional form. The only virtue he could plead was having turned down a prominent Republican senator's demand for an under-the-table bribe in exchange for an air force textbook contract.

Apparently hoping a sex bribe would persuade the senior editor to sign a book contract, my hoped-for New York misadventure told her fiction-writer lover, "I'll set him up with a young woman from where I work."

After some passionate kisses and secret assurances about an indefinite future, I flew to London, intending only solitude and devotion to writing my book, an intention I held to, except for time spent with a fashion-magazine editor, who lingered on leaving the airplane and picked me up, apparently liking my appearance well enough to select me out of a crowd and to spend four days with me before flying to her work—and doubtless to new experiences—in Paris.

"I know none of this will go any further," the drunken, big-city, big publishing house's senior editor had summoned enough executive manner to demand, back in New York, but of course I condemned him and all like him during my first poetry reading in London, and of course I condemn—and also, try to understand and forgive—myself for prolonging the sowing of my wild oats well beyond the season for tame oats planting.

My first time on the continent that I'd almost bombed, Europe, I flew to West Berlin and visited a friend from Drake University days. Controlled not long back by Hitler and surrounded now by Stalinist opponents of free speech, West Berlin was an appropriate place for my friend and me to reunite. Though without job security he and

I had joined older and better-protected colleagues in challenging the university president's attitude toward instruction. "The only thing that should limit class size is the size of the room," was one of the president's assertions, and "Tell those two young literature instructors that they have no future here," was the gist of what he proclaimed, by sending word through his network of administrators and through notice of next year's salaries. My friend quickly got a better job, at the United States' oldest institution of higher learning, the College of William and Mary. I got an offer from the University of Oregon, where I've stayed ever since.

Venturing into Communist-controlled East Berlin, I experienced the workings of a police state. Inside Check Point Charley two young couples were being interrogated by two border guards. One man said something mildly querulous, in German, to the guards, but then, in English, he told the women that he had called the guards stupid. The women laughed at the handsome braggart's self-proclaimed audacity, but the least loquacious of the two men looked worried, having noticed what I had also noticed, a slight change in one border guard's expression.

"Come with me!" that guard ordered and took the arrogant young man into a guard-post room and closed the door. The worried young man and the two women were told to step out of line and wait.

The next people in line were a U.S. Army major and his family. The major was impatient with the border guard, and he was told to step out of line and wait. I felt sorry for the major's family, especially a very old and frail woman who would suffer a long period of standing up on a hot day, because of the cruel guards, yes, but also because of the major's arrogance.

With my former colleague, his wife, and myself were a symphony conductor and his wife, all of us anticipating seeing statues and an ancient Greek temple, whose tons of marble had been looted from

Greece by Germany, then looted from Germany by Russians, and then ransomed back by the East German government. My companions and myself were talking in English as we walked from the museum parking lot. Accosted by four young men, the symphony conductor said, in German, that he did not speak German.

Immediately the four, all of them bigger than any of us, strode menacingly alongside. Perhaps the conductor's Southern accent had reminded the four of Lyndon Johnson's voice talking about his invasion of Vietnam, or perhaps they had had some personal experience with Southern-born American soldiers before the Russians took over. Thirty some years later I think of my father—and the generations of Southerners before him—disadvantaged, despised, and often endangered because of a Southern—a Confederate, a rebel—accent. At the time all I knew for sure was that I wanted to see statues and did not want to suffer a beating. I did as my companions did. We looked straight ahead, avoiding challenging stares, and continued across the street to the museum steps, where men in uniform stood. Their presence may have saved me and my companions from harm. All I know is that the hoodlums stopped menacing and left and that I got to experience an ancient civilization's war's slaughter brought under control by the ultimate policeman, Art.

In all of my days of teaching German students a few things about American Indians, I've taught in English, and I've learned only a smattering of German. *Kamerad*! Have I remembered correctly the word that would have enabled me to surrender if my bomber had been shot down over German cities — the word that World War I veterans said surrendering Germans said to try to save their lives?

My awkward smattering of German and Ingrid's more articulate and closer-to-grammatical German may have saved one life, the life of a German woman who'd taken a wrong turn on a trail in Natural Bridges National Park. Dusk deepening, the German tourist was headed into a dark canyon, and protected by a light jacket, she was headed for a night of exposure to an ice storm.

Ingrid and I were returning from Ingrid's month of teaching at the Bureau of Indian Affairs school near Aneth, Utah, and we had made an impulsive, last-minute decision to camp and see sundown at Natural Bridges, instead of driving on to camp at Capitol Reef.

While watching the slow, awesome, fiery disappearance of the star that gives all of us life, I noticed a man pestering a group of men and women, who ignored him, causing him to move anxiously on to another group. He accosted, finally, our apprehensive selves, his question, rapidly asked in barely understandable English, Did we own the Volkswagen camper van parked near the rim of the canyon where we were standing? I didn't want a distraught German hitchhiker, but I admitted that we did own the van. And was either one of us German? No. Could either of us speak German? A little. And slowly, after many repetitions, I understood that the man's friend was long overdue in meeting him and his wife at this trailhead above the canyon. His wife was terrified of being alone, and would we stay with her while he made the dangerous descent into the growing dark of the canyon? Yes, we would. For a while. But after we'd reassured the wife that there were no wild Indians or wild animals to fear so long as she stayed in the rental car—locked against, we didn't say, possible sexual predators—we drove slowly along the canyon rim road, sounding our weak Volkswagen horn at intervals to give the husband direction.

The ranger station was closed for the night, but guided first by the smell, then by the sight of woodsmoke, we found forest-surrounded living quarters and found a ranger, engaged in washing his four-wheel-drive vehicle to get rid of the mud accumulated during a rescue in the early afternoon. Another pain-in-the-ass lost tourist was not what a tired man needed at the end of a long, hard day, but the ranger said he'd meet us as soon as he'd finished with his car laundering.

We parked with our lights toward the canyon and sounded our horn and shouted and waited for the German man to come up at the next marked trail. It was nearly dark on the canyon rim, and there would be almost no light left on the canyon floor. The husband would be as lost as the friend he'd tried to find, we feared, but after a long time a cry answered our cries, and guided by our car lights' glow on the canyon rim, the German man emerged at the head of the trail.

We drove him to rejoin his anxious wife, and after the ranger joined us, we acted as inept translators, the only translators available.

Communication improved when a young woman doing a summer's internship at the ranger station arrived. She'd been an exchange student in Germany, and she did an admirable job of fulfilling the commitment required of all of us students and profs in the Fulbright program, "To promote international understanding."

There were no campsites left for the German couple, but we took them into the camp we'd made before going to admire the sunset. After helping them set up their tent, we shared our food and our bottle of wine. They were very worried about their friend and felt guilty about letting her go on a trail alone.

The ranger and the young intern came back from a search as unsuccessful as that of the German man had been. A rescue team had been alerted, but the distances were very great, and it would be a long time. We should get some sleep. As soon as there was news, we'd hear.

Sleep proved difficult. The first news was the spatter of sleet against our van windows, not good news for a woman with only a light summer jacket over summer clothes.

The first good news was the sound of the search team's arriving, at three in the morning.

The next news came while we were shivering around a breakfast fire at dawn. The German couple rushed out to meet the ranger and the young translator, and out of tact we waited, apprehensively, while some very serious talk went on. The bite of a rattlesnake, stepped on in the dark, a fall from the edge of a crumbling and sleet-slippery trail, the slow numbing of the senses in freezing cold — the lost woman was dead, we feared, but no, the clouds of breath did a dance, rising in the dawn. After two hours of searching, the woman had been found. An experienced outdoors person, she'd terminated her hike, fortunately, because her choice of trails would have taken her deeper into wilderness. She'd made a nest out of branches, and though she was cold, she might have lasted through the night. Being zipped into a sleeping bag, "with a great bear of a man," to be warmed enough to prevent hypothermia and be able to endure the hike to a road was the most animated part of the middle-aged woman's account, when we at last met her.

Did we own the German van? *Ja.* Did we speak German? *Nein.* Not then and not now, but *genuf,* yes, enough.

# 27

"Como se llama? What is your name?" our four-year-old daughter bravely ventured, seeking playmates on the Spanish beaches of Caldetas and Tossa del Mar.

I was on sabbatical, the release time granted professors for doing research and writing—in my case a book of poems—and I had brought my family to travel Europe, for Ingrid and for our daughter the first time.

Cruelty, kindness—the choice seems obvious, but I recall seeing, from a distance, an Austrian father choose to gruffly rebuke my child instead of gently correcting whatever small infraction of playground turn-taking she was innocently violating. Though remaining civilized and restrained, I felt quite murderous.

While waiting for our child to return from a Paris park carousel, we saw her running desperately toward us and saw a boy twice her size throwing her to the ground. I caught him just as he pounced on my child and pulled him back. He gave me an insane look and was about to try to pounce again when one of his apologetic caretakers caught him, the man and his wife explaining, as my limited French gradually caught up with what they were saying, that the boy was the insane son of rich parents. The two caretakers were extremely sorry and thoroughly nice, but all the time they were apologizing again and again for our daughter's fright and knees bloodied by gravel, the poor insane boy was staring at my daughter with unnerving hate.

Our child suffered loneliness for playmates, suffered from eating strange food at odd hours, suffered exhaustion from travel, and suffered the occasional — too frequent — natural and regrettable irritability of parents tired from long train journeys, from having to carry a little girl as well as luggage, from searching for restaurants inexpensive enough for the half-pay sabbatical budget, and from being forced to speak, far too awkwardly to satisfy poets, languages native to neither, not German, not French, and not Spanish, though Ingrid is the daughter of a Chilean father and studied in Chile as an eighteen-year-old college student and though I studied Spanish in college and have memorized poems by Federico Garcia Lorca, Cesar Vallejo, and Octavio Paz.

At night, during our travels, Ingrid and I cuddled and read to our daughter and made up bedtime stories, just as we did at home. In art museums we took turns at leading our four-year-old between rows of paintings that had meant much to millions, through centuries. Our daughter saw grown-ups and children slaughtered in painting after painting. She gravely asked questions, questions we could not answer and cannot answer. When she tired of great art and crowds of art viewers, one of us sat with her, and once, shamelessly irreverent in the presence of masterpieces, I cocked one ankle over one knee and, using upturned shoe sole for easel, began sketching in a small notebook, which I carried to write notes for poems. One arm around small shoulders, I drew princesses, queens, and kings, my studio a vast museum, whose monumental splendor had been designed by a famous architect, his patrons royalty.

To entertain my daughter, on a riverboat between Vienna and Linz, the birthplace of Ingrid's father's grandmother, I drew castles while we floated past real castles. Absorbed in the steadily appearing and disappearing green fields and villages, absorbed in glimpses of medieval architecture, absorbed in fatherly love and in the peace and fulfillment of creating images of kings and queens and princes and princesses, I was startled by a slight sound behind me, and looking up from dotting royal jewels onto the prongs of crowns, I discovered that every one of the half dozen or so children on the boat had gathered, fascinated by my utterly crude, utterly pleasurable attempt to please my own child. Castle after castle drifted past, and still the children preferred inept art to the cannon-ball-battered, moss-and-vine-adorned real thing.

The drama of hundreds of years of history around us, we experienced a personal drama when the tall young dock attendant locked our luggage into the check-room and then, in the course of what must have been a delightful lunch with a young lady, misplaced the key.

The ship's horn was sounding its final summons, the young dock attendant's rather amused superior officer had no duplicate key, and blushing with shame, the young man reared his tall body back on one leg—like an American football player preparing to punt his team from disaster—and launched a mighty kick against the door, splintering a little wood around the padlock—and releasing our luggage in time for us to catch the boat.

Hiking downhill, back from seeing the castle and dungeon where a defeated English king, Richard the Lion Hearted, had been caged, our daughter began chanting an account of abuse she'd suffered at the hands of bullies in a supposedly well-supervised church day-care center at home. The deep hurt of this was evidenced by repetition of the chant for the relief and release it gave. Iron bars and stone walls had been a prison for an English king. A church nursery school had been a prison for a small American girl.

On a train ride out of totalitarian Spain into more or less democratic France, our child repeated the chant about playmates' abuse we'd first heard in Austria. A childless young Spanish couple heard the chant and were visibly shocked as well as sympathetic. Once we'd crossed the border, they began a chant of their own, revealing the dictatorial strictures from which they were temporarily free and to which they must return.

Diarrhea is a problem for many visitors to foreign lands, and one day it was a big problem for a small child. My wife taking her turn at swimming, I heard our four-year-old daughter's urgent plea and rushed her to the beachfront "Damas," telling her I'd wait right outside. Seeing that she was afraid to go into a strange place crowded with women, none of them her mother, the grandfatherly toilet attendant told me that he would keep other men out of the "Caballeros" for a while.

Caught in the complexities of animal urge and human taboos, my child begged to go home, and with whatever fear of having to hose both of us off, I carried her on my sunburned shoulders, and, toilet tissue I'd bought from the attendant fluttering like a surrender flag, I ran seven or eight blocks, rushed up *our* stairs and reached *our* home—and *our* bathroom—in time.

We'd rented the small apartment to give our child a month of familiar surroundings after so much travel. The nightly sanctuaries we'd picked from those recommended in an inexpensive paperback book had not always proved reassuring.

A pleasant landlady was gracefully tolerating Ingrid's rusty Chilean-Spanish, my rustier Mexican-Spanish, and accepting the pesetas I was counting when our four-year-old ran to release little muscles cramped by a long train ride. The sound of her small shoe soles released the hunting instincts of a huge Alsatian dog, which lunged to attack. The landlady's shouted Spanish-Spanish halted the beast before it could reach two upright animals instinctively poising heavy luggage to defend their young.

Awakened by shouting from below the window of our room one night, we slipped onto our balcony and saw several gay Spanish men and American sailors playing leapfrog in the plaza and laughing, as gleeful as children on a playground.

We'd almost tried a restaurant recommended by our guidebook. It was only a block from our rather elegant hotel, but, we began to notice, it was in a red light district, its doorways filled with prostitutes and pimps, amused at the sight of a family. Sitting on our balcony one night, we saw a man run out of the red light district and heard him shouting that he'd been robbed.

In Barcelona young soldiers patrolled the streets surrounding a hotel where we'd reserved a room. The desk clerk was evasive, but we read in the evening newspaper that before our late-afternoon arrival a carload of men had done a drive-by shooting at the front of the police headquarters across the street. Confused in thick fog, police had later shot up a vehicle that was returning officers from their work elsewhere.

The next day we moved to a different hotel.

Explosions we'd heard a week before, in Caldetas, had been the fireworks of American tourists celebrating the Fourth of July on the roof of their hotel, but Spain was in turmoil. Pro-democracy groups were demanding immediate release of political prisoners. The state police were threatening to overthrow the monarchial democracy, which had replaced the Franco dictatorship.

Ingrid and I were having breakfast with our little daughter at an outdoor café in Madrid when two helicopter gun ships swooped down a few blocks away and began shooting, using, newspapers would say, rubber bullets. Only one person was killed, by a stray bullet when a policeman had felt himself endangered and had fired a warning shot, next day's news reported, perhaps truthfully.

Near the end of our stay in Madrid I phoned my brother Rex, who was commandant of the American Military Mission to Morocco. Despite my having published poems against the U.S. invasion of Vietnam—a possible embarrassment to a man in his position—my brother urged us to come.

We arrived in the southern Spanish port of Algeciras just at dusk, planning to take a hotel and continue to Tangier, Morocco, the following day, but when buses met the train, offering immediate free rides to the port in time to catch the last ship of the day, we changed our plans. The Straits of Gibraltar were smooth, the night pleasant, and we congratulated ourselves. Prematurely. No taxis met the boat, and the money-exchange cubicle was closed, as was everything else in the port. Our boat was already on its way back to Spain, and our only hope was that we could spend the night on benches in a lighted ticket area. Ironically, after feeling police were a menace in Spain, we looked for Moroccan police, but we saw none.

I recall a Hungarian hair-cutter's telling me that she and most people welcomed occupation by Russian troops because they put an end to the shooting being exchanged by rival pro-democracy factions. I read now that Iraqis, who first welcomed the U.S. over-throw of Saddam Hussein, are fighting a guerilla resistance to the occupation because it has brought rape, pillaging, and killings. I recall the apprehension of people in the far north of Norway because not far distant, across the border, unpaid and out-of-control Russian troops were raiding towns and taking what they wanted and doing what they wanted.

A good Muslim angel emerged out of the Moroccan night, a sixteen-year-old boy who was working as a runner, seeking patrons for the one Tangier hotel whose name we knew. Only he and we were in the vast ticket area. He telephoned for a taxi, paid the driver, and refused to take Spanish money for compensation, saying that we could pay him after we'd changed money. He offered to guide us around Tangier the next day and take us to the train we'd catch to Rabat. His fee was small. We hired our angel.

The apprehension we'd felt, amid the turmoil in Spain, returned when one of four Moroccan men angrily said something to our guide while we were sitting in a cafe drinking soft drinks. Our guide answered the man timidly, and his face was worried. I was afraid, but to show that I was not, I looked at the men calmly, hoping to show a confidence I did not feel.

Nothing happened. Whatever animosity the men had felt toward us was spent in their angry words, directed at our young guide. We finished our brief tour and boarded our train on time.

On the ride south I was back in Putnam Township School Number Five's *World Book Encyclopedia*, seeing donkeys, oxen, and camels pulling plows, and when the train stopped in a town as small as Aurora, Iowa, my family and I became an encyclopedia page for dozens of robed Moroccans, all of the men grinning, the women and girls too, perhaps, behind their veils. Seated in an air-conditioned train, behind tinted glass, I felt I was a zoo animal on display in a glassed cage.

A woman boarded the train and entered our car. Her robe was as blue as the haze obscuring the distant Atlas Mountains. She was veiled, but after our train had left the village, she removed the veil and revealed an attractive face, its expression poised and agreeable but possibly not friendly, I thought, but when Ingrid took our little girl to the toilet, the woman smiled and, in fluent English, engaged me in small talk. After my family returned, the woman took a book from her luggage, began reading, and remained silent for the rest of our journey.

Martina had a place to stay put for a week, and thanks to the efforts of my brother's late wife, Kathleen, Martina had playmates, the children of American diplomats and the children of military experts under my brother's command. She also had babysitters, the mothers of her playmates and their servants and, sometimes, my brother's fifteen-year-old son, a nice kid, though not long back he and some of his peers had gleefully hassled a Moroccan gate guard and had been whipped with a chain from the gate that was being guarded.

As a commander my brother had a diplomat's car, the traditional big long black one, though his was a Chevrolet, not a Cadillac, he told me, his proletarian-minded brother. The driver was also a bodyguard. One night he mentioned that we were being followed and turned to take a route that was better lighted and, presumably, policed.

"We Berbers are the Indians of Morocco. Your brother and I

understand one another," the driver told me, and he asked my brother's permission to make me a gift, a fireplace bellows, which I still have.

The driver was Muslim, and when we visited him in his family's vacation campout tent, on a beach, his wife kept to the kitchen, except to serve us. However, the daughter, a student at the Sorbonne, in Paris, was allowed to eat with us.

My brother's house was huge and luxurious, quite different from the farmhouse where we'd grown to manhood. There were two servants, a middle-aged gardener and a young maid. The gardener, married but forced to live separate from his wife during the work week, tried to seduce the young woman. He was unsuccessful, and consequently, when she was nearby, he was embarrassed and depressed.

The Soviet Embassy was an almost windowless, thick-walled mastaba, which harmonized with Moroccan architecture. It could also serve as a fortress or bomb shelter. The American Embassy looked like a Southwestern U.S. country club. Its walls were nearly all glass. At a garden party the American ambassador's daughter was enjoying her martini and enjoying regaling an obsequious group of Americans with her tales of Moroccan television's inept stupidity.

One of my brother's junior officers asked if he could take Rex aside and brief him on something secret. "I don't need to know it," Rex responded. "If I'm tortured, the less I have to reveal the better," he told me.

Surprised at some of my brother's openness in conversations with me, inside his house I asked him if the place might not be bugged. "Sure," he said, and when I asked him by whom, he said, "The Moroccans, for starters, the Russians, for sure, and if they're doing their job, the CIA."

I couldn't help thinking that married life would be difficult under such scrutiny.

Summer had begun, and Ingrid, our daughter, and I no longer needed warm clothes. When I gave these to the gardener, for his family, he thanked me in French and kissed my hand, a gesture I did not witness again until I saw Iraqi soldiers surrendering in the first Gulf War.

Let me live, please let me live beyond forty-six, my wife beyond twenty-eight, our daughter beyond four, I prayed, our homeward flight across the Atlantic barely begun when the plane shook as if it had slammed into something midair, something big, another plane, I thought, seeing a fiery blob as big as a coffin fly past our window. From the loudspeaker near us the pilot cried in a panicked voice, "Don't panic, don't panic, everything is all right, the aircraft is not in danger." A flight attendant rushed toward the rear of the plane, pausing to hastily lean across passengers to look out windows on either side. She demanded of one man, "Did you see anything? Did you see anything?" but he did not answer, his English probably unequal to understanding the question. Most of the passengers seemed reassured by the pilot's hasty words.

I heeded the pilot's command not to panic and heeded my own instinct not to say anything that might panic others. The flight attendant rushed back to the front of the plane and informed the pilot that our elevators and rudder were still intact. This freed him to announce that we'd lost one of our four engines but that we were "not in danger, not in danger." Ingrid and I dressed our child in all of the sweaters we had in our carry-on luggage, preparing as well as possible to survive the cold North Sea.

"If you're downed, forget the life preserver. Grab the heaviest thing you can find and drown before you freeze." That was a piece of advice I remembered from World War II, but determined to take any possible chance of survival, I continued, and Ingrid continued, to add layers of clothing to those already on our child's and, then, on our own bodies.

"As soon as I have finished jettisoning fuel to make the airplane lighter, we'll return and land at Frankfurt airport," the pilot announced, and for tense, terrifying minutes we continued circling, probably as close as possible to the coast of the Netherlands.

Our plane making its approach to an emergency landing at Frankfurt airport, I saw a sight reminiscent of my air force emergency times, the bright, rotating lights of fire trucks and ambulances between the landing lights lining the long runway.

The pilot made a safe landing and received loud cheers from the crowded passenger compartment. We waited for hours in the airport, presumably while the low-budget charter airline was trying to arrange for another plane. Near dawn a young woman appeared and told us in English, German, and French that we'd be driven to a hotel. Our layers of clothing back in our suitcases, we were checked in to an incredibly luxurious high-rise hotel and maybe got two or three hours sleep before being flown in a different airplane, landing to refuel at Ireland's Shannon Airport, an airport from which I'd flown after my first visit to Europe.

Eleven years later an Irish Republican Army assassin would tell my now fifteen-year-old daughter, "Always think twice before pulling the trigger on a man," the assassin separated from his family and missing his own daughter.

"Harkins? Ah, your people are IRA surely," a second IRA assassin would tell me, at that same party, in the Bastille neighborhood of Paris. The party, by the way, was not thrown by people who were IRA members or even significantly "political" on any basis. The two assassins were simply neighbors of our friend, in that low-rent neighborhood.

Not an Irish Republican Army man and not an American Republican but an effective liberal Democrat, Tom Harkin, the U.S. senator from Iowa, is my distant cousin. Ingrid and I met him once. We had just gotten off an airplane after some weeks, during which I had been researching the Mayan culture of Mexico's Yucatan. My sister, one of only a few Democrats in the bank — in which she had risen from teller to vice president — had conspired with my extremely conservative brother Rex's eldest daughter, Susan, to arrange the meeting with Senator Harkin, for whose reelection campaign she had been a volunteer.

"I seen 1,380 dollars worth of gold taken . . . in sight of disease starvation and death not that I seen any person die for real want of food at that time, but by disease brought on by the privations incident to gold hunting . . . Raise corn hogs wheat potatoes and babies and vote the Democratic ticket . . ." This is from a letter written in 1859 by Senator Tom Harkin's forebear, and my distant relation, Daniel Harkin, a letter my sister presented to the senator.

"Died from malnutrition and consequent illness" is how I understand my brother Leland's death and how I understand nearly dying, myself, in high fever from "winter sickness" at age three.

Let me live beyond eighteen, I probably silently felt without much hope, the ice-encumbered bomber I teetered inside jolted by another plane's exploding, explosion mercifully ending the suffering of those who'd been burning to death, their plane a crucifix shape blazing on the snow of the runway.

Let me die with dignity, l felt but could not say, only able to gasp, "Murderers," at ambulance attendants banging my stretcher and jamming my dangling arms against both sides of the bedroom door, the big cop looking the other way, only my future wife's scream ending the mistreatment, only her courageous protests speeding somewhat the slow pace of the ambulance to the hospital, where two white men — the age to have been Korean War medics — hoped to deliver a mixed-blood peace spokesperson from the ghetto to the morgue.

Let's be alive for as long as human generations read words, I say to my brother Ray. Even before going under the earth, he'd always been ahead of me in everything, everything, and beyond paying any attention to whatever a sissy kid brother might say. So I'd thought, but "Remember me when I am gone," his poem — scrawled on brown paper torn from a grocery bag — asks of friends and family, including his younger brother — the poem written the year Ray died of a heart attack at fifty.

"Remember me now I am gone," his ghost asked, shimmering like heat lightning above the boots I inherited, the boots he died in in the ditch he was digging to drain polar melt from the earth that Iowa had inherited from a glacier, the earth white Iowans had inherited from forebears who'd massacred Native Americans. "Remember me when I am gone," Ray's ghost asks each day, as I pray for him and as I try, humbly, inadequately, to write — an eternally, humanly incapable younger child trying to chip a memorial in the molten lava flow of time.

# 28

My brother Bob jumped out of our common bed, exclaiming, with unintentionally ironic appropriateness, "Oh, hell!" and it was only after he had pulled on pants and gone bounding downstairs to awaken our parents that I realized that our room was lighted, as if with dawn, but from the west and hours and hours and many, many dreams past the time when the sun went down.

"Oh, hell!" but it wasn't. Spontaneous combustion, a thunderbolt, or a careless hired man's cigarette had set our barn on fire.

Spontaneous combustion is the disaster theory of most interest to me because spontaneous combustion exercises my vocabulary and because the reality delineated by the words dramatizes the subtlety of some farm decisions. Leave the new-mown hay to dry in the sun too long, and rain will drench the harvest and cause it to rot. Put the hay in the hay mow too soon, and the green hay's spontaneous combustion will burn down the barn.

A thunderstorm was certainly witnessed the night our barn burned—and ironically, rain, lingering on the roofs of corncrib, garage, and house, probably saved them from burning.

Dad, a round-the-clock pipe-smoker, worried about hired men's cigarettes.

Spontaneous combustion. Lightning strike. A cigarette. Whatever the cause, the barn was certainly burning.

I pulled on pants and ran, shirtless and barefoot, downstairs and out, into an eerie, red middle-of-the-night daylight. Wind-borne swatches of hay glided, trailing flames, like mythic Cherokee raven mocker witches, flying to eat humans' hearts and the years they would have lived. Frantically, I swatted burning wings harmlessly to earth, which is where they would have ended up, swatted or not.

Arrived too late, the rural volunteer fire brigade was as ineffectual as I and equally excited, equally entertained.

Like books' besieged castle, frontier fort, enemy factory, cathedral, or home, the barn was going up into flames, up into smoke — going into family story, its hand-hewn shingles, its tree-limb rafters, its rough-sawed-plank loft floor and its tree-trunk beams, all collapsing, blazing, onto horse stalls, cow stalls, and the pen for cute little calves. It was a — generations-delayed — displaced forest fire. Our huge barn, constructed from trees that had shaded Ioway, Winnebago, Sac, and other Indians, was burning to pale gray ashes as fine as those Mom or Aunt Jennie shook out of the cookstove grate and the heating stove grate and shoveled into a rusty scuttle and dumped behind our woodshed.

I still bear the small scar a live coal left on my heel when, days after the burning of the barn, I waded its ashes and failed to find and bury the skeletons of my kittens. All that remains of a structure that had for a century withstood cyclonic winds — all that remains of the huge structure, raised so high, so hopefully and proudly — all that remains of a monument to the Irish-immigrant part of my family's part in westward-ho history — all that remains are glacial stones and concrete forming a rectangular foundation for a barn constructed of air, the air of my words, my small scar, and my grief for my kittens, inconsequential in a world where mothers search war-zone ashes for their children's bones.

The room in which I'd awakened to witness fiery destruction had been named "the Coon Room," a captured raccoon imprisoned there as a pet before I was born. A few years before the Coon Room became my and Bob's bedroom, a rooster pheasant had been imprisoned there in an orange-crate, through whose slats one could see: jungle-camouflage feathers and, thrusting out of zebra-stripe prison shadows, a white-ringed neck, a blue-black, red-wattled head, and a beak as yellow as the corn kernels it pecked out of a rusty tin can. The pheasant disappeared, probably into our hungry stomachs one winter's day.

Let me live, let me live, let me live, Leland, my parents' first child, could only say by shaping air into baby cries, and before he was one year old he had endured malnutrition and illness as long as he could.

At least twice that I remember, my father, drunk, came terrifyingly close to killing me, the second of his three living sons, but did I ever wish what all sons are said to subconsciously wish, for my father's death, knowing, feeling, fearing, and not believing that my wish would be reality? He looked up from leveling a wagon's load of oats, waved to someone, and suffered what I would years later suffer and live to write about, a heart attack.

He'd named me after a man who'd saved his life. He'd saved my life—by risking his life when thieves attacked our farm—by working hard for hours and hours for year after year so his children would not starve. Words of a poem repeated themselves in my mind, words I didn't know I knew, words written by Alexander Pope, "What is is right."

At almost eighty, after climbing a stair to her youngest son Rex's eldest daughter Susan's apartment, after a long car ride to attend Rex's next-to-eldest daughter Patricia's wedding, Mom died in her sleep, apparently "peacefully," I say, as most people say, not knowing what we mean but saying it for whatever peace it gives us.

"I'll go when it's my time to go," my mother told me during my childhood, youth, and after. The last time I visited her, some months before her death, she'd given me pictures of my two sons by my first marriage, Mom thinking compassionately, self-sacrificingly, and correctly that I might not have copies after my divorce. The last time I telephoned my mother, days before her eightieth birthday, which she did not live to celebrate, she seemed apprehensive about the forthcoming long journey by car, and I sensed that she felt her time was close. She lived with great courage. I failed her often, and, the best words I have not enough, I am failing again.

The red roses I wired before her last journey may be the best I will ever be able to do for her. She loved roses, but during most of her life she had no money for anything beyond necessities, and she worked so many hours she had no time to tend flowers.

Grieving and distraught, my sister Ruth hoped the roses I'd sent would live, though rootless. To ease Ruth's grief, her loving husband, Bob Walker, planted the wilted roses, and though or because they were doomed, as all living things are doomed, to decompose and become a part of the earth, they grow, they bloom, they flourish, year after year of my beautiful and long and—for how long?—lengthening life.

# 29

Public Television informs me that that, mystery of mysteries, the Egyptian Rosetta Stone and most other surviving ancient writings are not sacred texts and not artistic evocations of an age but lists of goods to be sold. For today's huge cargoes — of food, oil, troops — the rosetta recorders are tiny computer chips, but still, on marble or some humbler stone, chiseled letters and numbers record the consignment of a few dollars' worth of human chemicals to earth, and still tongues chisel, on air in ears, consignment of a secret cargo to an unknown destination.

In my midtwenties, following the example of Salvador Dali and other surrealists, I minimized my sense of my body and freed my mind by reclining on a cot between shelves holding jugs of bubbling raisin wine, with which I was trying to reconcile my need to be frugal, for my family's sake, and my need to party with friends. Body weight propped by pillows, forearm of pencil hand at rest, only wrist and fingers moving, I wrote spontaneously page after page, letting a notion fade midsentence whenever another notion emerged.

Like the great Mexican writer Octavio Paz and like the great Peruvian Indian writer Caesar Vallejo, I was exploring the land between sleep and waking. I became adept at remembering dreams. My sleep was often broken by nightmares of violent deaths I'd seen in air force crashes and of childhood traumas. I'd wake sometimes from benign dreams too. Sometimes the two seemed mixed. Right after my father's death I dreamed I was in his body, not as a sperm, struggling for survival, but as a sentient, living person, entering a luminous tunnel, which was the throat of my singer father.

One night I lifted from the sea gold letters gold-chain-linked to form a page-size poem, but I awoke, and not one moon-reflecting word illuminated a pillow as wrinkled as a human brain.

Usually my Spirit Dreams do not involve writing. Often my people return from the Spirit Land, and sometimes I wake in the night, flesh vibrant with the sense of visitation. Two nights ago my mother returned, and I was bidding her farewell, in our home, on the farm, before going to teach in Europe. In one memorable dream, some years ago, I was in a sinking ocean liner, with Ingrid, Martina, my mother, and Aunt Jennie. With none of waking's concern for the bends or other realities, I gathered my loved ones close to me, and we floated, many fathoms, to the surface.

I don't often try to interpret dreams, but I try to be alive to their possible implications. Awake, I hunt my dreams as I once hunted for food. I keep very still. Once I aimed my rifle at what seemed a shadowy tree fork amid sun-bright and shaded leaves. The tree fork became the spread of a deer's ears. The slight sounds of my careful breathing shaped a killer's body in the ears of the victim, and in imagination the victim was already venison in my mouth, already a poem's image in sound waves traveling from aimed gun, and my best poems are sunglowing pollen lifted by a bullet's trajectory's wind.

For whatever reason, I have had recurrent dreams of escaping from lions and dreams of defending others from lions. Last night I climbed my childhood home's stair, going on my hands and knees, like the child I once was, playing at being an animal, and I came face to striped face with a huge tiger. I said something to show I was unafraid, and then I spoke soothingly, as I would to our small tiger cat. The second decision was a good one, I guess, because the tiger left.

I have dreamed fairly often of shooting at enemy soldiers and of being shot at.

I am often beautifully in love and ardently, erotically loved in return.

I dream of fishing, sometimes successfully, sometimes disappointingly. I dream of hunting.

I have hunted dreams, not to kill them but to keep them alive, to make them a part of my waking life, and to realize their essence in poems.

In the waking world killing another part of Creation is awesome, always, but sometimes the awe is relieved by a few laughs. Once my brother Ray and I crawled, for dozens of yards, over icy pasture, stalking wild ducks, which had landed on a marsh-surrounded pond. Many times we had endured cold, only to see flocks detect us and take flight.

This time we were nearing the feeding quacking of ducks on the pond when another flock materialized as the sound of powerful wings beating overhead. Let's guess that I was confused, still focused on the first flock. Let's guess that Ray was similarly confused.

He was the first to react. He was older. He was a superb hunter. Though maybe jealous and surly and resentful, I always tried to wait for him and to take his leads.

His rickety shotgun was a bomb, waiting to explode in his hands and kill him, as many had warned him it one day would. It was an old-fashioned twist-barrel single-shot, the long tubular barrel constructed of spirals of wire, welded tight into a tunnel for dozens of deadly lead pellets. The steel welding was strong enough for old black-powder ammunition, but the more powerful new smokeless powder might explode the shotgun barrel into deadly shrapnel. My brother's gun was one he could afford to buy from a pawn shop. He risked his life every time he shot it.

I was right beside him, endangered by explosion, as he rose on his knees as if in Christian prayer, raised the gun almost straight up, and, without taking time to press it tight against shock-absorbing shoulder, squeezed the trigger.

Frantically trying to get my gun awkwardly into aim at the ducks overhead without aiming over my brother, who might rise from his knees into my line of fire, I heard the explosion of smokeless powder right beside my ear, and I saw the potentially murderous old shotgun recoil down to slam its steel butt against my brother's groin.

It wasn't funny to me until my brother finally recovered from shock and pain and started laughing.

We had failed to bring home a single mallard or blue-winged teal. Our family would be hungry. We'd failed our dad, who nearly always brought home meat, and who had gone on forking hay to hungry cows and had trusted my brother and me to go after an elusive V of black dots crossing sky as drifting frogs' eggs cross the clear currents of a pond.

Ice crackling in soggy jackets, we trudged home through the dusk. Our hunting bags were empty, our mother's meat platter would remain empty, but we were laughing at our story, a story that relieved our feeling of disappointment and humiliation. It eased our fears of castration, which we and our father had inflicted often on domestic animals. The incident reminded us of what all hunters instinctively know—and forget, and forget—that ultimately the hunted always get away, and the hunter, becoming the hunted, escapes into the sacred Earth.

Months later Ray left the old twist-barrel shotgun leaning against a tree, because the sound of a car might be the game warden checking on licenses — and, the woods so vast, the maple boles so similar, Ray failed to remember where he had left the gun. Losing it may have saved him from a fatal explosion.

"American history is, for the most part, false, because historians are paid better for promulgating favorable views of the American past," a distinguished American historian I met in Germany lectured, "and," he added, "the true history is only available in literature."

A writer and a reader, I naturally agree; however, today billionaire advertisers control what commercial publishers can print, and the wordswordswords of propaganda persuade millions, while literature reaches only a fraction of the U.S. population.

This is not a novel that a rocket-booster thrust of publicity will propel through the "best-seller" troposphere into orbit around a movie-gold "Oscar," and this is not Great Literature. What this is is the source of all literature. My mom and my aunt Jennie are talking — "visiting" — while serving to friends Mom's home-baked bread, spread with butter — from our own grass-or-hay-cud-chewing cows, the butter fresh from the churn whose creaky handle I have been allowed to turn and turn and turn, and feel big. Inside the two thick bread slices would be, quite possibly, spicy, flavorful headcheese, made from meat scraps off the head of a pig, a pig that Dad had fed until fat, then shot between its little eyes, then butchered.

A neighbor's wife is enjoying being waited on. The neighbor and my dad are greedily enjoying, without a thank you, the treat and the pampering treatment that local farm folkways have ordained to belong to men. They are passionately, optimistically talking about "one hundred bushels per acre" corn — "Indian corn," red and blue ears and, yes, often white, among the dominant gold, in those years before hybrid strains were developed. There is talk about foxes hunted successfully and about those that were so smart they got away. My eldest brother, Bob, and his three scrawny little siblings, my sister, my two brothers, and I, and maybe some equally scrawny neighbor kids are sometimes listening, sometimes not.

After 1932 AD — after Democrats were elected — there was, for the first time I can remember, enough to eat.

Too late for my brother Leland, his infant bones under stone.

Too late for millions of ordinary, good, hardworking people, and, ironically, too late for some whose greed had caused so much suffering for so many. We ordinary people said "millionaires" — in the same awed tone in which we said "God" and "dead." When I was three years old, my undernourished body fighting against fever to stay alive, some millionaires, those awesome beings, had been photographed plunging off buildings called "skyscrapers." Former "highflying" monopolists were, sadly, ironically, flying, expensive clothes fluttering like the robes of angels, their destination maybe heaven or maybe only the earth, the sacred earth, which they and their fathers and their fathers' fathers before them had plundered from nature-respecting Indians as if it were the source of endless wealth. Unbounded greed had destroyed the greedy by causing a disaster called "Depression," which little kids could scarcely pronounce but could suffer. And did.

"I wonder if I could get you to write down that recipe for chow-chow."

"I'd be glad to, but I wish you could tell me how to get my kids to eat it. My oldest boy, by my first husband, rest in peace — my oldest remembers what it was like to have next to nothing to eat, and he still chews and sucks chicken wings down to the bone, like he used to do because he took pity on the little ones, who needed the better pieces more than he did, bless him, bless his good heart, but it breaks my heart to see he got the habit so deep he still takes those scrawny wings first, even now when there's enough to eat. These little ones they've forgotten already what they lived through, what their brother they never saw didn't live through, rest in peace, bless his innocent soul."

"I see you burning your cornstalks again to make the plowing easier, but I keep telling you to plow them stalks into the earth so's your next crop will do better." The old way. The Indian way. Put back to make up for what you take.

I think now of my father's commanding his family through the starvation years of the Great American Depression, teaching us to work hard. He also taught us to enjoy our lives. For a time, before marriage, he'd made his living as a gambler, and by the light of a kerosene lamp we played simple card games, "blackjack, hearts," and, with no sensitivity toward our mother's unmarried sister, "old maid." Our father told us stories, played his banjo, and sang for us. I think now of the years of his boyhood, spent hoeing hard clay of the hills to grow food, spent mining coal, spent felling trees.

My family's stories were my oral tradition — stories of the old times and also stories of recent experience. One of our milk cows bled to death after trying to get through a barbed-wire fence. It being warm weather, there was no possibility of our family's eating so much meat before it spoiled. Dad drove our horse-drawn wagon seven or eight miles and tried to sell the cow to a butcher. When the butcher would not go higher than a ruinously low price, Dad butchered the beef right on the back of the wagon and sold it to shoppers for less than the butcher was getting in his store.

The butcher threatened his competitor for selling without a license, but Dad faced him down with the declaration that there was no law against a man selling his own property to whoever wanted to buy it.

Was a license required? Was Dad correct in his assertion of an unshakeable legal principle? I'll never know, but Dad's was a story of triumph, the butcher finally offering a fair price and Dad driving home to his farm work. As memorable as any victory march, the pride in Dad's storytelling voice became family pride, still a part of my life, in these times of mad cow disease and E. coli despite hygienic standards for meat.

On another occasion my father hauled grain to sell in town, but the scales showed the weight to be far less than my father judged it to be. This was before the New Deal's "socialist" notion of providing government inspectors to insure that scales weighed correctly.

My father spent half a day driving his horses and his wagonload of grain to another town, and there the scales were honest.

"If the corn goes a hundred bushels an acre, and if Roosevelt meant what he said about fair prices, maybe you and me we can hire us this trench-digging machine and lay some tile lines to drain our sloughs on down to the creek and then go to farming what's now just too damned wet to grow anything but quack grass and thistles."

I write, the best I can, what feels like the cadence and essence of my parents' conversations, their "visiting" with friends, and now I remember something my father often said, something so impassioned, so simple, and so strong, from years of hard work and hope and conviction, not even a little kid could forget. "If they'd just stop trying to starve the American farmer to death on his own farm, by God he could feed the world."

# 30

Eighty-one years of age, I feel as I felt, age twelve, at this time of day, 5 AM, dawn soon to come, when I proved, to my solitary self, my worthiness of another day, hour, minute, second, breath of life by running each morning faster and — by the space between one, two, three, four fence posts — further.

My only audience the highly intelligent mongrel herding dog and watch dog and affectionate pet, old Rover, I was winning race after race, my belly satisfyingly empty, the emptiness masochistically pleasant because it proved my manliness and had only to be endured till breakfast. Nostril-shriveling ice, the mingling of rot and growth under melt, the fragrances of mown clover and mint, wild in the pasture slough, and the smell of corn just before harvest — I ran season after season nearly every day.

Eleven years ago, while staying with the Danish scholar of Native American literature Bo Scholer, I found and read a chapter from *The Son of Old Man Hat* and learned one similarity between the memoirist's Navajo upbringing and my own, the daily practice of demanding the utmost of your body. Last September, when my wife, Ingrid Wendt, was teaching in a Navajo boarding school, Aneth, I found and finished reading the book I had only had time to begin reading eleven years before. I learned that the Son of Old Man Hat went on herding sheep for all of his life. I left the farm at eighteen when I went to train for flight duty in the air force. There, after my years of body-building exercising and body-building farm work, I passed the most rigorous physical tests with scores higher than the military's highest standards.

Here, in northern Norway, where I am now doing research, I watched my friend, the Sami scholar Harald Gaski, chase a huge buck sheep that had strayed onto Harald's mother's farm. In his thirties Harald still runs like a boy. He runs nearly every day, he tells me, as he has been doing all of his life, as I did, as long as physically possible.

Did I ever feel, through anesthetic more potent than oxygen deprivation in a Cherokee sweathouse, the blade of scalpel, the teeth of surgical saw, and the stitching, which left a scar like a six-inch centipede to crawl over wired-together breastbone? A young man decided to become a medical student. Memories, disciplined into his brain and his hands, saved my life and released my fingers to tap plastic and form, in electronic impulse in silicon chip, my memories of big people, who labored to help me grow big — who probably, at least partly, did not want me to grow big but to, forever, stay as small as they'd once been.

I am a more ignorant than not human with a bad heart and God knows what else, but I feel healthy, feel youthful, vital, energetic, vigorous, and intensely creative. Will I live to touch one more key on the keyboard of this computer? Now nearing eighty-two — seven years since I began this a hop-skip-and-jumps-and-maybe-some-dancing memoir — I believe that all of us live only so long as the Creator has reason for us to live. I try to be as alive as I can each day, and that means to me awakening as much of myself as possible and strengthening my verbal capabilities as I used to strengthen my growing muscles. I write so that I will be as much myself as I can be at the moment of death, whenever that may be.

Last night a Sami ("Lapp") publisher was talking about the corrupting dangers of Sami writers going on TV and getting large commercial publishers and becoming celebrities.

When I was a young writer, my huckstering Beat and Black

Mountain coevals were vociferously rebelling against Gutenburg's printing press, and the young rebels were exploring the oral tradition of orators and preachers, reading or reciting their poems from a podium at the head of the room and aiming to reach large audiences. Having grown up in a family tradition of story meant for a small, intimate audience, I write to reach my own essential self and to reach other imagined individuals, one at a time. I think I have, by instinct, sought the Spirit Voice that has spoken from within me since my earliest childhood memories, and I try to stay close to my people, not so much to speak to and for them but to listen and try to discover the invisible borders between my inner self and the inner selves of people who are listening to their own inner voices.

"Why are you always writing about those red Indians, man? Why don't you write about your Irish people?" an American professor asked me, and I could only wish that I had written more about my Irish American mother.

Having lost, at age twelve, the guidance of her own mother, my mother told and told and told her children whatever they might not learn in time, to keep out of trouble and stay safe. She told us and told us, but I learned more from seeing her working, hour after hour, beside my dad, to milk, feed, and clean up after cows and then to feed and scoop out a window and onto a manure pile the waste of pigs—pigs she'd later help Dad kill, bleed, disembowel, scald, scrape, and hang to freeze, out of reach of rats, foxes, coons, and wild dogs, in our laundry shed, to see us through winter, if we were lucky. If not, we'd survive on rabbits and pheasants and potatoes and bread or pancakes fried and flavored in lard.

By now I am so modern I have become addicted to a computer keyboard for creating prose, but for poems, elusive as deer among dawn mists, my rifle is a stub pencil, like those with which I first drew cowboys and Indians and other combatants and like those with which my father recorded the days the bull was observed in the act of creating calves.

Am I still, these years from my upbringing, still an Indian?

Applying the Rez Test of authenticity, it is true that, like most Cherokees, I have never lived in North Carolina, never lived on our single reservation, one that a kind white man bought for a few oppressed Cherokees after so many had been robbed of their fertile plantations, hunting grounds, and population centers, including the sacred city Echota—after so many had been ethnically cleansed, been massacred, been death-marched west.

My protein source was often, in my early days, wild animals killed by me or others of my family, but I was civilized enough to use, as toilet paper, pages from last year's mail-order catalogs or the *Des Moines Tribune*'s assessments of labor unrest, the Abraham Lincoln Brigade, and the New Deal. I utilized the traditional Cherokee hygienic material, broad leaves, only when seized with one of the inconveniences of malnutrition while stalking game miles from rural America's Dream Book crammed with necessities and fripperies—miles from words telling me what the *Tribune*'s publishers, investors, and advertisers wanted believed.

My mother told me that her first husband's German American family didn't approve of his marrying an Irish American. Also, with whatever concerns about relatives back in the fatherland, the parents were against their son's being in the American army. I guess his was a familiar story of a generation gap and the rejection of cultural roots.

I taught my two sons something of hunting, and my eldest son, Jeff, liked hunting in the mountains and forest to bring venison home to our table. I told all three of my children stories, and I soothed them with chanting when they were ill or frightened by dreams in the dark. However, my children don't feel Indian, having grown up geographically removed from any Cherokee influence other than my own.

"Write of what you have lived or have witnessed. Don't let the conquerors' whims turn you into a tourist-grade museum exhibit,"

I have told young Indian writers, but—"Do what I say, not what I do"—I too have slid into the trap I've warned of, trying to give some substance to my Indian people's past and thus sometimes taking others' laboriously arrived at scholarly suppositions and turning them into fiction.

I am my immediate family's last-ditch Indian survivor, as I guess my writing about mixed-race confusion and loss of identity suggests. In Luigi Pirandello's short story "War" a bereaved father says that a father does not give half of his love to one child, half to another, he gives all his love to each of his children. I am a Cherokee-Shawnee-English-Irish person, not part this part that but all everything, whatever it is.

I have, by family consent, inherited my father's banjo, which, ironically—father-son hangup or basic inability—I cannot play. Old now, I see, around brass frets, the wooden banjo neck, worn from years of fingering, and I see my father, dawn turning the clouds of pipe smoke around him into colossal pale blue petals, the four silver strings of his banjo gleaming, the ceaselessly quivering copper bass string glowing like a single ray of the full sunlight, soon to come.

Greed destroyed the greedy in the Wall Street crash, and greed for food he'd never had in his near-starvation childhood destroyed the lean, handsome, mixed-breed Indian man my father had been. He died while harvesting oats—died by his own hand, one could think, the fork hand lifting, one time too many, potatoes and gravy from his plate. He suffered a fatal heart attack while raising one hand in friendly greeting, signaling a salesman, just wait while I finish filling this wagon with oats. The salesman was prepared to wait, but death was not.

Ray began mouth-to-mouth resuscitation—the kiss of life—and where he'd learned that I'll never know—maybe from his wife, who had been a hospital ward helper. Bob ran to get a car and to get our mother, who could not take in the reality and, true to her image of herself as a lady, wanted to change out of work clothes before going to town. "A man dying—it's a hell of a time to think about changing your clothes," her combat-infantry-veteran eldest son told her, his anger, if it was that, maybe as much an evasion as Mom's not wanting to go to town in her kitchen clothes.

Bob rushed our mother, food-stained kitchen apron and all, into the car, Ray continued "the kiss of life" during the twelve-mile, high-speed drive, and Dad reached the hospital alive—but, sadly, not for long. The doctor, a friend of Dad's, wept—"A few miles closer. A few minutes less. I almost saved him as it was."

For a time, for a time, for a time, but only for a time, Ray had given breath to the man who had joined with our mother in giving us ours, but my father had gone into death—gone into breath, the breath of whatever stories would outlive him. Two hundred miles away I got the news by telephone, from my sister's husband, who wept. My father had treated him like a son, and my brother-in-law had loved my father. "The hell of it is, there's nothing you can do, there's nothing you can do," he said to me, a truth every human knows and understands and, devoted to life and wanting life to go on and on and on, refuses to believe.

"This is hard for you," had been my first response on the telephone. Saying something compassionate and perceptive was maybe characteristic of the writer and professor I'd become. It was true and something I felt, but it was also a denial, an evasion. As I left to be with my family in mourning, I glimpsed a red Irish setter like the one I'd given my dad, and tears, the first of many, made it difficult to drive through city traffic without endangering my life and the lives of my then-wife and two little sons.

I read "retired" on my father's last driver's license, and I felt the terrible anguish of love that death had wrenched into grief. Retired or semiretired all these years since a heart attack gave me warning, I feel grief and love for my father now.

"I didn't know this man, but from all I hear, he was a good man," a kindly preacher, hired for the day, could honestly say of my dad, who had not been a Christian let alone a member of a congregation and had probably died as he had lived, sensing the Great Spirit over us all in Creation, so far as I can guess, still trying, still trying, to be able to truthfully say more than, I didn't know this man — of my dad — of myself.

"Occupation: Retired."

My father was sixty-four — let's see, oat harvest, yes, less than a month before Social Security would have begun — affidavits having convincingly, legalistically confirmed the family Bible's scrawled assertion that Charles Salisbury — or berry — had been born, something no one had doubted in all those years Dad had paid taxes.

I was standing alone, eight feet from where I'd been born, when I read "retired" on my father's driver's license. The license was on the piano, which, for lack of leisure and tuning, was never played, my overworked mother the only one who knew how. The piano was of use for putting losable or breakable valuables, such as family photographs, out of the reach of five children.

My father and my mother's first son, Leland, dead of malnutrition and illness before he was a year old, Ray, my father and mother's second son, dead of a heart attack at age fifty, while working at his job, digging a drainage ditch, a Vanishing American, with only a heart-bypass operation and a cancer treatment to thank for not vanishing altogether, I pray, God bless my people in the Spirit Land and let them know that I love them, my father, my mother, my aunt Jennie, my brother Ray, and my brother Leland — and, by now my brother Bob, my sister Ruth, and my brother Rex.

I am aware of the years my father labored, in 100-degree heat, in 30-below-zero cold, to keep his family alive. He never lived to retire. I have retired, officially, though I go on working as I have done since childhood, when I carried pails filled to the limit a child could lift, for the feeding of animals. I have worked full-time ever since I was big enough to be of use in the fields, at age twelve, also the age at which, for the first time in my life, I'd hunt for hours and kill meat our family needed to stay alive.

Now I feel sadness, feel the held-in tears, for the years gone, for the loved ones gone, for the reminder of aging, of my death — maybe what my father felt when he wrote Retired.

# 31

I was destined to write stories in which I'd try to render others' stories. My role in war was inconsequential, but my grief for friends remains — maybe more vivid because their deaths were not so numerous that I became callused, as a battle-shocked soldier has to be.

The commander of Kirtland Field, Albuquerque, New Mexico, was Colonel Frank Kurtz, who'd flown General Douglas MacArthur out when Japan defeated the U.S. Army, then occupying the Philippines, and Kurtz had published a book, which I'd read at seventeen, *Queens Die Proudly*. *Kurtz* means "short" in German, and apropos, his book was shortened to fit into the *Reader's Digest*. The book told millions of Americans how to feel about war, and it indirectly told something about a society where an ill-prepared general, who'd just suffered humiliating defeat, could command a badly needed warplane to fly him, his family, and servants to safety, while thousands of ordinary Americans were forced into the Bataan Death March.

That's history. For me the Battle of the Philippines has become the stories and poems of my friend Myrna Pena Reyes. She was a small girl during the war. Her botany professor father knew what plants were good to eat during the years he and his family lived as jungle nomads, to avoid Japanese soldiers. Myrna's memories include being machine-gunned by U.S. planes. That's not history. That's war. That's life.

At the end of the Four Freedoms War, which had followed the War to End All Wars, I was told I should enlist in the air force inactive reserve because we'd soon be at war with our heretofore much praised ally Russia. All I'd known about communism before World War II was the newspapers' approval of somebody's being thrown into prison for being a communist. During World War II communism was smiling Uncle Joe Stalin, whom American propaganda lauded as the savior of his nation. All I knew about China was Generalissimo and Madame Chiang Kai Shek's being lavishly entertained and praised in Washington. All I knew about Mao Tse Chung's guerillas was that our bomber crews were instructed to parachute into guerilla-held territory, if going down over China, because the guerillas would protect us, while Chiang Kai Shek's Nationalists would sell us to the Japanese.

A buck sergeant, my last "command" was a dozen aerial gunners, headed, as I was, for military discharge. I received vouchers to feed us all. I had a bed on the train. No more sleeping sitting up or sprawled in the aisle. I'd never heard of Korea and its centuries of suffering under foreign oppression. I was twenty. With no notion that I'd get some education, some history, and risk prison by resisting my call to duty in the Korean War, I signed an eagle-emblazoned piece of paper and joined the air force reserve.

The intervals between friends burning, the last two of my teenage years — and the intervals between the whippings, shootings, and terror of my childhood years — those intervals were blessed times, more blessed because of unpredictable danger.

Destined to fly in airplanes, higher than any bird can fly, I first flew as high as my father's arms could reach and strained my little body full length and kicked both bare feet up against a magically warm sky, our living room ceiling, and descended through thinning clouds of pipe-tobacco smoke and landed safely against a warm chest, from which, magically, breath would later issue, telling the scary and somewhat funny story of two men who hunted a really really big, really fierce bear because they and their families were as hungry as the dickens and they wanted to skin the big bear and eat it, and they found some hair and some blood in the late and last snow of winter, where the bear had waked up from its hibernation and starvation and done it some eating, probably a rabbit or squirrel, and the men found big tracks in mud where their bear had had a good drink from one of the springs that trickled out of ice-fringed stone, and they found white claw marks in pine bark higher than any man, including them, could reach, and resin was still oozing from the bark, the amber globules glowing like — like globules of honey. Some big tracks further on, the hungrier and hungrier men found a bee tree and had to run, the bees still mad because the bear had stolen some of the honey the bees had worked so hard and so long to make, and here it was still more winter than it was spring and no blossoms for more honey for months, and then the two hunters found the bear fast asleep in sunshine high up in a tree, and it was even bigger than they'd thought, up there like a big black storm cloud amongst other clouds as white as sheep, a whole lot of eating for each of the men and for each man's wife and little kids and the glossy black fur for a robe to warm the bed of whichever one shot first, and, BangBang, they both shot fast at the same time, and they put down their guns and climbed to be the first to push the bear loose from the branches to make it fall down where they could skin it, and the one who'd climbed the fastest and done the pushing could claim the skin, and then the two friends would divide the meat and leave the guts for the varmints and birds and trees of the forest to eat.

Feeling a foot a-stomping on its own two front paws, the foot a-trying to kick a-loose the grip claws had on wood, the bear roused up, and the sharpsharp teeth clamped down on the foot, and the man he grabbed a branch and held on for dear life, and his friend grabbed the bear by the tail so it couldn't go no higher to get a better bite, and it was tug of war, tug of war, tug of war, while's they was hoping the bear it would bleed some more, give up, and just die, and the one with his foot in the bear's teeth he was a yelling, "Hold on Hold on," and his friend yelled back, "I'm a-holding, but if tail hold breaks, you're a goner" — tug of war, tug of war, tug of war, and the two men they'd been in a war together, a real war, one of those so-called Indian wars, on one side or the other, or the so-called Civil War, or the so-called War to End All Wars, and the one man he couldn't get his foot, all bloody and hurting inside its stiff leather brogan shoe, a-loose, and the bear it couldn't climb to do its biting no higher, and the friend he just kept on holding on, and the sun it went down, and the sun it come up again, and it just goes on, goes on, goes on, tug of war, tug of war, and Daddy's little boys and little girl fall asleep.

Or they whine and they plead for one more story, just one more, and they get one, while blue gray clouds of pipe smoke slowly replace the oxygen in little lungs, the pipe smoke meant to be breathed only by men, Indian men, who smoked pipeful after pipeful in the small space of their sweathouse and let spirit visions come, the smoke thick but not so thick men would starve for oxygen and die. But lung cancer? Another story.

One more story, just one more, but no, no more stories and no more whining and yamping or the black dog will get you, and like centuries of children before us, my sister and brothers and I were scared off to bed, because the neighbor across the road's black dog always barked and snarled at our two good dogs, Old Shep and Old Fido, who liked me to pet them and pet them on their smooth warm heads until the three of us dozed and dozed and dreamed dog dreams and little-boy dreams on the dog pad on the porch in the midday sun.

Another neighbor's bad dog barked at a little girl who was walking to school, and when she ran, it caught her and bit her on the leg, and she had to have stitches, like my Teddy bear, but the stitches tore out, and my mommy and my aunt Jennie were working so hard to can vegetables in jars to feed us in winter they didn't have time to make new stitches, and the sawdust all ran out, and then I had a one-legged bear, with one white underwear button for one eye and just some loose threads for the other, loose threads as black as eyelashes, like those of my brother Bob's one-eyed friend, whose rifle Bob borrowed to defend himself after I ran and warned him that Dad was drunk and threatening to shoot him. And another neighbor's bad dog caught another little girl walking to school, and there was nobody home to kick the dog or hit it with a stick and make it stop, and there was a funeral for that little girl, just as if she'd been big and old.

And bears and coyotes and cougars are moving into urban neighborhoods and killing cats and dogs, and there have only been yay many fatal attacks on humans, in yay many years, more chance of being struck by lightning, and people are reminded and look up to make sure their lightning rods are flashing in the sun and forget about wild dogs and wild animals until the next need for news, and war is on again and again, and there are "acceptable losses" from enemy action or from misdirected "friendly fire," and those of us still alive feel, we are told, the need "to heal," from the most recent TV combat footage before the next TV combat footage starts, and there is "collateral damage," and there are "unavoidable civilian casualties" but only to somebody else, in some other country, on some other continent, other channel, other network, and an airliner crashes again and again, and as sure as death and taxes, there are ongoing official investigations again and again, enough for several newscasts, and there are airline profits to make, and Hold on! For God's sake hold on, day after day, year after year, generation after generation, tug of war, tug of war, tug of war, and when tail hold breaks you're a goner.

It's a good day to die, Sioux defenders chanted, and here I am, like the Sioux nation, defending a smaller and smaller perimeter of years, days, hours, minutes, seconds yet to live, defending whatever future is in my aging and doubtless dwindling mind.

It's a good day to live, here, where I am now, in Germany, a nation divided among conquerors, now becoming one nation again after massive destruction, oppressive occupation. It is a good day to live, the sun seeming to have a chance of shining through smog onto earth, a seminar in Memory and the Native American Tradition for me to meet this afternoon, some thinking to do, about the stories and poems of others, after some time this morning with my own writing.

I have said my dawn prayers, to the Creator and God of All, to the spirits of the Four Directions of Creation, to the Spirit of the Earth, from which growth comes, and in which my loved ones lie. I have prayed that my loved ones may be well in the Spirit Land and know that I love them, and I pray that they may live a life of beauty and happiness where they are now.

# 32

A university is a place where people who've sold their souls do their damnedest to kill the souls of others.

"If I hired you, would you be serious, or would teaching be just a way of putting food on the table so you could go on writing poems?" an English Department head asked me, himself a self-declared poet who'd never published, I'd later learn.

"Are you serious about teaching, or is it just a way of putting food on the table so you can enjoy reading and writing articles about writers?" I could have asked but instead said something equally undiplomatic and did not get the job.

A university is a place where individuals can discover themselves by discovering other individuals, including those centuries dead.

A university is a place where you have to struggle and fight to survive as an individual, resisting the powerful, who keep power by destroying.

"Why should one avoid bad company?" a psychology test, itself being tested, would ask a would-be psychologist, me, and, deaths witnessed having shocked me into an earnest regard for truth, I would answer, "So as not to waste time better spent in good company."

A university is a place where I've found sanctuary and, despite some opposition, have lived for truth and beauty. An administrator who'd low-salaried me for years was forced to report that "an overwhelming majority" of full professors had voted to promote me into their ranks. That and years of seeing former students' achievements gives me pride and reminds me that I have lived and worked among some of America's best minds, best citizens of the human community.

"Why do scuba divers make so much more money than professors like Dad?" my younger son, Brian, asked his elder brother, Jeff, who replied, "Because scuba diving is more dangerous," a response that made the three of us and a young woman standing at the meat counter near us laugh, the four of us realizing that we were only half a block from a university branch bank that civil rights activists had bombed the night before. A thick drape had absorbed shattered window glass, and thus a university student hired as a night watchman had not been killed.

A university is a place where young women have to walk in groups when leaving a night class because, just as bank robbers know that banks are where money is to be found, rapists know that a university is where young women are in abundant supply.

A university is a place where politicians do their damnedest to restrict freedom, I discovered when a state legislator demanded and got the expulsion of one of my students from the editorship of the student literary supplement to the student newspaper. My student had published a piece of fiction that contained some mildly sexual details. I was interviewed and denounced the censorship and was consequently myself denounced by a right-wing journalist.

As a young reporter, twelve years before, I'd resigned from the student newspaper after the editor was forced to suppress my story about discrimination against a Jewish professor. I'm a writer, and my stand for freedom of expression isn't only idealistic; it's also a matter of self-preservation, preservation of the best self I'm doggedly trying to become—and hopefully to clutch, with my desperate words, some of my fellow humans and to dog-paddle them back to where they can wade ashore and walk for themselves.

An entire issue of a literary quarterly was suppressed because a character in one story had used the sort of language used by soldiers, during my time as a soldier and probably still. The university president demanded that the author of the story agree to change his story's "offensive language" or the story would not be distributed. The author agreed, and at considerable expense the original edition of the magazine was cut apart and revised—except for two copies, one kept by the editor and one that he gave me.

The magazine was again attacked, this time for publication of something by Antonin Artaud. The editor was fired, and I was asked to assume the position I'd been promised when hired years before, the position of editor-in-chief. I refused to edit and censor the magazine and became one of three faculty members who wrote a freedom-of-the-press manifesto for a vote by the entire university faculty. The vote was overwhelmingly favorable for free press. The president then offered to give the editor he'd fired ownership of the issue for which the university had paid. The editor accepted and published the material in a new magazine called *Coyote's Journal*. With the backing of a faculty vote to guarantee freedom of the press, I accepted the editorship of *Northwest Review* and worked at that job unhampered until I published a "Protest and Affirmation" issue during the Vietnam War, after which I was fired, the second time in my life I've been fired from a job. The first time I was fired for finding a better job and not showing up for work on the steel gang of a manure-spreader factory, which—a further irony—had gone into bankruptcy.

A university is a battleground, on which the struggle for human freedom is ceaselessly being waged.

A university is a place where some professors and some students go mad.

A talented young poet in one of my classes telephoned to tell me that he was going to kill himself, then, when I tried to convince him to stay alive, hung up.

He had tried to do without sleep for days to induce disorientation, his University Health Service psychologist told me, and I uneasily worried that I'd mentioned Rimbaud's doing that in his successful quest for a vision not constricted by the ordinary. Police had found dozens of empty aspirin bottles in my suicidal student's empty apartment. Telling me that I was the only person my student trusted, the psychologist asked that I be available at either my university or my home phone as much as possible twenty-four hours a day while police continued to search.

I was already committed to be at Oregon State University, thirty-nine miles up the road, attending a panel, but I phoned home every hour. It was difficult to concentrate on the panel. I only remember that an acclaimed critic tried the sadly familiar trick of treating the featured speaker, Susan Sontag, contemptuously, intending to advance his own career by verbally destroying a distinguished, and seemingly rather fragile, opponent. After a scheduled intermission Sontag began by saying that the personal attack had made her give way to tears and decide not to return, but strengthened by colleagues' encouragement, she had gained the strength to reply. Her carefully articulated counterattack devastated her pompous opponent and forced him to falteringly apologize.

My sensitive, fragile young student phoned my home while I was gone, but he did not phone the emergency contact number my wife gave him. Again it was a time of tense waiting.

During my regular conference hour, in my third-floor office, I finally got the call everyone had been waiting for. My student wanted to come right over and talk with me. I said fine, let's meet downstairs and sit on a bench in the sunshine and talk.

"No, I'll come up to your office," the big, muscular young potential suicide and potential murderer said. As I started to close the window, on that hot day, I saw the concrete three stories below, and realizing that glass would do nothing to prevent my student from falling and/or throwing me to my death, I left the window open.

My student was nervous, apprehensive, and tense, pacing around the small office while he talked. He desperately needed to be famous, and he'd had nothing but rejections from magazine editors. I don't remember what he said, and I don't know what I managed to reply, but he agreed to go and talk with his psychologist if I went with him. I went, trying to keep up with the young man's long, manic strides as we went down three flights of steep steps and then crossed campus to the University Counseling Center. After all those days and nights of cooperating with the police and carefully planning for this moment, a receptionist, who had somehow not been informed of the situation, said, "You'll have to wait."

For a quarter of an hour or so we waited, my student becoming increasingly tense, rocking back and forth, big body creaking chair; then he bolted, disappearing into the masses of students outside.

The next opportunity for intervention came two nights later, when police surrounded a suspected hideout and the psychologist phoned for me to aid in the capture.

"No," I decided, "I am not going to destroy whatever I might mean to him as he tries to regain the best self he was trying to be. I'm not going to put myself in his mind as part of a police raid."

"I respect that," the psychologist said, "and I think that you are right."

The supposed hideout was empty, and again there were days and nights of tense waiting and readiness, and then a policeman, as ignorant as the psychologist's receptionist about the days of planning, saw the nervous behavior of a young man waiting for a bus and captured him and maybe saved what was left of his life.

What kind of parents would have such a son? They came to see me, and they seemed to be serious, intelligent, and normally devoted parents.

The young poet survived, but despite treatment he was sadly deranged, I judged, from the letters he sent to my university address, his own address a state mental institution. I answered as insightfully as I could, and I dutifully wrote the institution's psychiatrist that his patient had written, "I'm going to kill my psychiatrist."

I next saw my former student years later, when a kindly young woman in the registrar's office asked if I would change an incomplete so that my mentally fragile protégé could be awarded the degree he'd been just days short of receiving. Receiving the degree was an obsession, and his psychiatrist felt that finally getting the diploma would help to "establish a plateau of stability." Again weeks of insightful effort by well-intentioned strangers came up against institutionalized madness. When I went with my mentally shaky former student to file for graduation, a grouchy man behind a desk insisted that further red-tape requirements had to be met.

Luckily I was able to find the young woman who'd first phoned me, and she gave what the grouchy man had refused to grant, a permission-to-graduate form for my student, for whatever good it might do.

What good it did I cannot judge. What good any of my years of efforts as a teacher have done I cannot judge, though I am soon to face a final judgment myself, I am told and am ready to believe.

"All I have tried to teach my students is that I don't know anything," Socrates is said to have humbly said, and the state killed him.

# 33

Loose dogs chase children running as if fleeing, and loose dogs attack, one from either side, a seventy-five-year-old man so crippled in one leg he is easily dragged down, after landing only one kick, and he lies, stunned, arms protecting his throat until the dogs' owners are startled out of their marijuana torpor and drag the dogs back, and most of our lives it's happening to—not me and not you—dogs attack and maim or kill—somebody else's child, sweetheart, spouse, parent, friend—and one pack of humans wants the dogs "put to sleep," and another pack wants the dogs kept awake, and someone wants dog-control laws enacted and enforced and enforcement paid for with someone's taxes—not one's own—and the million-dollar TV ads sell billions of dollars' worth of food for Walt Disney doggies, who are nicer and more human and more humane than most of us are even on our best behavior on our best days—and, let's see, in between the ads there're new wars and new atrocities and some new massacres but across an ocean or across a continent or across town and so distant, so unreal, they are found enjoyable on TV again and again, and what's new again for the news again? and—as sure as death and taxes, as sure as you're born, as sure as God made little green apples, put your mitt into an apple bin and out an apple comes, out of the pile of wire stories you'd have a yesterday thrown away: "DOGS ATTACK"—and maim or kill somebody else's child, sweetheart, spouse, parent, friend. And now the weather for the weekend family romp at the beach—with your pet running as free, free, free, as TV history's Caucasian Americans have always supposedly been—as free as you and me and other civilized, nuclear-armed Americans can be persuaded to pretend that we are.

And today, as I review what I wrote days ago, news comes of terrorists hijacking American jetliners and crashing them into the World Trade Center and the Pentagon. Our daughter, Martina, phoning that she is okay and in her apartment, three miles from the explosions, I am full of relief and gratitude.

If—John Kennedy a few months dead—I were thirty-five again, I might be writing of accepting a job "only forty miles from the center of publishing" and following my publication in the *New Yorker* to a teaching job in a college in New York.

Actually, my seventy-fifth birthday seven weeks away—I am writing that Ingrid and I decided, last night, that we would visit our daughter in the city where six thousand humans died.

I hear that the rubble of two towers—not of Babel but of World Trade—are the rocks upon which a new building may be built—as cathedrals were rebuilt from rubble after World War II.

I may not reach New York. Devoutly religious and true to their cause, terrorists may turn the airliner into a bomb.

Will my death be like the deaths of centuries of millions burned by religious zealots throughout centuries—like the deaths of friends burning in a crucifix-shape bomber—a bomber designed to fly through subzero, high-altitude air to burn men, women, and children in their homes? Or will my death be sinking into sleep, to wake up—where? how? and as what?—natural to wonder, natural not to know.

Loneliness and terror—they are what I think I saw when I visited what proved to be the deathbed of a man I've known for many years. I remember his wife's spunkily insisting on a brisk walk after eating Thanksgiving dinner last year, unwilling to lapse into feebleness the last year of her life.

"I just don't know why God let's us suffer such pain," another friend gasped and pumped more morphine into his blood. Months later the miracle cure, death, released him from suffering, and I joined other friends in offering words that might be a consolation to his widow and sons.

Eighteen years beyond my birth I buckled on a parachute that might save my life. Fastened to the chute harness was a medical kit, inside it a needle—no bigger than those with which Mom patched pants and made them last for one boy more—and a silver tube the size of a bullet for slaying a vampire. The tube contained maybe enough morphine to ease pain until rescue or death. Holstered on my belt was a pistol, for protection against any seeking to avenge bomb-obliterated families. Some of us young bomber crewmen promised each other that we would put a merciful bullet into the brain of anyone trapped in burning wreckage.

A dear friend of many years suffering and dying of lung cancer asked, "Have you had to endure such pain?"

Edges of three fractured ankle bones grating against each other as I was carried a quarter of a mile or so—a hole rotting in my heel inside a cast—"I have suffered," I could honestly say, "but not as much as I see that you are suffering."

As I embraced for a last time flesh that cancer had eaten down to ninety pounds—what my brother weighed nine months after escaping from a prisoner-of-war camp—I heard, "There's nothing left of me," and wanting to be as kind as my friend had been to me, to my wife, and to our daughter, I said that all that mattered was in my living arms right then, meaning what I do not know and do not expect to know.

Ray, my brother, is back at the farm, our home, and it is night, and he is dead, without having had children, but he tells me that he and his new love, not his wife, have had a little girl, "with them for over a year," is how Ray puts it. It's a good visit from my brother, happy altogether, as far as I can remember, but I feel tears now, asking myself how I could have fought with him, failed to remember how generous he was and kind, really kind, though tougher than I was. When he told me he had cancer, I tried to get him a job close to a hospital, but he let it go. He had a grudge maybe, though it never showed when I visited him. Maybe he was jealous, feeling that I'd moved on into the big glamorous world, as he'd failed to do, when my father stopped him from joining the navy.

Ray's widow — long since dead herself — told me that my envied and admired older brother had shouted that he was Ralph, the writer of books, poetry, and fiction, Ralph who'd persuaded Dad and been allowed to enlist in the air force and venture out into the world. Ray's widow told me that my brother had scribbled poems and had sung — not the old ballads Dad had sung but the then-popular country-western hit, "Too Many Years with the Wrong Woman." A friend told me that Ray had taken up with a blond young woman, quite pretty. She came to my brother's funeral, accompanied by her husband or ex-husband, I think. It was a time of intense grief, and I can only remember details through the confusions of emotion.

Even in death he knows how to fix this car, whatever car this is, whosever car this is, and as he does the repair, he explains the work to me, his younger brother — as maybe he did in life more than I can remember.

In my dream last night I knew that my brother was dead, but there he was helping me with a car, and it was perfectly natural, no unhappiness, no grief until I awoke. This has happened before, our mother, our father, and our aunt Jennie with me in a dream but dead, as I will be.

My competitor and family enemy during childhood, Ray was also my admired, loved, and envied heroic older brother. He did a man's hard and dangerous work early in his short life and took no crap from anyone, fighting and defeating opponents bigger than himself. He was kind and generous, often spending his hard-earned wages to buy me and my teenage buddies hamburgers, soft drinks, candy, and other treats we had no money to buy for ourselves.

In my recent dream he is dressed in white satin shirt and pants, and he is riding, standing, aloof and tranquil, on the back of a galloping white horse, riding from our farmyard, across the road and across the fields of our neighbor. He is leading a troupe of horsemen, who are riding their white horses astride. At the crest of a mild hill, in the distance, they go on riding in a circle, and in memory they are happy, they are content, they are living in the dimension that humans fumblingly call beauty.

My heart doing the best it can, okay so far with what is left alive of it, I want to live as long as possible, I think, I want to experience more love, for my wife, for my children, for my people still living and for my people already in the Spirit Land, and I pray that the God of the Universe will allow me to live long enough and well enough to fulfill my Medicine Path, my destiny, in writing, in teaching—in becoming as good a person as I can be.

# 34

A couple of decades or so ago I joined the annual tour of Eugene, Oregon's, historic homes. In one lay a very old man, his eyes open but motionless, his face without discernible expression, his presumed breathing undetectable.

I felt embarrassed, quelled. None of our group bowed over the invalid bed to say, "Hello, I am your neighbor. Thank you for allowing this visit."

The ten or twelve of us being instructed about an architectural style averted our eyes from the old man's motionless, terribly defenseless face. What were we thinking? Oh, God, there but for a few years or days, minutes, moments, few breaths, few good dinners, few sex impulses, lie I, my superbly architected house no more than a casket, decomposing somewhat more slowly than its occupant.

Back in sunshine, with others hastening to stay in line, to not wander and enter, unwelcome, the wrong door, I asked a university colleague younger than myself about the presumably living presence we'd just departed. He knew no more than I and was, furthermore, discomfited that I'd not let him quickly forget.

I did not know if I had joined in easing somewhat the boredom of a helpless man or if I had disturbed his peace. I felt that I might have committed a desecration. I felt as I had felt in a Mayan temple—as I had felt when, despite a Christian ritual's taking place, tourist chatter turned a European cathedral into a Tower of Babel.

The stone structures of vanished civilizations—Celt, Roman,

Mayan, Athabascan — and the stones of living Christians are scattered like glacier detritus under a bomber's wings. For a time the bombardier, a young person, feels triumphant, the names and numbers on his family's pitiful accumulation of meaningfully carved stones transcended in an illusion of godlike power — for a time, but only for a time, and always the awareness that another stone awaits another name.

A few years ago I was invited to join the National Aeronautics and Space Administration's on-the-ground follow-up to what an earth-orbiting satellite was informing a part of the world about global warming and the state of life-preserving forests. My job was to maintain my friendship with the project director and to fire a shotgun, to bring down twigs for future lab inspection.

The work began with dawn, and the first day I saw Old Man Coyote, the Trickster, trotting ahead of our government-seal-emblazoned vehicle, an interesting omen, I thought. For several days I performed my simple task, shooting down twig after twig from canopy, midsection, and low growth, as instructed by deeply educated men who would take vegetation back to the laboratory and check it against what satellite instruments were showing.

One of the sharply focused scientists sat down to put selected foliage specimens into plastic bags. Poison oak was outside of his area of study, and he was earnestly working in cool shade, unaware of the days of itching ahead. Too late to tell him, the others and I agreed. He'd find out soon enough, and he might as well enjoy sitting and working in shade.

In the last hours of the last day our crew drove up and parked alongside the road and found our last experimental site devastated by loggers. The U.S. government signs were all in place, but the trees they'd been meant to protect were gone. Years of human knowledge had come up against a few hours of human ignorance and had lost.

Old Man Coyote laughed and trotted toward the end of his own day.

On my desk are books of poems and fiction, some mine, their shapes rectangular, like the shapes of buildings glimpsed from a speeding bomber. Among them lies a recently rediscovered photo album, which shows a nineteen-year-old bomber crewman, his black hair, high cheekbones, and tomahawk nose evoking awareness of wars older than the one for which he is being trained. With him, a tennis racquet in hand, is one of his girlfriends, her name the name of the town from whose high school he has recently graduated, Aurora, her name one of the names for the dawn, half of one of the names for the Northern Lights, which he has witnessed from the ice-jeweled north window of his Iowa farm-home birthplace and will witness again, standing with his wife beside a fjord in the far north of Norway.

His wife, coincidentally garbed in a robe the color of snow, comes from the kitchen to wish him a good morning. World War II — two of how many to come? — ends.

A beautiful, eighteen-year-old girl, her complexion evocative of Hispanic and Pueblo history — and evocative of youth, of youth, of youth — yields to her older, more experienced, more intelligent, better-educated, accomplished, glamorous poet rival, named Ingrid, Nordic and Germanic for Daughter of the Chief.

A nineteen-year-old bomber crewman, only a year from beginning his writing career, yields to an eighty-two-year-old writer of poetry and prose.

"An aged man is but a paltry thing . . . unless soul clap its hands and sing and louder sing," wrote poet, playwright, and politician William Butler Yeats, winner of the Nobel Prize in Literature, and his poem "Sailing to Byzantium" goes on, his soul singing, for the mortals of Ireland and of all the world.

An aged man, what should I think of my worth or worthlessness as I live on toward whatever may be said over my grave? "An elder," is what some younger Native Americans have said of me, and some have praised the example I set for them as they were making their contributions to the world as writers and teachers. "An old coot," I have overheard, from the mouths of some mortals living and fulfilling or wasting the beautiful years of youth. "A medicine man," some have said, because a thunderbolt, hurled by one of our principal spirits, Red Man, the Big Thunder, touched me but left me alive.

Fifteen, I regained consciousness and breathed the scent of warm rain in grass beneath my face. Then I noticed the smell of burning in my hair, in my shirt, and in the pants I'd been reaching to unsnag from barbed wire when lightning blazed along the fence, seethed over my flesh, and became thunder I could not hear.

Ears again functioning, I'd listen to my father's story of Ralph, a know-it-all kid, impatient as usual — impatient or not willing to endure the itching of stiff oat stems under his collar and not willing to endure dread of spiders crawling down out of an oat bundle, which roofed a temporary one-person oat-bundle tepee erected against rain.

"Lightning left us as blind as hogs in the whiskey mash a minute or two, and then we seen Ralph jump up from where he'd been throwed. He ran hell bent for election, sloshed through the slough, ran up to the next fence, backed off a dozen steps or so, and ran again and slid like one of them baseyball players on his belly through mud under the bottom barbed wire. He ran on to the lane and got into the car we'd bought new — after all them damned Hoover years. Mud on his pants, he sat there on that brand-spanking-new car seat, shivering like a wet hound pup until we could catch up to him and drive on home."

My experience of being struck by lightning has become, after fifty-three years, a Spirit Awareness. I say a prayer, and during thunderstorms I keep as far as possible from tall conductors of electricity, but the danger of being killed by lightning is a danger to which I feel reconciled.

The fear of falling—the best I can say is I've endured it when I had to: flying in bombers, keeping a thick-mittened grip on bomb-stanchions and inching cumbersome flight boots along a slippery, narrow catwalk over thousands of feet of air, bomb-bay doors flared open like the lid of an army-camouflage-color coffin, clouds its satin lining. Hanging by one hand from a second-story window, I nailed boards with the other hand. Working for hours after a grueling university day. I was building an affordable home as a way of feeding my wife and child and surviving the 1970s, when powerful men were manipulating university budgets to destroy freedom of expression and commitment to egalitarian democracy.

My fear of writing the wrong thing or writing the right thing too long or in the wrong way—it's partly like my fear of heights—I say a prayer, and I start to write.

My fear of falling—I struggle against it as best I can.

Making a hard decision in 1992 — which we Indians remember as the five hundredth centennial of the Columbus Invasion — a narrow trail behind us maybe by now washed away in hard rain, Ingrid walked an eight-inch-wide slippery path five hundred feet above the Ligurian Sea's rocky shore. I might have drowned in the sea that drowned Percy Bysshe Shelley. I might have ended as a bloody blob on the shore, but after Ingrid crossed safely, my mind set against my phobia of heights, I concentrated on digging shoe sole edges into slippery clay, dug my fingers into the muddy slope above the trail, and crossed.

Thunderbolts striking the mountain around us were frightening to Ingrid, but the relief of not having plunged to my death was all I could feel.

Twice since beginning this memoir I have gone into seemingly peaceful unconsciousness. The first time I was sitting at my computer, a medicine container clutched, unopened, in one hand, a pill inside, fumbling out the container the best I could do in my fight against death. Ingrid came home and found me inarticulate. The computer keys my head had sunk onto had created page after page of scrambled alphabet, my incapacity putting to the test the philosophical assertion that enough generations of monkeys slapping typewriter keys long enough would — law of chance — write all of the works of Shakespeare.

After the ministrations of ambulance attendants and emergency room personnel, I am as okay as one can expect in old age, so the grim wisdom of old age informs me.

When — *if* — you read this, I may be dead — my — your — human destiny.

His brain beginning to atrophy, a friend sixteen years younger than myself has just lost the teaching job, which he loved.

In my own first year of teaching and in the same classroom where I persuaded a bright enough young racist to face the fact that he was not as good a nuclear physicist as a highly educated black man, I heard, in an adjacent classroom, the cruel jibes of a class making the last month of a colleague's teaching miserable, that professor stricken, in his midfifties, with what all called senility. Car crash, illness, drug overdose, war wound — "a human vegetable," we hear in the news, and anguished, loving survivors reluctantly decide that the body should be allowed to join the brain in death — or decide the opposite — or politicians seeking the votes of sadists decide that a human organism no more aware than a jellyfish must be expensively sustained election after election.

What is death? What is life?

To live a life that is not one's own is a suicide that many fearful people accept. To feel like God, not like God the life giver but like God the destroyer, gives millions the illusion that they have transcended their own deaths. "May I live well enough and long enough to fulfill my destiny," is my prayer. May I fulfill my Medicine Dream. May I follow my Medicine Path to its end. And may I and may my loved ones live a life of beauty and happiness after death.

# EPILOGUE

Simultaneity. Access to one's entire life in any moment. To see or to feel the universe in a grain of sand, eternity in an hour. To live, not by the calendar, so useful in sentencing criminals. Ontogeny recapitulates phylogeny. Which meant—to my twenty-one-year-old simple-mindedness about what it does to my eighty-three-year-old simple-mindedness—that what went on for generations of adaptation goes on in each new child—and human embryos still have gills and tails in the womb.

Dream recall. Meditation. Dianetics. In 1951—yet another imperialist war killing thousands in Korea—a fellow university graduate student in Iowa City, Iowa, said, "I spent last night in my mother's womb." Time travel all the way back through the faunal scale to the beginning of life. Science fiction. Religion. Simultaneity. Fascists shooting at my brother as he escapes prisoner-of-war camp while my brother is aiming a gun at my father and going to kill him if he doesn't stop abusing our mother, while someone is enduring a winter night to shoot the glass out of a window above my baby bed. Simultaneity. Simple-mindedness. Why not. Simultaneity, spontaneity—why not. What other word pattern is so sensible that it should preclude—Rosetta Stone, Rose ate a stone—spontaneity, simplicity, simultaneity? Our noble allies and comrades in arms, in World War II, our Evil Empire enemies the Russians—and hypnotic media propaganda deludes millions from perceiving the military-industrial takeover of the government, which President Eisenhower served for eight years and then condemned.

TV, the repetition of a few enslaving phrases until they become the Amerikan language. TV, on which you can't tell a mother from her daughter, ostensibly because expensive chemicals keep the mother looking so young but possibly because the tyranny of always having had to spend so much of her young life in trying to look like a machine-age courtesan makes the daughter look as lifeless as plastic derived from fossils. TV, on which you are told again and again, slyly, that what's good for those enslaving you is good for you. Fear words. You'll be playmateless, friendless, loverless if don't have the TV-approved toy, air-ballooned breakfast cereal, soft drink, hard drink, harder drink, garment label, music group label, shampoo, hair conditioner, soap, deodorant watered, "scientifically moisturized" so you will smell like fake flower chemicals, not smell of animal sweat and secretions — toothpaste decreed by actors in white laboratory smocks to polish to mating-season-luster enamel to frame enticing tongue, framed by TV-approved lipsticked lips, enamel that, in name-recognition restaurants, tears apart meat. Pit-bull dogs are maiming or killing your children. Happy Dog dog food makes your dog happy and is EZ on your family budget. Unamerican, communism, socialism, Arab terrorists. Arab oil.

An elderly person, no longer able to keep up with family and tribe, decides to rest, meditate, and starve beside the trail so that loved ones may survive and bring new generations into the world.

For my aged self, this Christmas month, life has been a loving, significant, fun-filled reunion with children and grandchildren.

I cannot imagine a post-nuclear ice-age audience gasping, "Wow! This writer dude was utterly — utterly cool!" It is, however, good to think that some fraction of my words might help some fraction of some population to live better or might give solace in the human suffering all of us live. It is good to think of my words possibly being of use in the ongoing lives of my children and grandchildren. A thousand or a mere hundred years from now someone may stumble onto some words of mine fallen off the splintered shelf of a maybe bomb-blasted library, I can think, this moment when my memories of life are flowing onto a computer screen — to evaporate into clouds and rain, to fall, or not. This moment, when my death is at least the medically estimated four minutes from the next breath, it is good to think of my body's adding to the earth's scant supply of fertilizer.

Why am I not walking in the sunshine of my eighty-third spring, a spring I would not be seeing out this or any other window had not medical skill progressed to the ability to transplant a blood vessel from my aging left leg to my aging heart? My heart, receiver of stolen goods, thriving — leg still okay, like any living thing robbed of anything short of life — why am I not walking, my eyes stealing the beauty others have labored to create, in front yards most will labor one-third, approximately, of their lives to own?

Why are my feet and my mind not tagging along with my gaze and my mind into the reality of this day's, this instant's, inexpressible splendor?

My mind unites with the hand clutching this pen — same tool with which bored clerks were busily recording their century's piracy's booty and inhumane worship of wealth. Gloriously, transcendentally "mad" William Blake experienced the world in a grain of sand, eternity in an hour. As mad as Blake, whether gloriously and transcendentally so or not, I am trying to experience again and again at least some of my past, in a computer chip, and to translate it into ink, in the hope that others may experience a tiny piece of a time I would like to call mine — a time I try to save from those whose love of power threatens to destroy our children's children's children and render humans extinct. I hope to feel myself fifteen again and again and afraid of death and trembling and trying to do what a son and a man, a man, should be expected to do, defend his home. I hope to sense again and again the fragrance of fallen maple leaves, the bouquet of a stranger's perfume, an island of impossible dreams in an arctic ocean of air, the brilliance of sun in daffodils, the daffodils I would give my wife, my complex, fascinating wife of forty years, when, tired and beautiful, utterly, unutterably beautiful, she returns from her workday—eight hours of William Blake's eternity. Unaware that I am trying to destine her to live the rest of her and William Blake's eternities in a computer chip—itself, so I understand, a grain of sand—she will suggest, I hope, a walk, a walk through sunlight finding fulfillment in forsythia—forsythia seething like terribly beautiful—and reassuringly distant—lightning, forsythia a molten thunderbolt hurtling toward sky and into two aging lovers' delighted eyes.

So, enough of this purple poeticized prose, somebody, somebody with a body still as young as a newly created poem, may say, hurling youthful flesh — past my awed, admiring, aged eyes — toward no place else but bed.

"Forsythia," by God, I affirm, in my eighty-third spring's hours and hours of eternities. "Forsythia," yes, by God, "forsythia," by God, and by chance or by hook or by crook or by a poet's warped way of looking at facts, but by God, whatever else, by God, by God, by God!

And wild ducks, yes, rain or shine, raincoat or t-shirt, hundreds and hundreds of wild ducks so numerous and varied I couldn't even begin to count the jewels the force of their landing will scatter across water shining like a silver platter, yes, ducks, wild ducks, mallards, like the ones I'd get soaked and shiver and shiver for hours to harvest from blue or gray sky for my family's often bare meat platter, wild ducks, bless their beauty, their forgiving, fearless, and greedy gabbling enjoyment of life as intense as my hopefully equally forgiving own.

Trumpeter swans, for sure, straight lines of black-marked white flowers, growing in a blue or a gray sky garden and trumpeting, yes, creating a music—presumably about arduous effort and anticipation of food and of mating—mating for life, I am told, for life—and whatever each swan may feel about death and ongoing life is all, I believe, that Beethoven could express.

And now, again and again, snow geese, a great, white, incredibly beautiful blizzard descending on the gray waters of the bay—a beautiful blizzard to these aging eyes—soon, too soon, to close—a blizzard a beautiful reminder of winters gone and winters to come and to melt again into forsythia blossoms under egg-yolk-color sun.

To order or obtain more information on these or other University of Nebraska Press titles, visit www.nebraskapress.unl.edu

CPSIA information can be obtained at www.ICGtesting.com
Printed in the USA
BVOW082353030213

312228BV00002B/2/P